Vietnam as if...

Tales of youth, love and destiny

Vietnam as if...

Tales of youth, love and destiny

KIM HUYNH

PRESS

Published by ANU Press
The Australian National University
Acton ACT 2601, Australia
Email: anupress@anu.edu.au
This title is also available online at http://press.anu.edu.au

---

National Library of Australia Cataloguing-in-Publication entry

Creator: Huynh, Kim, 1977- , author.

Title: Vietnam as if ... tales of youth, love and destiny / Kim Huynh.

ISBN: 9781925022308 (paperback) 9781925022315 (ebook)

Subjects: Youth--Vietnam--Conduct of life.
               Youth--Vietnam--Attitudes.
               Youth--Vietnam--Social conditions.

Dewey Number: 362.709597

All rights reserved. No part of this publication may be reproduced, stored in a retrieval system or transmitted in any form or by any means, electronic, mechanical, photocopying or otherwise, without the prior permission of the publisher.

Cover design and layout by ANU Press

This edition © 2015 ANU Press

Contents

Acknowledgements	vii
Foreword: The Turtle	ix
Chapter 1: The Sticky Rice Seller	1
Chapter 2: The Ball Boy	47
Chapter 3: The Professional	83
Chapter 4: The Goalkeeper	103
Chapter 5: The Student	159
Postscript: The Other Turtle's Tale	183

❝ **Kim Huynh's accounts of social life in Vietnam never back away from difficult topics and themes. Importantly, he neither exoticises his birthplace nor commoditises himself in crafting this exceptional work of Vietnamese diasporic writing.** ❞

— Mariam Lam, University of California Riverside

❝ **These portraits offer a confronting vision of a society that's surging in many, often contradictory, directions. The Vietnamese brought to life in these pages represent a generation of youth who are ambitious and idealistic, but also insecure and aloof. Imaginative, well-researched and intricately crafted, this work should be read by anyone who is studying or travelling to Vietnam.** ❞

— Philip Taylor, The Australian National University

Acknowledgements

- David Adams
- Philip Taylor
- Marian Sawer
- David West
- Erica and Will Taylor
- Andrew Watts

- Asialink Arts Residency Program
- Arts ACT
- Australia Council for the Arts
- ANU Press
- ANU College of Arts & Social Sciences

Foreword
The Turtle

Sometimes it feels as if one thousand years goes by in a single day. Perhaps it's just me, slowing down in my old age. But from what I can tell, everyone else is also moving faster, trying to squeeze more into every second, eager to get from one point to the next without ever wondering what might be in between or beyond.

Often I watch people go by with their ears pressed up against their phones or staring into those shiny little screens. I gather that they are liking, messaging, tweeting, posting, following and tagging. I don't pretend to know what any of this means exactly, but suspect they are connecting with people down the road, across the city, or on the other side of the world. Being connected doesn't mean what it used to mean in Vietnam, but it seems to be more important than ever.

I'm old fashioned – more concerned with the quality of connections than the speed or number of them. If I had my way, we would all apply the brakes ever so slightly so that we could be with one another and be in the moment.

Don't get me wrong. Slowing down is not the same as being lazy.

In fact, if you pay close attention you'll see that I am never idle. In the mornings I paddle to the side of my lake where the marsh lands used to be, or to the spot where there was once a stream that ran all the way to the Red River. Even though my lake was closed off to the world more than a century ago, these are still my favourite places to search for worms, plants and algae.

Once the sun has risen I like to swim up to the surface to see who's about and let others see me. Visitors and children often gather to gawk and take pictures.

'Is that really him? He's even bigger than I thought he was. Why's he swimming so slowly? Is he okay?'

'How many turtles are there, anyway? Just one? He must get lonely.'

'Is he really real? How can anything live in that?'

'He's real, all right! Really old and really ugly.'

The locals walk by, do their exercises and go about their day. They've seen me before and have no reason to see me again. I know that many people find me odd, perhaps even gruesome. But I'm too slow, my shell is too soft and my claws are too worn to threaten anyone. I suppose I'm a spectacle, but one that's easy to grow accustomed to and then ignore.

In the afternoons I sink down to the bottom of the lake to escape the heat and noise. It's there in the silent darkness that I find myself thinking back to all the turtles who came before me and who passed on that yolk of wisdom that allowed me to emerge from my egg ready to watch over a nation.

Constantly, I taste the silt that settles down from the air and through the green water. My lake is not like it used to be. Strange morsels and substances are always being deposited. Most of them I tolerate – even if they are not to my liking they do not turn my stomach. You don't get to my age without being able to adapt.

So I'm comfortable with Vietnamese moving from rice paddies to apartment blocks and flying far from these shores. And I have no problem with outsiders coming to Vietnam. When I hear people speaking in alien tongues I rarely feel frightened or out of sorts. I've witnessed Chinese, French, Japanese, Russians, Americans and many others march into this land and stay for a while before moving on. All of these visitors have challenged us to change and yet somehow remain Vietnamese.

And then there's that perpetual struggle between youth who are intent on making their own way and older folk who are determined to preserve their legacies. I'm in step with both, having seen many of the former turn into the latter. Change and struggle sit well with me. They ensure that every day in Vietnam is different. It's just the speed of that change and the ferocity of the struggle that I'm inclined to question.

One thing about moving so slowly is that I don't need to sleep very much. And so, after the sun has set, I do gentle circles of the lake, clockwise and then anti-clockwise, leaving plenty of time to stop and float. When I look up, I can't see the blanket of stars anymore. Instead for hours at a time I gaze in wonderment at the city lights flickering like so many synapses in a mighty brain.

So now you know how I fill my days. You know that I'm relaxed but never at rest. Whether swimming, diving or floating, I am always connecting with people, networking you might even call it. The oxygen that fills my lungs and the water in which I'm immersed allow me to keep in touch with people all over the country, people who breathe the same air and are born of the same fluid. My spirit enchants them. And I, in turn, am enchanted by their spirits. As if in a dream, I see what they see, feel what they feel, while watching and assessing them from the outside. I am at once master and slave to their stories.

But because I can't be in more than one place at a time, I must be selective. I tend to connect with youth. Not just any youth, but those 100 or so hatchlings of each generation who help me to fathom the character of the nation and divine its destiny. They are not like everyone else. You could call them heroes, figures worthy of glowing swords, magical bows and riding atop elephants. Whether they fulfil their potential is a matter of resolve, judgement and fortune, and remains uncertain to me even after all these centuries.

Ultimately, I keep moving because my time, like everyone else's, is short. Nowadays it is nice to get a little help from others. I'm grateful to the scientists who treat my earthly ailments, who build me special cages to protect me from the elements and who encourage me to slow down that little bit more. And I appreciate those who dote on me as if I was a great grandfather or some creature that's suddenly deemed rare and therefore precious. What I really need, however, is for people to believe in each other and in me. Belief is what gives me substance and purpose. While the nature of that belief is bound to vary and its level ebb and flow, the thought of it dwindling away is one change that I find hard to swallow.

With respect,
The Turtle of Hoan Kiem Lake

Chapter 1
The Sticky Rice Seller

'Take a seat! Take a seat! Don't stand there thinking about it. Make a choice. Trust me. Everything is tasty and cheap. Only seven sickles a serve. Ten clams if you're hungry or five twigs if you're on a diet. But you're already so slim, you don't need to worry about that. In fact, why don't you buy a jumbo serving with extra dripping for 15 Uncle Hos? It's enough for your breakfast, lunch and dinner. And I bet you'll be back tomorrow for more.

'Take a seat! Here's a serving with pummelled mung beans. Eat first, pay later, you won't be disappointed. It doesn't get better than this.'

I learnt a long time ago that you can't afford to be timid when it comes to selling sticky rice.

That's not to say I'm pushy or think I'm better than I am. My stall is small. Fifteen little stools and an old market umbrella – that's all the style and comfort I have to offer. I don't pretend to be a skilled chef or aspire to own a restaurant. Why would I want to do all that training only to make food that people don't know how to eat? And even if I had the money to open a restaurant, why would

I want to pay rent and taxes, fill in forms, follow regulations and manage people? Better to be my own boss, work in the open air and make the most of what the heavens have given me.

I know my place and it suits me fine.

I'm forever grateful to my grandmother, who started teaching me how to make and sell sticky rice when I was six.

Gran took great pride in rubbing people the wrong way. My mother says that her mother could cultivate curses like they were bean sprouts. She swore at the competition, at customers who did not treat her with respect, and at strangers she didn't like the look of.

'Put some clothes on, hussy!' she once hollered to one of my high school classmates who was walking by. 'Yes, I've heard about how you could seduce the Buddha in all 28 of his manifestations. Your mother was no different. Go home and slip into a pair of pants or a long tunic – that skirt's so breezy I'm catching a cold looking at you. And while you're there, clean that syrup off your cunt before a wasp comes along and stings you!'

Another time, before I left Gran to go north with my mother, I gave some money to a beggar with only one leg and one arm. I don't usually give to beggars but it was the New Year and he said he was a war veteran who needed the money to return to his village. When Gran saw what I was doing she called the beggar a drunken retard who didn't know a fart from a shit. With lightning speed, she snatched the money back, put it in her shirt pocket and told the beggar he had two more limbs than he deserved.

Last time we spoke on the phone, I told Gran I was doing well enough in Hanoi but I still missed her and didn't have many friends.

'Your problem is not a lack of friends. It's that you don't have any enemies', she exclaimed. 'You're too abiding. People piss all over you and you smile as if it's perfume. A good woman needs enemies. That's why I am not rich and respected, because my enemies have been sub-standard, too easy to overcome. You're even worse-off because you don't have any at all. You have to learn to push back, make people fear and hate you. Otherwise they'll screw you over.'

Gran is really something. And I suppose she's right. I'm not one to swim against the current. I like to float along. And I can't hold bitterness in my belly and hurl abuse at others like she does. I prefer to be sweet-scented and supple, like my rice.

Gran and I are a little alike in the sense that both of us can't help but make up stories about people. The difference being that while she insults others, I try to identify with them. I also keep my stories to myself.

It's usually less than a minute of inactivity before I am conjuring up tales about strangers on the street. For me the traffic is a procession of warm and wonderful characters. As the parade rolls by, I marvel at the drama of each character's life. In my mind I follow them home at night to peer through their windows and listen through their walls. From my street corner I discover people's heartfelt aspirations and deepest secrets.

There's 'Mr Binh', license plate 29-Y2-6258, who some days wears a white helmet with 'I love lipstick' on it and on other days a yellow one branded 'Versace'. Both of them, I imagine, were chosen by his wife sometime in 2008 after motorbike helmets became compulsory. They were newlyweds then and his wife couldn't decide whether to get the white one – because it had a hole in the back for her ponytail – or the yellow one, because it was cosmopolitan and sassy.

Mr Binh insisted they buy both. His wife protested because they were trying to save money to set up a sushi stall and move out of her parents' house. 'I don't need one for myself,' Mr Binh asserted, 'I'll just wear whatever helmet you're not using.'

When she said it would not be proper for him to wear a woman's helmet, he responded: 'What could be more manly than for me to look after my wife?'

Now I imagine that they have a son, their business is up and going and they have a second motorbike. Over the years, Mr Binh's wife routinely suggests that they buy a new, more befitting helmet for him. But he's always maintained he would not use it: 'Sharing these helmets reminds me of our humble beginnings and makes me pay attention to how you do your hair each morning.'

And there goes 'Mademoiselle Trinh', licence plate 56-A1-2344. She is younger than I am but has seen the world and encountered both triumph and heartache. I am drawn to the tiny butterfly tattoo on her right ankle and envisage her having had it done in a Parisian parlour near the Sorbonne where she attained her business degree.

After going to work for a British finance company, she met and fell in love with a young law graduate who had a black camel tattooed on his right arm, a tribute to his father's Moroccan homeland. He adored Trinh and called her his *petite papillon*, despite her having grown five centimetres taller and six kilograms heavier from eating creamy sauces and croissants.

When the global financial crisis hit, Trinh's company went bankrupt and she decided to return to Vietnam, where she had been offered a prestigious consultancy position with an oil company. Before settling upon this decision, Trinh and her boyfriend stayed up through the night discussing their future over red wine and kisses. On several occasions Trinh's lover had said he'd like to move to Vietnam. She told him that her country was at once developing and struggling, and that there were many opportunities for someone like him to make a difference. But in the morning they agreed that he should stay behind to pursue a career in politics, as they were convinced he was destined to become France's Barack Obama.

Sometimes I wonder what would happen if Binh, Trinh or one of the many characters from my daydreams stopped to talk to me.

They would surely be friendlier and more fascinating than some of my regulars, especially the ones who are always complaining. Not about the quality of the sticky rice, of course. Usually they object to the prices, which they seem to think go up for them alone.

'My costs are rising too', I remind them. 'Do you think I'm in the sticky rice business to make it big or something? Look at my clothes! Hardly high fashion. Look at my waist! Where's the fat? The only thing thinner is my profit margin.'

Old people pine for the days when a serving of rice cost a 100 su coin. The ex-neighbourhood cell leader says he preferred it when he had to line up for rations and didn't even have to think about what to eat or how much it cost – it was all on the ticket. University students moan because they don't have enough for rent, books and food, although soon they'll be making much more money than me. Even rich people sometimes complain about the prices, but I suppose they wouldn't be rich if they didn't know how to pinch their pennies.

Fortunately, most of my customers don't complain – most of them don't say anything. I have served some customers more than a thousand times without ever exchanging a full sentence. Sometimes I don't even know their faces. They pull up beside my stall with their facemasks on and their engines still running: 'Corn rice, 10 clams worth' or 'Same as before', is as much as I'll get.

I like to identify them by the pattern on the facemasks they wear to protect them from the pollution and dirt. Mr Red Tartan comes at 6:45 every weekday morning and has black bean rice wrapped in a banana leaf, no condiments. Mrs Paisley Green and her Yellow Love Heart daughter like deep fried shallots on their peanut sticky rice. When I see my reticent regulars coming I begin preparing their parcels so they're ready to go before they have even stopped. I leap up, loop the bag over the hooks on their motorcycles, collect the money and wave them on. That's what I call service.

The morning exercisers who come to my stall in groups and bark orders are also locked into my memory by their clothing: badminton player short shorts, tango dancer heels, tai chi buttoned tunics, and walkers in their matching cotton tracksuits.

And there are the junior high school students who have eaten my rice since they were spoon fed it by their mothers and their maids. I feel like an older sister to many of them, but while it was easy to chat to them when they were happy toddlers, now most of them are dark and burdened. They grunt more than speak and stare down at the ground as they eat, resenting the sun for bringing another day.

'Have a seat, little sister', I said to one young lady the other day.

'Got sticky rice?'

'Every type and in any way you want it.'

'Got egg?'

'Aye yah, I'm out of boiled eggs. Do you want some pork? I'll get you a nice juicy piece.'

'Whatever.'

'Do you want some gravy on the top?'

'Okay. Whatever.'

Sometimes I also wonder what sort of stories my customers and passers-by make up about me.

'She's nice enough', I guess they would say. 'Honest, never misses a day's work. She's from the countryside for sure; there's no way she has a residency permit. Not much schooling by the look of her. She's done fairly well given where she's come from. Probably makes just enough to get by and sends home whatever she can. Poor dear. She would have been pretty were it not for the birthmark on her face.'

They would be right about me working hard and of course about my birthmark, but wrong about everything else. While I am not from Hanoi, I've been living in the city now for seven years. And I have a permit because my father is a property-owning resident. He's a professor of fine arts, or was before he retired. My mother was once a famous lacquerware artist and, although I don't really know them, I have a half-brother in Germany who is a famous sculptor and a half-sister in Finland who is married to a fashion journalist. Obviously, I'm not rich; but I make a steady income, enough to pay my way and save a little for the uncertain future. I can even pass on some money to my father each month, which he calls his 'fund for green tea and mung bean sweets'.

And although I am not brilliant like others in my family, I too have a talent, one that I prefer to keep hidden.

I'll never forget when I first discovered this gift. Mother and I were pressed beside one another on a little wooden desk and bench set that my father had bought for me on one of his visits. She was teaching me the alphabet. My mother liked to draw each letter so that a B was never just a B, but also a butterfly or a bouncing ball. Every Â she wrote was a picturesque snow-topped house from a Hans Christian Andersen fairy tale. At that stage I didn't know that my mother had been a celebrated artist; I didn't really know what an artist was. So while I liked her ornate pictures, I sometimes took them for granted and on occasion was frustrated when her doodling stopped me from moving on to the next letter. Once when I grumbled that I wanted to draw the letters by myself, she snapped and told me that people would have paid a great deal for the creations that I brushed aside or scribbled over.

Shortly before my fifth birthday, I was copying letters my mother had written for me when I told her that 'I like writing Ds and Đs the most. I like how I can change a furry brown letter into a slick and shiny one with just a single little line.'

My mother froze. I knew I had done or said something horrible. It was as if I had suddenly transformed into a monster before her eyes.

My mother slapped the lead pencil from my hand. 'Heavens above! Isn't the birthmark enough punishment? How many possible ways can this child be cursed?!'

She regained her senses and stood up to retrieve the pencil before returning to the desk and looking straight at me. Mother said I was not a bad girl, but that there was something bad inside me, a seed planted in a previous life by nasty spirits that could not be allowed to sprout. She said that my senses were confused, my wires all crossed.

'Letters are letters – and that's that. If they're black, then they're black. If they're on paper then they feel like paper. Simple as that. Normal people don't see them as colours or feel them. That's how it is. That's the way you should be.'

Mother held my hand, the one she had just slapped, and said to me in a slow and severe voice: 'It's important, Mai, that everyone thinks you're normal. I'll try to help you fix this, but you can't tell anyone about it, not even your Gran. Otherwise people will not like you and they'll say horrible things about me.'

As I grew up and went to school, I gained a better idea of how different I was to others. I realised that even if I tried as hard as I could, I could not help but associate letters and also numbers with colours and textures. It was and still is inescapable to me that 1, 10, 100 and so forth are red and rough like gravel; 2, 20, 200 are blue and puffy like clouds; and every u' is gunmetal grey and wet like fresh rice paper. One of the first things I did was to find a red pencil and write '2' after '2' after '2', thinking that this might somehow reset my senses. I could see that it was red on the paper. Yet no matter how hard I tried, '2' was still puffy and blue.

But in truth it was not long before I stopped trying to fix myself, largely because my gift had benefits and gave me comfort, even some pleasure.

Whereas other children had to repeat letters and words many times over before they could spell them, I only needed to hear or see them once or twice to remember them forever. I also learnt arithmetic much faster than others because there was always a multicoloured abacus floating in front of me that I could manoeuvre in my mind in a fraction of an instant. In history and science class I never had to cram or use crib notes because recalling dates, facts and formulae was a cinch.

The major difficulty that I had at school, along with being lonely, was the crushing boredom. I dealt with both by thinking of my favourite numbers and progressions – multiples, exponentials and Fibonacci sequences – which enveloped me in a warm, familiar haze. Even today I find myself constructing this shield around me whenever I am anxious.

But of course I never told anyone at school about my condition. This was not hard given that no one was interested in me. I was the pitiful girl with the birthmark on her face. I never put my hand up in class, and when the teacher called upon me to respond to a question I often answered incorrectly. Usually this was because I was not paying attention, but there were also times when I gave the wrong answer because it seemed like the right thing to do. It was what others expected of me. And it would've made my mother happy to know I was doing my best not to stand out.

Mother occasionally encouraged me to tell her about my gift and how I coped with it. I suspect this was not to support or console me, but rather to monitor it in the same way that she might a disease. But I don't mean to speak unkindly of her. She always tried to keep me safe and do what she thought was best.

When I was older and after much prodding, Mother told me that I was not the only one in the family with special abilities. My father had an older sister who saw numbers as colours and smelt letters. When my father's mother discovered her ability, she did everything possible to cure her. They made regular trips to the family communal house and church in the hope that the ancestors and the Almighty could help them to drive away the evil spirits tormenting my aunt. They tried acupuncture and all manner of concoctions from simple rice and onion soup to expensive bear bile and Western elixirs. One or some of these measures was apparently effective, but the side effects and stress made my aunt giddy during the day and kept her from sleeping at night. Because everyone knew she did not sense things properly, my aunt didn't have any friends and never found a husband despite being very beautiful; no man wanted to risk catching her affliction let alone having children with her.

I would have liked to meet my aunt and have always thought that we could have helped one another. After I moved to Hanoi, I asked my father about her and he told me she had passed away in his home village not long after his mother. Father said that he didn't want to be reminded of his sister, so I never mentioned her to him again.

A few years ago when my neighbour bought a computer, one of the first things that I searched for on the internet was whether there were other people out there whose senses were jumbled. Back then I didn't know anything about the internet and computers, so I asked my neighbour to look it up for me and told her I knew someone who knew someone who had that affliction and thought it eerie but also a little cool. I was curious to know more.

We found a story about a 43-year-old man in Kien Giang province who claimed to be able to see and feel time as if it was a colourful spectrum that spanned out and up ahead of him. As a consequence, he had a stopwatch in his head accurate to the millisecond. The story began by claiming that the man was possessed, but it ended with some facts and figures that made me feel at ease. Apparently, babies are born into the world with their senses mixed, but quickly learn to discriminate between touch, taste, sight, smell and sound. One per cent of the population hold on to part of this trait and associate colours with letters, numbers or days. There are others who smell words, see music and even taste names. Most importantly, I learnt that my condition had a name: 'synaesthesia', which as a word is honeydew melon green and feels like a plush rug rubbed the wrong way.

When my neighbour called the guy who could see time a freak, I agreed. But in my heart I felt connected to that middle-aged man from Kien Giang. I wondered if, like me, he had experienced sensory overload the first time he entered a train station and was hustled and bustled by all the colours leaping out of the timetables and notice boards. And I have always been grateful to the journalist who wrote his story, as it gave me hope that there were people out there who might understand and accept me.

Today I'm more accepting of my gift and do not hesitate to use it, especially at work. On busy mornings I can handle several transactions at once without getting flustered. And I take great pride in never giving the wrong change. I'm not all that good with faces, but am excellent with everything else – number plates, names, dates, clothes, songs and colours – so there is always enough information for me to recognise my customers and give them that personal touch.

Of course, I don't want them to know about my gift and don't expect them to care where I've come from, what I can do or who I am.

But there are times when I wish they could judge me by something more than just my humble trade and the birthmark on my face. What bothers me most is when people glance in my direction and whisper to one another with belittling sympathy, as if I had just arrived from the rice fields and had never seen my reflection … as if I had not once imagined what my life would be like if I was unblemished … as if the sight of me had never brought my mother to tears because my face reminded her of all the wrongs she had committed in this life and others.

> To know the seeds sewn in former lives,
> Behold the fruits reaped in this one.
> To know the fruits of future lives,
> Behold the seeds sewn in this one.

My mother has long been guided by this folktale about the origins of watermelons, and is forever reminding me to heed the weighty presence of karma in our lives.

But Mother has never really got beyond the first two lines. For her the past is rusted on to both the present and the future; she is convinced that wrongdoings accumulate across lives and down the generations, so that the most people can ever hope for is to stop our karmic condition from getting worse.

I take a more positive approach to my destiny and focus on the last two lines, which tell me that by avoiding evil and doing good, I can enrich my soul for an eternity.

But I don't blame Mother for being the way she is. And I know from speaking to Gran that my mother was once a lot like me.

My mother was one of the most promising and beautiful lacquerware artists in the South. She was so talented that she received a scholarship to study at Can Tho University when she was only 16. This is where she refined and developed her unique style, producing work that was praised for capturing the joyous soul of the Mekong. She adored how each layer of lacquer is a fresh start. With every wash, Mother once wistfully told me, she could incorporate new colours and apply different techniques. At the same time, previous layers were ever-present, so that strokes of both folly and genius could never be totally glossed over.

Mother had learnt the craft from her father's brother, who was a well-regarded lacquerware artist in the North. Their family had moved south in 1954 because their priest had told them Ho Chi Minh's Vietnam was no place for Catholics. For a time they slept in makeshift tents on the streets of Saigon, receiving handouts from the church and the government before moving to my home town in Long An province, where my mother was born. My great uncle eventually opened a successful shop, Thang Long Pty Ltd, specialising in evocative images from the North: one-pillar pagodas, Co Loa spirals, Temples of Literature and misty Fansipan Mountains.

He also trained apprentices, the most talented of whom was my mother. My great uncle conveyed this to me not long before he died. 'Her varnish was as shiny as a cockroach's wings and elusive in the sense that you were never quite sure if they were red, black or brown. She had amazing instincts. There are many vagaries when it comes to lacquerware. For most artists it takes years for them to judge how their paints and lacquers set, particularly when the humidity and temperature fluctuate. Even the oldest master is prone to errors that result in undesirable shades and sheens. But your mother picked it up very quickly and never got things wrong. To this day I don't know how she did it, and fervently wish she could have taught me.'

My parents met in 1986, not long after my father became a professor at the University of Fine Arts. As one of the youngest professors ever appointed, he made his reputation as a prolific sculptor during and after the American War who had published pamphlets, articles and a much-respected book on the function of art as a binding and mobilising agent in revolutionary societies.

It was for this reason that father caused a great stir when, after being awarded his professorship, he declared that he had outgrown both sculpting and socialist realism. In what is now regarded as a historic lecture to faculty and students, he pronounced that the time for war was over and therefore wartime art should be confined to the dwindling twentieth century. A new and renovated creative spirit, he asserted, was needed to connect the people to their past and inspire them to march forward. And so he had chiselled his last square jaw, and all of his tools along with his extensive collection of casts in the shape of hammers, sickles and stars were stacked outside the door of his studio for anyone to take.

But this did not mean that my father was no longer an artist-patriot. On the contrary, as he explained in his speech, he was heading across the 17th parallel to study Southern culture and explore ways to bring it together with the North and the Centre.

He was especially keen to see how lacquerware had developed since the Vietnamese marched south from the Red River Delta. Previously he had thought that only Northern art, with its longer and purer history, could be truly Vietnamese. Now he suspected that his Southern brothers and sisters had fashioned something distinctive out of their contact with the French and Americans, and that these vestiges should be preserved rather than eradicated. The North was of course the cradle of Vietnamese civilisation, but this didn't mean that Southerners were barbarians. My father recognised that the Southerners knew how to make money, which after the war was a most valuable skill. He sensed that the export market for lacquerware was about to mushroom and generate much wealth for the people while also promoting their culture overseas. Many regarded my father as a radical, others called him a revisionist, but it was not long before he was celebrated as a visionary.

My mother played a large part in his success because it was her artwork that my father first brought back to the North, where it was met with much acclaim. Their relationship, however, was thorny from the beginning. Mother was frightfully cold towards my father's advances. It took two separate visits to

Can Tho University and over four days of constantly watching her at work and asking her questions about her life and art before my father could even coax a sentence from her: 'So, you're the professor from the North are you?'

But for all her aloofness, Mother was impressed by him. My father enchanted her by recalling trips to China and Eastern Europe, and inspired her by speaking of the changing seasons in Hanoi and all the places up and down the coast of Vietnam that he had visited.

He was far more suave than anyone she had met. Mother once told me that she had hardly ever seen a man tuck his shirt into his trousers until my father came along. Now, as he did then, my father ensures that the colour of his shirt matches his socks. His out-and-about shoes always have buckles because slip-ons, in his view, should never leave the house and laces are only required for sport.

Even today, when he is well into his sixties, Father can charm people with only a few words. He has an air of esteem that allows him to look down on others, even though he is a little shorter than most men. I've always noticed how my mother stays close to him when he talks to other women and looks wary, as if she would prefer it if he did not.

If there was one thing that finally warmed my mother's heart, it was the feature article that my father wrote for *Van Nghe* magazine, in which he recorded his encounter with a Southern belle who had mastered the art of lacquerware – an article which now occupies a prized place in his library. In the article he describes my mother's astonishing gift for turning two dimensions into three, such that the first time he saw her pictures any doubts he harboured about giving up sculpture dissipated. He felt as if he could reach out and touch her images in the same way they reached out from the wood panelling and touched him. Her human figures were sometimes abstract and a little romantic, but always revelled and sang. And he was sure he could smell her dazzling yellow apricot blossoms and *mai* flowers that reminded him of spring. What impressed him most was her mix of precision and improvisation when inlaying mother-of-pearl and crushed eggshells into her pictures; as if each speck had been placed on the picture by a swallow that had grown tired of building nests.

Looking back, I am certain that my parents were brought together by fate. It did not matter that Father was twice Mother's age and that he lived a thousand kilometres away – neither of them had a choice. And ultimately it didn't even matter that he was already married and had two children. Although my mother maintains that she did not know until it was too late, my grandmother insists otherwise: 'There's no goddamn way a man like your father would be single and it did not take an artist's eye to see the impression the ring left on his finger.'

I can also thank my grandmother for a more recent revelation that, while my parents' union was foretold in the stars, my coming into this world was not.

'Your mother was very young – much younger than you are now – and so very frightened', Gran disclosed to me. 'She was afraid of what people would think about her and what it would mean for our family. I knew it would be hard, but said that she had done the deed and had to face the consequences, and that I would help her. After all, I had a fair bit of experience as a war widow and single mother. And I assured her that I would slap senseless anyone who spoke poorly of her or our family. I don't think this helped. And so for a while I thought I would have to tie up your mother and force-feed her until you were born. But in the end, it was your father who came to your rescue with his pandan-sweet words. Apparently he was, for perhaps the very first time, honest with your mother. He too was a Catholic and although he had hardly been to church since he was confirmed, it still meant something to him. It was an anchor that weighed down his soul. It meant that he could not leave his wife and family in Hanoi, nor could he take her on as a second wife. Above all, it meant that neither of them could risk eternal damnation by aborting their unborn child.'

Father said he knew Mother's suffering and shame would far surpass his and that she would have to give up her scholarship and return to her home town, at least for a while. As penance, he promised to send whatever money he could to her every month and promote her career, so that in time she would not need his help.

With newfound steeliness that she had built up over tearful nights, my mother told my father that he could keep his money and favours, and that he should not overstate his powers of manipulation. It was *their* mistake and *their* weakness and not his alone. Moreover, he would need the money to visit her and the child every year. This was the first of her three conditions. The second was that he was never to commit adultery again, especially with her, and that she in turn would know no other man. This was because they could consider themselves betrothed with the wedding ceremony set for one month after the first anniversary of his wife's natural death. The ceremony would be civil or Buddhist because this whole affair had given her the reason she had been seeking to reject the Almighty and condemn Catholicism as fit only for those who are either totally bereft of power or intending to abuse it. The final condition was that my father tell his wife in Hanoi everything and in so doing pass on my mother's deepest apologies.

My father agreed, and their contract sealed my entry into the world, with the stain on my face serving as evidence to all that a mistake had been made.

After I was born, my mother tried to revive her career. But her pictures were gloomy, almost macabre, and did not appeal to the buyers of the late 1980s and early 1990s who were looking for uplifting images.

New technologies also arrived, polymers that hardened in minutes rather than days and were easier to work with because their colour and sheen were predictable under all conditions. The factories that replaced the family stores in my home town could produce dozens of pictures a day: exact copies of girls in long tunics riding bikes, egrets in lotus ponds and boys on buffaloes playing the flute. Mother insisted that natural materials were far superior because the richness of their colours improved over time, while the artificial products would fade. But this only made her look outmoded and desperate.

It was not long before she turned to the factories for work. But her heart was not in it, and it became impossible for her to copy the same image over and over again. To make matters worse, she was castigated by her boss whenever she introduced the slightest creative deviation. After a few months the new polymer toxins started to sear her skin, causing sores on her hands, which meant that she could not hold me when I was small.

Eventually, Mother gave up and began helping Gran sell sticky rice and volunteering at the pagoda. When I commenced school, she relented and accepted some money from my father, but it was sent to my grandmother so that she would never have to see or touch it.

It was not until I was 17 that we moved north and my parents were finally married, although my mother maintained that she would have been just as content to wait longer. Only a few of my father's friends and colleagues were present at the ceremony and reception. I remember it was more solemn than romantic or celebratory. Everyone knew it was a marriage of redemption. To this day my mother refuses to lie in the same bed as my father, asserting that there is no room for both her and the spirit of his first wife.

Mai – she has the same name as me – lives in a serviced apartment two districts away, but once a week comes for my peanut sticky rice. She says she likes it because it is a little sweeter than others and because my sesame garnish reminds her of the old country. I always stock a few Styrofoam containers for when I run out of bowls or banana leaves – Mai insists on eating out of one because she believes it's cleaner and more modern.

Although I would never turn anyone away, sometimes I wish Mai didn't come as frequently as her once-weekly visit. She sits at my stall for up to an hour and has a knack for getting on my nerves and embarrassing me in front of customers. I hardly get a word in with her and when I do, she reminds me that more and more I sound like a 'hiccupping and hissing Hanoian' who's lost her Southern roots.

'Let me tell you, I'm sick to death of these Northerners. I'm sick of their stinginess and uncivilised ways. There's money and opportunities everywhere in Vietnam and yet here I am living in a city of beggars and bumpkins.'

I was glad that everyone in earshot chose to ignore her.

'You know, if it wasn't for Joe [she never neglected to mention her Canadian husband] there's no way I would be in this swamp. Of course Joe doesn't want to be here either. He says that no one really wants to do business up here; there's too much red tape and Northerners have a no-can-do attitude to everything. He doesn't trust them. Neither do I. They're never straight with you. They're polite and official to your face, but stab you in the back at the very first opportunity. Joe says that Southerners are much better to deal with because they are used to Western ways and expectations. He tells me the only reason anyone does business in the North is the government compels them to. You know, the Northerners are dragging us Southerners down and taking advantage of us. My German friend Gertrude says the same thing about the East Germans, except the difference here is we lost the war and are forced to prop up the victors!'

I didn't say anything, but tried to make apologetic eye contact with my customers and somehow convey that I did not agree with my namesake.

Mai is not the only Southerner I know who is suspicious and scathing of Northerners. Before we left for Hanoi to join my father, Gran informed me that I had no chance of selling her rice 'up there' because Northern tastebuds were poorly evolved.

'Their tongues are caked in buffalo dung', she said. 'They don't know what good food is and never will because they're so closed-minded. And I should know. After all, I married one!'

'Your grandfather was from Nghe An province, where people are wiry and proud – they're wooden carp eaters. It's true, you know, people from there were so poor and proud that they used to put a wooden fish in the middle of the table to fool passers-by and perhaps even themselves that they could afford meat!'

Gran had never been beyond Nha Trang, but was resolute that there was no one worth meeting and nothing worth doing in the North.

She compared the *cai luong* operas of the South, which we often watched on video discs at home with the *cheo* musical plays on television. The modern *cai luong* operas were filled with light, emotion and beauty, while the primitive *cheo* folktales were in her view closer to re-education than entertainment.

'The Northerners don't know anything about spontaneity, fun or romance; everything is a lesson for them about the nation's 5,000-year history or the glorious Uncle Ho, blessed be his name. Give me a break! Those Northerners, they might be able to mobilise for war, but that's all they're good for. There's no reason for you and your mother to move up there: I pity you for doing so.'

I like to think that that was Gran's way of saying she would miss me.

Despite Gran's warnings, I was optimistic about moving to Hanoi and thought I would fit in okay, or at least I would not be any more isolated than I was in my home town. I had just finished high school and was not sure what to do with myself – I'd considered opening my own sticky rice stall as a tribute to Gran, but also to get away from her. My father told me over the phone that he could put up the money to get me going and that he even had a corner in mind in front of an underpants store owned by his friend. The store didn't open until 9 and its owner did not mind me occupying the pavement in front of it because I would draw customers.

After arriving in Hanoi, I set about establishing my little business without delay and planned to market myself and my rice as distinctively Southern: 'Mai's sticky rice, all the way from the parrot's beak peninsula.' It took me a few weeks to locate all the ingredients that I needed, and was shocked to find that the prices were much higher than they were at home. Nonetheless, I hoped that people would be willing to pay more for something a little exotic and, in my view at that time, better. My first few days of business were an utter failure. After that, I tried to lure customers in with free samples. Most people were polite enough to try it, but moved on without making a purchase. A few kind souls bought my sticky rice out of pity and no doubt discarded it soon afterwards. Others were openly critical. One woman said my Chinese sausage rice was far too oily and that by adding garlic and coriander to it I was trying to poison people rather than feed them. Another customer said my orange-coloured rice garnished with desiccated coconut made his eyes sore and his teeth fizz – eating my food reminded him of the time he accidentally swallowed a cigarette butt. Most depressing of all was the unveiling of my majestic durian-flavoured sticky rice, which cleared the pavement of pedestrians like a bomb scare.

During those early days, there were moments when I thought Gran was right about me and the North. Maybe I belonged here even less than in my home town. And maybe the Northerners were sadists, just like Gran said, only liking foods that are excessively sour, horrifically salty or numbingly bland.

My father was more constructive, suggesting that because my rice was too sweet for the Northern palate, I might have more luck selling it in the evenings as a dessert. This too, however, was unsuccessful because people in Hanoi by and large saw sticky rice as a morning food, just as vermicelli with grilled pork strips and paddies or deep-fried tofu dipped in fermented prawn paste were for lunch alone. That was simply the way things were done and, even if no one knew why, there was no good reason to do otherwise. As one fellow commented, 'your rice is special' – he was using this word to be kind – 'but not so special that I want to eat it for dinner. I'm far more likely to crave sticky rice at 3 am than I am at 6 pm.'

And so I caved in and did as Hanoians do, selling just three types of simple sticky rice in the morning: corn, peanut, and pummelled mung bean.

Even then, it took some time for my business to get going. At first the only reason customers came to my stall was that it was convenient: the sticky rice was much like everyone else's. Once I was established and making a small profit, I began to think about how to make my product more of a drawcard, not so much by introducing alien elements, but rather by enhancing what was already there.

In this regard, all my efforts to find the ingredients for my Southern-style rice were not in vain, as it meant that I knew almost all of the city's wholesalers and markets. On Wednesday afternoons, I would catch the number seven bus to a warehouse over the river, not far from the airport, which sold 25 kilogram bags of Three Chrysanthemum brand glutinous rice at a good price. Hauling the rice home was always a challenge, particularly in the afternoon on a crowded bus. But that rice and my attention to detail have helped me to get along.

I also buy banana leaves from a woman who washes them very carefully – who understands that any customer who finds grit in their rice will not come back for at least a month and that encountering a grub is the end of the relationship altogether. For a few weeks in summer, I change from banana leaves to lotus leaves, which add a delicate nutty scent to my rice. There are other products like soy milk and eggs that I have delivered to me each morning, but even then I am demanding of my suppliers – anything substandard or late is sent back without payment, with an occasional curse that would make my Gran proud.

One of my important innovations came four years ago when, to my great fortune, an elderly cousin of the woman who runs the underpants store behind my stall came to the city for a visit. She was from the village of Phu Gia, which is famous for its sticky rice. Because I had grown close to the underpants store owner, her cousin was happy to pass on to me a few trade secrets that had been in her family for generations. She taught me the value of steaming my rice twice: the first time until it is 80 per cent cooked – no more, no less; then it has to be sprayed with water so the grains contract and retain their freshness overnight. In the morning, I steam the rice again until the aroma is sweet but not syrupy and the grains are soft but not gooey. There are practical benefits of this technique too because, while it takes up more time, most of the cooking is done the day before and not in the early hours of the morning. Most importantly, however, the result is delicious, which my customers attest to, even if they don't know exactly why. And of course when they ask me, I do not let on.

The strange thing is that in the last two years, after mastering Northern-style sticky rice and coming to appreciate its gentle flavours and textures, I am rediscovering my Southern cooking. I think that the time might now be right for my customers to try something different. After all, if they can manage Indian, Japanese, Korean and Taiwanese food, surely they can enjoy popular dishes from their own country? And so on weekends I have begun selling stewed pork and boiled eggs cooked Southern style. And I am proud to say that it is selling well, with some customers requesting a sprinkling of sesame sugar or the occasional sprig of coriander with their meals.

Even more peculiar is that the last time I returned to my home town, Gran's sticky rice did not live up to my fond memories of it. It was a little too sweet and oily for me. Of course I never told her this. But it made me wonder, not for the first time, whether I would ever find a place to belong or, for that matter, a husband.

For a long time my mother did not want me to have anything to do with young men, who she collectively referred to as 'defilers'.

After I had my first period, Mother explained to me that my body was developing so that I could have babies, but also that I had to be very careful. Until the time was right for me to start a family, I had to protect my chastity with all my might. For her, however, the corrupting touch of boys was not the biggest problem.

'There's a voice that many women begin hearing at around your age', my mother told me. 'It tells us that we can do anything and make our own choices, that we are no better or worse than men, that our desires exist to be fulfilled, and that the world is there for us to conquer and enjoy. Don't listen to that voice, Mai. It's the voice of maniacs and floozies.'

I understood her concern, but have never once heard that voice or found it hard to avoid young men. For this reason, by the time I turned 20, mother's attitude towards me and men changed. And in recent years she's become convinced that her primary responsibility is to find me a suitable husband.

Naturally, Mother would prefer it if I left it up to her. But while I know that she has my interests at heart, I have made it clear that the thought of committing for a lifetime to someone whom I hardly know is more frightening than dying alone. My father agrees with me, largely because his first marriage resulted from an alignment of families rather than of souls and, as far as he's concerned, this was the major cause of hardship in his life. Unfortunately, he has no say in this matter.

Of course I don't want to be alone, but I've always thought that there is someone out there who has a place in his heart for me. And in the story I make up about us, we come together by good fortune and not by my mother's design. So lately, when there are no customers and I have nothing to do, instead of making up stories about strangers I find myself searching through the throngs of people for him. I guess that a fifth of the men who pass by are of an acceptable age, and that a fair proportion of them are single. And among all of those people I sense that he is out there, running an errand for his family, going to work, perhaps even studying at university. But at the same time he is searching for me as fervently as I am looking for him. Sometimes I even feel a little sorry for him and worry that his yearning might be more angst-filled than mine.

Lately, Mother has not been content for me to watch and wait.

And so, my mother has been praying to as many spirits as possible – except for the holy Catholic one – to bring forth my soul mate or indeed anyone who she considers acceptable. Most of the time I have simply followed her instructions in this regard, even when it seems pointless or embarrassing. Often I've had to remind myself that we're united in our goal even if our ideas of how to get there are different.

For a time I considered joining an internet chat site or taking up tango classes to meet people. I also made an effort to cover my birthmark with makeup. But Mother assured me that the problem was not physical.

'Look at your cousin Thao. She is as fat and sweaty as a swine, has a pock-marked face and is wildly over-educated. Yet suitors are tripping over themselves to get to her.'

By my mother's account, both the mark on my face and my un-marriageability are symptoms of the same malaise: a heart that's chained to a past life.

And so, we appealed to the ancestors for assistance, first at the altar in our home and then at my father's family's communal house, which is a three-hour bus ride from the city. These visits were tense and uncomfortable – my father's family have never really accepted us.

When this did not yield results, we turned to a diviner who my father had recommended, a one-time calligrapher who had almost died of rabies after being bitten by a monkey on Cat Ba Island. Master Zin, as he had become known, had well and truly stopped breathing and was pronounced dead, but somehow came back to life. More miraculous still was that he remained connected to the other side. Master Zin thus gave up his calligraphy to focus on soul calling, and established a highly successful consultancy specialising in finding the skeletons of long-lost soldiers. Such was his industriousness that he developed his special ability by studying Chinese astrology and numerology, which allowed him not only to tap into past lives, but also to predict the future.

Master Zin gripped my wrists and stared into my pupils with such intensity that I dared not move, even though my instinct was to squirm free. Then he wrote down my name and birthday in Chinese characters on a large piece of paper, from the corner of which he tore off a small square. Master Zin commanded me to wait until he and my mother had left the room. I then had to write one word in capital letters on the square scrap of paper before scrunching it up into a small ball. It was important, he stressed, that I drop the paper ball back on to the piece of paper exactly ten times, each time marking where it settled. Finally, I had to swallow the paper ball before calling for him to return.

I thought about what to write for some time before settling on '*DAT*' [to attain], a simple word that's milky white and granular like MSG, and which captured my heartfelt desire for companionship. The tiny ball fell off the paper twice, so I repeated the step before swallowing it as instructed. Master Zin returned with a cup of green tea and turned to the piece of paper like a surgeon examining an x-ray. He connected the dots and closed his eyes as he considered my place in the cosmos. Then he picked up the pen and began writing in a slow and deliberate fashion as if he was receiving a message by Morse code.

I watched on in awe as he wrote '*DAT*' in my handwriting. He showed me the piece of paper as if the result was never in doubt.

Master Zin then turned to my mother with his eyes downcast. 'She has a heavy debt to pay.'

'I knew it! Please tell us. What else do you see?'

'Her "spirit root" is tied to a man from a previous life, a jilted lover who seeks revenge. Under these circumstances, she has no chance of finding a husband. The solution is not yet clear to me, but I have no doubt that this is the problem.'

My mother thanked him profusely and offered him a box of dried plums and an envelope with money in it. He took the plums, but refused the money, saying that it was a favour to my father.

As we left he whispered to me, 'Good luck, young lady. And by the way, steer clear of young men named "Dat".'

With the diagnosis established, our next step was to visit the local pagoda, where my mother explained the problem to one of the senior nuns. She looked me over, all the while shaking her head with a mixture of pity and disapproval before convening with the other nuns. I was then led towards the main altar in the pagoda and instructed to sit before the statue of the Buddha in lotus position. My mother knelt beside me and, before I knew it, a red satin sheet was thrown over me. I later learned that this would make it harder for the vengeful spirit to seek me out and sabotage the procedure. 'Stay still and be silent!' I heard my mother urge as she placed a board on my head and held it steady. The board was stacked with boxes of my favourite treat, Choco-Pies.

I closed my eyes, smelt burning incense and listened to the striking of the wooden fish-shaped drum and rhythmic chanting of the nuns.

> Blessed Buddha Amitabha,
> Repel the spirit of the jilted lover
> That haunts this poor girl.
> She and her mother have suffered enough
> For the sinful desires of their past lives.
> We beseech you to grant her happiness.
> We beseech you to give her mother peace of mind.
> Witness our humble offering.
> Bless us with your infinite light.

A week or so after this, an aunt from my home town sent my mother a wooden amulet that had been soaked in porcupine pheromones and blessed by a Khmer shaman. Mother instructed me to wear the amulet on the outside of my clothes to repel the evil spirit, but it looked so gruesome that I tucked it under my shirt. The only outcome of that effort was a rash that took several months and 300,000 dong worth of ointment to clear.

Finally, at great expense and effort, my mother enlisted the services of a spirit medium who was famous for his ability to remedy women's problems. This involved my taking two days off work and travelling to Nam Dinh province with my mother, where we met eight other women who would also take part in the ceremony. The medium's assistant told us he always conducted ceremonies for nine women at a time because this was a feminine and maternal number – for me nine was tan brown and feathery. Five of the women were struggling to conceive and the other three had baby girls but dearly wanted to give birth to a boy. As Mother and I spoke to them it was clear they were stressed and desperate and, while I was sorry for them, part of me was even more sorry for myself: all of them had husbands and some had young daughters to love. Who did I have?

I had read a little about spirit mediums and had even witnessed a similar ceremony in Hanoi from a distance. This medium was a dainty fellow who was about my age, perhaps a little younger. He was dressed as Princess Lieu Hanh, daughter of the Jade Emperor, who since ancient times was renowned for her power to control men. He was beautiful in a way that made women jealous and men uncomfortable. His skin was perfectly smooth and clear, his plump eyes were highlighted with mascara, and his silky black hair was tied back in a neat ponytail. The medium's lips were painted deep red, but he did not look lustful or comedic like many of the Thai ladyboys I had seen on television. I suppose he looked the way a woman ought to look: elegant and assured.

The nine of us sat in an arc with the medium standing in the middle. In front of him was an altar dedicated to the Four Palaces made up of earth, heaven, water, mountain. Then the assistant turned on a CD of traditional music and pop songs to which the medium chanted and began to sway. A few minutes later, his movements became frenzied – he began kicking his feet out and spinning around at great speed so that his red satin gown flew up in the air. The fake gold and jewels he was wearing jangled so vigorously that I worried they would come loose and hurt someone.

It was half an hour before I could relax and forget about how much the spirit medium was charging my parents and how disappointed my sticky rice customers would be that morning when they didn't find me on my corner. Not long afterwards, I was surprised to find myself having fun and clapping along with the music. Some of the other women even hollered and whooped as if they were in a nightclub.

After two hours the medium had fully transformed into the Princess Lieu Hanh. Her eyes were rolled back and her sentences were slurred and old-fashioned. She had a regal, haughty pose; occasionally she giggled and at other times she wept for no reason. Near the end of the day, the Princess stopped and knelt before each of us. She clasped our hands in hers – despite all the physical activity, they were cool and dry – and then presented us with a small enchanted charm that would ward off the evil spirits: a cigarette holder, a comb, a candle and, for me, a yellow wooden bead from an old necklace. The entire process took five hours and by the end of it I am sure something supernatural had occurred because the medium never once looked fatigued until he broke out of his trance, collapsed in his chair, and told the assistant to fetch him some mineral water and two bottles of beer.

In the end, I'm not sure whether the charm worked or whether it somehow combined with our exertions and prayers. What I know for sure is that less than a week after encountering Princess Lieu Hanh, Dat came into my life.

In fact, I knew of Dat before I went to see the spirit medium. He had recently joined the pack of motorbike taxi drivers who worked next to my stall. Some of the drivers had been on that corner for much longer than me, but I never spoke to them unless they were buying my rice.

There were five of them before Dat came along. As custom demanded, they parked their rear wheels to the kerb so that customers knew they were for hire. But from what I could see they did little to attract business and much to discourage it. The drivers seemed to think the best way to bring in customers was to badger and harass them, particularly women.

'Where are you headed with that nice fat arse? Hop on to my machine and I'll take you for a bumpy ride.'

'Hey little sister! What are you studying? Put your books away and I'll teach you a few lessons I picked up on the internet.'

Their crassness no longer bothered me, but I've never understood why they were surprised or even offended when their advances were ignored.

'Syphilitic whore! You'll come back begging tonight.'

When there were no customers around, which was most of the day, the drivers lay across their motorbike seats napping or reading the paper. They discussed football games with such urgency and expertise that it was as if they were coaching the national team. And they were constantly betting with bookies and each other on everything – from how many medals Vietnam would win at the ASEAN games to how long it would be until a backpacker walked by.

When it came to the intricate science that was the lottery system, the drivers were forever on the verge of a breakthrough that would allow them to predict the results and never have to work again.

Whereas I saw the street as my workplace, they treated it as their home, which meant they had no qualms about shaving or popping blackheads in their motorbike mirrors, or urinating in the gutter – sometimes in teams. Once the neighbourhood cell leader politely asked them to use the public toilet, which was only a short drive away. He tried to reason with them, explaining that this would be far more hygienic and civil for everyone and might improve their business.

One of the older drivers sardonically thanked the cell leader and responded that 'it is natural and refreshing for a man to piss outside. That's how our ancestors have done it ever since the Dragon Lord stuck his sword in the Alpine Princess. As a man and patriot, I consider pissing outside to be our sacred right and national pastime. If we stopped doing it then we might as well cut off our pricks and plant magnolias in the holes where they used to be.'

The two youngest drivers were heavily tattooed and assumed to have gang connections. The cell leader did not press his case.

Dat was a distant cousin to one of the young drivers. He had a rumbling voice and was never discrete, so it was hard for me not to find out about his background. Indeed, he recounted his life to the other drivers in daily instalments as if it was a soap opera. His mother had abandoned him as an infant and he grew up in the motorbike garage where his father worked. Dat could ride a motorbike before he could ride a bicycle, and by the age of 17 was competing in illegal races under the name of 'Night Storm'. He had had many victories and by his own account was the most skilful driver in the city. But Dat was also reckless and prone to accidents, and had recently become embroiled in a race-fixing scandal that resulted in an outburst of gang warfare. For now he was lying low, but was still on the lookout for a way to return to racing. Dat lived by the motto that if he made it to the age of 30, then something had gone wrong.

I remember after he first arrived one of the older drivers sneering, 'What sort of hotshot drives a humdrum piece of shit motorbike like that?'

Dat replied that the Honda Future was the only motorbike worth racing, and he was grateful that so many people didn't know this because it allowed him to buy them cheaper. Apparently, the Future was perfectly balanced, ever reliable, and offered more power than other standard machines without much more weight. To be sure, the bike was made to appeal to family men, but it could easily be stripped back and modified. Anyone who knew anything about motorbike racing could tell you that, in the right hands, a Honda Future was to be respected and even feared.

'Much respect to you and your scooter, though, older brother', he said to his colleague. 'I've ridden a few nice automatics like that. They're ideal if you need under-seat storage for your purse and want to keep your knees together so that people don't see your panties. The only problem I found riding them is that it feels like your genitals are turning outside-in, so that if you don't get off quickly you'll end up with a vagina that gapes more than your helmet hole.'

The other drivers quickly grew fond of Dat and came to see him as both their leader and mascot. They admired him for being tough and dangerous. His collarbone was shattered when a competitor kicked him during a race, causing him to crash into a light pole. Another time he fractured his tailbone while driving home drunk from a victory with three girls on the back of his bike. A branch speared his thigh in an off-road race, and there were burns across his arms and legs from skidding along the asphalt and being pressed up against the exhaust pipes of his opponents' bikes. He readily showed his scars to the other drivers along with anyone who was interested, taking off his shirt or pulling down his pants with pride as if he were displaying wartime wounds.

The drivers were also impressed by his tricks, which Dat was always eager to demonstrate. He drove across the street balanced on his front wheel; leapt over sleeping dogs and homeless people; and once zipped in and out of the traffic with a bowl of steaming green bean pudding balanced on his head. His favourite stunt involved placing two cups of my soy milk an inch or so apart on one of my stools and then driving towards it at high speed before screeching to a stop so that his front tyre tenderly nudged the stool and the cups clinked without falling over.

Whenever he pulled this trick off, Dat would grin at me, expecting applause and adoration. 'Just make sure you give me four clams for the soy milk', is the most I ever gave him.

Dat was especially admired because of his sexual conquests, which he recounted in graphic detail. Apparently, there was always a supply of groupies at the finish line of big races, most of whom Dat had hooked up with at least once. Of course he had had many girlfriends, but none of them were steady or serious. I heard him say that motorbike racers referred to these girls as mufflers because they were hot, easy to replace, and preferably silent.

He often talked about 'couples racing' in which scantily clad young women rode on the back.

'Those motorbike babes are amazing, ab-so-lute-ly crazy. Some are poor sluts who need the money for their addictions or to pay back family debts. But there's also plenty of good girls from respectable families. They spend their days studying at some big university – marketing, international business, whatever, and it makes them desperate for a thrill at night. Just last year one little number told me how fed-up she was with chasing grades, listening to her parents and taking the safe option. When she sat behind me she whipped me like a racehorse to go faster and faster. As I was pushing the bike to the limit she reached down and grabbed my tool, waving it in my pants like a windscreen wiper. Those are the girls to go for – it's all about the four virtues and three loyalties during the day, then after dusk anything goes. No helmets or protection for them, motorbike or hotel room.'

And with this he gyrated and thrust his hips as the other drivers hollered.

As much as Dat appalled me, I couldn't help but notice that he had a positive impact on the drivers. He suggested that during quiet times they play Chinese Chess rather than cards and split into teams so that there was always a substitute when someone was called away. This made for less gambling and bickering; as did his simple idea that they set up an informal taxi rank rather than hustle every customer – young women and tourists remained hotly contested. I knew they had tried this before, but there was no one with Dat's charisma to make it work. And the more I watched him, the more I realised he was in some ways an exemplary taxi driver. He didn't drink on the job, always wore his helmet – a silver full-faced one embossed with golden lightning bolts on the sides – and he carried a spare for customers. He drove very slowly with elderly clients and anyone else who asked nicely. I must admit I even considered hiring him myself.

So, eventually, I too fell for Dat. And to this day I am not sure whether I chose to yield to his charm or, like untethered sampans in a rushing stream, we were destined to crash together.

At first Dat tried to court me using phrases from *Kieu*, the epic poem about a star-crossed heroine who has to sell herself to save her family. With a yellow rose in each hand he proclaimed that we were 'two kindred spirits tied together in a knot that could not be yanked loose' and compared us to 'blossoming flowers waiting for the moon to rise'.

'Do you think I don't know those lines?' I told him. 'I'm surprised they ever worked on your groupies and cheap whores. They've got no chance on me. Next time try reading the poem before quoting it eh? The flowers show how true love is expressed through restraint and sacrifice – things you have no idea about. And one more thing – yellow is my least favourite colour!' My grandmother would have approved. It was important for Dat to know I was no pushover. And I took more than a little pleasure in deflating his ego.

Dat gave up on classical poetry, but not on verse. 'What you have to realise', he asserted one week later, 'is that we are like a pair of flip flops.' Apparently, he was the right one and I was the left, but we had been imprinted by the same master and were destined to travel the same path. If one of us was broken or lost, there was no hope for the other; but if we moved together we could go as far as we wanted.

I told him I knew that poem from trashy women's magazines and asked what he was doing reading them.

His next strategy was to assert that I, indeed both of us, had no choice in the matter: our coming together was as natural and necessary as David Beckham and Posh Spice's; Tommy Ngo and Linda Trang Dai's; or Lee Byung-hun and Lee Min-jung's. It was a matter of when and not if. The earth would not spin smoothly until we two were finally one.

Dat apparently adored my lingering Southern accent and the South generally. 'You see, we are not really coming together like most young couples; we are being reunified; like the country was in 1975, but with more amity and good will.'

I asked him what his zodiac sign was. 'I am a horse, born at high noon in the hour of horses', Dat said with his chest protruding.

I could have guessed as much; like so many horses he was proud, fast-talking, fun-loving, and prone to disaster.

'Hah! I'm a cat and was born in the feline morning hours. How could someone as reserved and thoughtful as me get on with you? So much for our union being written in the stars. And I'm older than you. We're hardly compatible at all.'

And probably because I enjoyed being on the front foot, this is when I revealed to him that I had been warned by Master Zin to beware of men named 'Dat'.

'That's no problem because "Dat" is only my middle name. My full name is "Vu Dat Kim", but I gave up the "Kim" a long time ago because it's a girl's name. But honestly, older sister Mai, screw all the fortune tellers, superstitions, cosmic signals and what other people think. Do what I do. Follow your heart. Go with your gut. When you are true to yourself, you'll come up with the right answer: that we would be really good together.'

The other drivers couldn't understand Dat's persistence. 'Why waste your time with the sticky rice girl?' I overheard them asking.

'She's a frigid bitch who hasn't flashed us a nipple in all these years. There are thousands of plumper and easier birds to snare.'

'I've never seen her with a man. She's probably a dyke', another one of them said. 'One thing's for sure, she's a prawn: her body's nice enough but her face is frightful and her head's full of shit!'

I gasped with outrage and that's when Dat realised I had overheard them. In retrospect, I wonder if he had staged the whole scene.

'Shut your fuckin' noodle hole! You're talking about my future girlfriend and who knows what else?' To all who cared to listen he pronounced that it was *he* who was out of *my* league and that the mark on my face was a beauty mark that was sometimes shaped like a butterfly and at other times reminded him of a tender steaming pork bun broken open and ready to eat.

It was around then that I started to wonder whether Dat and I might after all have a future together. However, it was not long afterwards that his advances started to wane. 'Remember, Mai', he said, 'those who are coy with their suitors end up sleeping alone. Would you rather hug your pillow at night or me?' To this question I had no good answer.

So in the end I said yes to Dat because he made me feel desired, and I was worried that if I did not give him a chance I would never have that feeling again.

Dat took me to a new Vincom shopping centre for our first date. While I had gone past shopping centres many times, I had never stepped inside one. He did not have to know this of course, and so when he asked me whether I had been to the centre before I replied, 'No, but I've been to others much bigger and better.' And while admittedly I was excited as we passed through the entrance and I felt that blast of air conditioning, my excitement was easily contained and short-lived because I had seen shopping malls on the television and heard people talking about them many times. The cavernous lobby, the thoroughfares soaked with fluorescent light and aisles of merchandise did little to impress me.

It was also the first time that I ever rode on an escalator and had been in an elevator, which I also kept from Dat. He assured me that he often went to malls, but still seemed to find a boyish thrill in such expeditions. On the escalator, he pushed his foot along the side railing as if he was on a skateboard and wanted it to go faster. And in the elevator he repeatedly pressed the button to close the door even though people were still trying to rush in.

While going to the mall was not an earth-trembling experience, it was an enjoyable enough beginning to our relationship. Dat was keenly interested in the electronics stores and waited impatiently as I examined the food prices in the supermarket. I took satisfaction in seeing that I could buy just about everything for less at the market. Some of the items on sale, however, were much cheaper, and so I was heartened when Dat offered to carry around a 10 kilogram bag of washing detergent that I had my eye on.

When I saw him shifting the bag from one arm to the other, I suggested that we take turns holding it.

'Not on your life. No girl of mine does the heavy lifting. Just make sure you pay attention to my bulging muscles. And at some stage I'll expect a thank you kiss.'

Dat had intended to buy us dinner at the food court, but I found both the offerings and prices unappetising. Much of it was premade and the place smelt of ammonia. 'Let's go somewhere else', I suggested. 'Take me to a favourite place of yours. That way I'll get to know you better.'

He insisted he was no cheapskate and that he wanted to treat me with something more than just washing detergent. I suggested we share a drink at the mall and then move on. He agreed but refused to share, ordering a beer for himself and lemonade for me.

Upon leaving the mall we made our way to a workers' outdoor buffet that opened in the evenings for young couples and families. Although he had been there before, Dat was wide-eyed at the sight of all the dishes before him. When they asked us what we wanted he greedily pointed to the crispy silkworms, deep fried egg, omelette, stewed pork and chicken drumsticks, so that he needed a separate plate for his rice. Even then he insisted on getting the complimentary crab mince and spinach soup, along with a healthy scoop of peanuts.

Both of us were a little startled by the price. 'Are you sure that's right, lady?' Dat asked. 'Didn't cost so much last time.'

'Inflation', the woman responded.

'A "rip off" is what I'd fuckin' call it. How much did you charge that guy over there with all the prawns and liver?'

'Share it with your girlfriend if you don't have enough money or give it back for all I care, but decide quickly, son. There're people waiting in line who aren't so tight.'

I clasped Dat's forearm to pull him back slightly. 'It's okay. She's telling the truth. My prices are going up too and you've chosen all meat dishes so it's bound to cost a little more.'

I ordered some steamed kohlrabi, bean sprouts and pickled cabbage and then lied to Dat that I was not eating meat that day.

'Do you want some tofu in tomato sauce?' he asked. 'Tofu's good for women, you know, dampens their desire. On second thought, maybe you're better off without it!' And with that he was smiling again, showing off those incandescent teeth. He even gave the woman a small tip.

He munched away at his dinner and would have finished much faster than me if he was not talking at the same time, mostly about his motorbike racing and how he wanted to win a few more titles so that he had enough money to open his own garage.

'I thought you had a death wish. What happened to not making it to the age of 30?' I said to him with a wry smile. He seemed surprised and embarrassed that I already knew so much about him.

'That was just a bit of chest-thumping for the lads. I'm no different to anyone else really. I just want a little more money in my pocket so that I can save up for an apartment of my own. And you know what? I want to have a family someday, be respectable and all that. I could really make something out of myself. I just need someone to give me a chance, for the wheel of fate to turn in my favour. There's no way I'm going to be taxiing people around all my life. But don't make this all about me. Tell me about you, Mai, your favourite colour, singer, your dreams …'

I couldn't remember anyone asking me to talk about myself. And for the first time that evening, I was taken aback. When I finally started talking – about my grandmother and my home town, my talented parents and step-siblings – I was surprised to see that Dat was listening. His dark, shiny eyes were focused on my face, which made me more than a little uncomfortable at first. But by the end of our meal I was used to his gaze and even welcomed it. I felt as if I'd spent my life looking down at the ground, embarrassed about my birthmark and my past, and all of a sudden I had reason to look up and at someone.

We climbed back on his motorbike and bought some sugarcane juice on the way to Long Bien Bridge. This time I sat a little closer to him so that the inside of my thighs touched his body ever so gently. To be honest, I was giddy with elation, but did my best to ensure he did not know how glad I was to be close to him. There was no way that I was going to be just another motorbike groupie. My mother used to say that she could tell a good young woman by how she sat on a motorbike. 'A decent girl rides with her back straight and her head pinned back, like a lioness on the watch. Most girls bend forward to hug their boyfriends with their spines bowed like a dog taking a dump.'

'Lioness, lioness, be a regal lioness', I reminded myself, 'not a crapping dog.'

At the bridge we parked far from the other couples and rowdy groups of youth who were snacking on dried squid and sipping energy drinks. On the railing I could make out a few padlocks with initials scratched into them that had been fixed to the bridge by lovers. Couples marked their commitment by casting the keys into the river. Why had they bothered, I wondered, given the widely reported 'locks of love' debacle in which hundreds of youth had secured their locks to the bridge, only for the authorities to decide they were an eyesore that threatened to bring down a structure that had survived American bombs. I wondered how the bridge master felt as he did his rounds with a monstrous bolt-cutter. Did he relish breaking the bonds that held together so many young lovers? Or perhaps he was a romantic and riven with guilt? Maybe there was a special room in his house where he glumly sifted through his treasure trove of broken locks.

Dat's lips and hands were expectant. I saw how his front teeth reflected the moonlight as they moved in towards me. I suspected even then that most of his teeth were fake, the originals having probably been broken in a motorbike accident.

'I've had a magical night. Let's not risk ruining it. No kissing for now, okay?'

'What makes you think I even wanted to?' Dat said. But I could see he was wounded.

I slapped him playfully on the shoulder and let my hand linger. We hugged. Perhaps it was too forward of me – no doubt my mother would not have approved – but I am sure that I was the one who initiated the embrace. I could have stayed like that all night, but Dat grew bored just hugging and broke free to suggest that we play a game.

He took out his mobile phone. 'You said you like listening to music. Let's see who knows their songs better. I've just loaded almost 1,000 new songs onto my phone. I'll put it on shuffle and we can see who can guess the song first.'

The speaker on his phone was small, so he had to hold it up to our ears with our cheeks pressing together and my hair blowing sideways tickling his neck and shoulders. Most of his collection was made up of rap songs and grunge, with a few rock ballads and K-pop tunes that I was more familiar with. When I heard the pop singer Only C's hit 'I Don't Want My Gifts Back', I couldn't help but think of the salacious film clip in which the singer's ex-girlfriend strips down to her underwear in the street. And I was surprised to catch one of Thuy Linh's songs from her 'No Hurry' CD, which I think Dat was self-conscious about because it clashed with his tough guy image.

'No idea how that song got on there', he said, before quickly shuffling to the next one.

Despite not liking Dat's music, my special abilities allowed me to identify them after just a few seconds. At first Dat was impressed. Then his competitive spirit kicked in and he insisted I was fast, but often got the songs wrong. A quick glance at his phone proved this was not the case. Soon I was enjoying the game so much that I didn't notice his frustration until he remarked, 'Are you cheating or something? It's like there's some scary Bluetooth connection between your brain and my phone.'

I let him win a few in a row which seemed to lift his spirits. 'Smart, beautiful and talented – what else could a man ask for?' he said to me, just before his phone ran out of charge.

We sat silently for a little longer as other couples set off home, wispy clouds passed over the moon and the city lights dimmed. In the darkness and with my fringe falling over my face, I sensed that it was impossible for passers-by to identify anything distinguishing or different about me and us. They would see Dat and me sitting there and guess that we were like any other lovers. They would think we belonged together.

A week later we ate dinner hastily and rushed to the bridge, where I kissed him. Of course, I let him think that he was making a move on me; but in truth I orchestrated the entire affair, inviting him first to place his lips on my forehead, then on my cheek and finally on my mouth. At first I was so self-conscious of whether I was doing it properly that my kisses were rigid and thirsty. It was not until I relaxed that I tasted the peanuts on his breath and felt how the salt had made his lips a little dry but still plump like the flesh of a pomelo. I think Dat was surprised by my enthusiasm, although I'm sure he had been with far more assertive girls.

I clung to his shoulders and escaped into the creases of his shirt where I put aside all my concerns about what my parents would think, especially about his background and him being younger than me. We must have kissed for two hours, only intermittently talking about music, our work and our dreams. Even today, after all that has happened, I still cherish that night.

In fact, I adore much of the nine or so months – three full seasons – that we spent together. Dat was dashing and attentive. He opened doors, helped me pack up my stall, and bought me gifts: a hairpin in the shape of a seahorse, and a necklace with a lightning bolt pendant to match his night storm helmet. On International Women's Day, he twice gave me flowers as I sold my sticky rice. He took me out for Southern food – stir-fried beef and vermicelli and crepes filled with pork, shrimp and bean sprouts – and pretended to like the dishes even though I knew the fish sauce was too sweet for him. I remember late one night when we were eating beef noodle soup and there was only one vinegar-soaked chilli left in the jar. We both reached for it but Dat got there first. He smiled and then delicately placed it in my bowl. I bit the chilli into two and gave the larger piece to him. It was then that I knew we were a couple.

However, as the weeks and months went by it also became clear to me that Dat was the one who needed looking after. As much as he was gallant and strapping, he was also hot-headed and childish. He seemed to be driven by a conviction that the world had it in for him, so that when events did not go his way he took it personally.

This was most evident when Dat was on the road. Everyone and everything seemed to stop him from reaching an imaginary finish line. If there was a traffic jam then it had been somehow pre-programmed to ruin his day. When he was pulled over and fined, it was always the fault of the police, who had him in their crosshairs because he was young and dangerous looking. Even shards of glass had been placed on the road to cause him flat tyres at the worst possible time and place.

What bothered me most was that, in Dat's mind, being aggrieved gave him the right to do what he pleased to others. When he was stuck in a traffic jam he reached out and grabbed the luggage racks of other bikes so that he could inch forward. If he got caught, Dat offered either an impish grin or menacing snarl depending on the mood he was in. Like everyone else, Dat knew there was a three-second gap between when a set of traffic lights turned red and the other set turned green. For him this meant that all red lights were effectively shortened by at least six seconds and all green lights were extended by the same amount of time. Sitting on the back of his bike, I was astounded by his skill at weaving through intersections and petrified by what felt like a death wish.

One Sunday afternoon I asked Dat to take me to the supermarket where we went on our first date because I had heard they were selling extra-large bags of prawn floss. The shop was about to close and people were scurrying to get to the checkout and home to their families. We were relieved to find a register with only one person in front of us. However, just before my bag of prawn floss made its way to the front of the conveyor belt, the attendant called for assistance because she couldn't price an item. When that was resolved, we had to wait even longer as the elderly woman ahead of us rummaged through her purse in search of her loyalty card – to no avail. Added to this, she didn't have enough money because she had brought a 100,000 dong note thinking that it was 500,000.

Throughout all of this I could feel Dat's rage building and so I slipped my hand into his tightly folded arms and stood right up beside him in the hope of somehow absorbing his ire. As the old woman sorted through her groceries trying to decide what to leave behind, he broke free of me in the same way a horse might its trainer.

'Can't you see that there are people waiting, venerable grandmother?!' Then Dat turned back to me and hollered, 'She's so close to the grave you'd think she'd be in a hurry. What are we doing in this cattle yard anyway?! We're never coming back here again. No fuckin' way!'

I came up close to him again and whispered, 'Try to relax, please, it won't take much longer. We're in no rush anyway. And I thought you said you were going to stop swearing? You said you would do it for me.'

'I wouldn't be motherfuckin' swearing if we hadn't come here, come here for you and your fuckin' prawn floss!'

He grabbed the bag and with the same muscular arm that had carried my washing detergent on our first date, hurled it over my head and back into the store where it burst open on the floor.

After cleaning up the mess and paying for the floss, I eventually found him in the basement parking lot where he was lying on his motorbike looking up at the ceiling.

'Why are you always so calm?' he said without sitting up and looking at me. 'How can you put up with all of that ... that stuff, without saying a word? It's all so unfair.'

I didn't know what to say without hurting Dat's feelings and creating another scene. I wanted to tell him how ashamed I was to be with him that night. I wanted to say that back in the supermarket I had felt, not for the first time, frightened of him.

'I suppose things have never really gone my way. I've never expected to come first at anything or even beat anyone else. As I see it, the world's not meant to be fair so I don't worry about little things that go wrong. I just do my best and accept things as they are and take people as they come.'

It took a few seconds, but Dat responded with a pomelo kiss which I had no choice but to accept as his apology.

'I can help you. In fact, you can help me too. We'll do it together.' I said to him with as much enthusiasm as I could muster.

'No way, never. I'm not going through that again. What if I fail? I couldn't live with myself. And we both know that my chances are slim. They've got my number. The whole thing's rigged against me.'

Dat had been pulled over again. He had been speeding back from a job and in addition to paying the fine he had to grease the officer's palm because he did not have a licence. Most of the other motorbike drivers were also unlicensed and managed okay. But for Dat it was a big deal, largely because of his pride, but also because he broke the rules often, which meant that the traffic police were on the lookout for him.

All of this added a sense of urgency to my quest to reform Dat's ways.

Somehow, the idea had lodged in my head that if Dat could get his licence then he would also follow the rules, if only because he would not want to lose it after going to all that trouble. And perhaps I was being too hopeful, but I also thought that once he was licenced he would see that the authorities and everyone else were not always against him and that it was better to stay in line than to be always wrecking fences.

'I'm sure we can do it', I said to him. 'It will be fun and it'll bring us closer together. I can help you study for the theory section. You said yourself you hardly read the rule book last time, so it's no wonder you didn't pass. And you can help me with the practical test. You know, I'm very unsteady on the road.' This was true, although the main reason for my lack of confidence was inexperience. I never needed to ride a motorbike.

'Okay, but I can tell you what will happen now. You will pass and I will fail and then what will people say?'

'Then I will become a motorbike driver and you can sell sticky rice', I suggested.

He was not amused, but agreed to study with me that evening.

Dat was not good at written exams. It was not that he was stupid; but rather, deeply unsure of himself. 'You should have seen the examination room', he said with a shudder. 'All that tension, the prowling supervisors and the ticking clock on the front wall. It was too much for me to handle. I couldn't breathe let alone think. But you probably don't know what I'm talking about. What do you know about being stupid?'

We caressed and kissed many times that night, hardly reviewing a single page of the traffic rule book.

I reasoned that it was probably better for him to teach me first as this would build his confidence. And so the next day he took me to a parking lot near the old citadel lined with grand old Pacific walnut trees that dropped giant leaves and tiny white flowers.

Dat sat behind me, his arms and hands stretched over mine. I had told him that I knew how to ride, but he insisted that we start with the basics – what and where are the brakes, gears and indicators? I pretended to be interested as he went into far more mechanical detail than necessary and recounted anecdotes from his workshop and racing days. When he was done we held each other for a little before he allowed me to take control of his motorbike.

We began with accelerating and braking, using clumps of leaves on the ground as markers. Admittedly, my gear changes were jagged, I often missed the leaves by a wide margin; we almost ran into the gutter at the end of the parking lot, and Dat had to put his foot down several times to ensure we did not tip over at low speed. But this was largely because I hadn't ridden a motorbike for years. I needed some time and patience. It didn't help that I could feel Dat growing frustrated behind me.

'This would be much easier if you just got off the motorbike and let me try by myself', I suggested to him. 'I have ridden before, you know. I'm touched that you want to be right here to help me, but you're too heavy. It's hard for me to steer the motorbike – I'm just not as strong as you. Anyway, it's not like you can sit the test with me, right?'

He relented, and I improved immediately, so much so that I moved on to practising my figure eights, which were the first and by far the hardest part of the examination. I thought I was going well, but Dat shook his head, commenting that my figure eights were far too big and that I was going too slow. He demanded his motorbike back and showed me how fast he could do it, obviously expecting me to swoon over him like one of his groupies.

I tried again, but was still not up to his approval.

'It doesn't look like you're going to get much better', he said. 'Let's practise hugging and kissing instead.'

He couldn't understand why I was not in the mood.

Our studying for the theory component of the examination was also strained. Dat was always fidgeting and finding excuses. We couldn't study when the other drivers were around because he would lose face with them. My house was out of the question because I hadn't told my parents about us, and so was Dat's place because he did not get on with his uncle and aunt. One café was too crowded and noisy with truant students playing cards, and at another there was a waitress who Dat said unnerved him because he recognised her from his racing days and thought she might have connections with rival gangs.

The test was only a week away and Dat hadn't learnt a single rule or regulation. It was almost fortunate that he was pulled over by the police twice in one day, as this gave him the motivation he sorely needed.

And so we studied on a park bench during the day and at a frozen yoghurt bar at night, which was all but empty because the weather was turning cold. I encouraged him to envisage the faces of the traffic policemen as encouragement – 'Don't let them beat you!' And we developed a few tools and tricks to help him hold on to information. We associated series of answers with playlists of songs on his phone or the assembled parts of a motorbike. I reminded him that the licence was for life so that he never had to sit a test again provided he didn't get into trouble. And when no one was looking, I gave him a kiss for every answer he got right.

One night once we had closed our books and all that remained of our frozen taro yoghurt was a thin layer of lilac liquid, Dat told me that he was amazed at how good I was at storing things in my head and then somehow transferring them to his and making them stick.

'You are the smartest and most beautiful girl I have ever known', he said. 'No one has ever given me more.'

I raised my head, which was resting on his shoulder, and looked into his almond eyes before giving him one more gift. I told him about my special ability. I told him why I had kept it secret from him and everyone else. I told him about my mother and what had happened to her and rambled on about why it wasn't so bad, about how it helped me to remember things, about how nowadays it gave me more confidence than it did concern, and how it was a relief finally to tell someone. I told him that I was a synaesthete and asked him if, by any chance, he was one too.

Dat shook his head, vigorously. And of course it was silly of me to hope that he might be like me. Perhaps it was even too much to expect him to empathise with me given that I had sprung it upon him so suddenly. But I felt wounded and alone when all he said was, 'It's okay. I don't mind. If your birthmark doesn't bother me then neither should this.'

When the day finally arrived, I was exhausted from the many late nights studying with Dat before getting up in the early morning to sell sticky rice. The night before he had declared that he was not going to sit the examination because, while he may well survive past 30 years of age, life was still short and there was no sense in wasting another second of it looking at books and taking notes. We quarrelled, negotiated, reviewed a few questions and embraced. He said he would do it for me, but as I collapsed into bed that night I was far from certain.

We drove to the test in silence. I was just about the oldest person at the examination; the vast majority of the 206 people on the list of candidates were 18 or 19 years old. Most of them were clearly nervous, but comforted by being with their friends. They all looked middle-class and well educated, used to doing well at tests. We were corralled into a common room where the national anthem was played before we were given instructions. The theory exam would take place in six smaller rooms. I knew that Dat was haunted by the memory of his first failed attempt and the shame of having to leave before he could undertake the practical examination. As we filed off to our different rooms, I was far more concerned for him than I was for me. And in that moment I loved him as much as I would ever love anyone.

I had studied so much with Dat that I was done in less than 10 minutes and was surprised to see that I got one wrong, probably because I had filled in the wrong box accidentally. No one in my room seemed to fail.

Dat took his full allotment of time, and I imagined him looking up at the roof with thought lines on his forehead as he mouthed the titles of songs from playlists on his phone.

He finally emerged with his characteristic grin framed by two deep-set dimples. 'It's almost as good as winning a race', he said as he picked me up and spun me around.

But with Dat's troubles out of the way, I realised that mine had only just begun. Having focused on the theoretical examination, we had neglected the practical side. Failing was not really my concern; after all, I didn't need my licence. What petrified me was the thought of all those *Proactiv*-skinned youth scrutinising me.

As the instructions were explained to us again, my mind swirled and my stomach churned. I had never had so many people looking at me, mocking me, pitying me. My birthmark seemed to grow darker and larger under the glare of the mid-morning sun. I wanted to quit, run away.

Dat could see that I was queasy. 'Don't worry Mai. This is the easy part. I could do it with my eyes closed, which is not such a bad idea.'

I probably would have snuck out of the gates had I not been one of the first to be tested. At least the ordeal would soon be over, I reasoned.

There were two Honda Alphas to choose from. 'Take the red one, darlin'. It's much luckier', said the elderly attendant. He could see how edgy I was. 'Relax, remember to breathe, you can do it. Keep it in fourth and you'll be fine.'

After thanking him I climbed onto the red one, but only took it up to second gear because I knew that bunny-hopping might only result in a penalty, but stalling meant an immediate fail. It was a bad mistake, because I could not manage the sensitive throttle and as I stuttered around the figure eight my front wheel crossed over the guiding lines several times. As I stared down at the dashboard display I could just make out my reflection and thought of all those people looking at me. I tried to focus on the road as Dat had had mentioned to me minutes before, and totally forget about the motorbike as if I was just walking along. The number 8 was a warm, yellow-orange with the texture of coconut husks. The second time around I went up to third gear, which was far smoother, and although I was still slow and uncertain, the result was close to perfect.

After emerging from the figure eights, I had to ride along a straight line right past a panel of judges, which was nerve-racking, but when I looked up I was encouraged to see that they were barely paying attention. My arms stopped wobbling by the time I turned around and was weaving in and out of the chicanes. Finally, I passed over the series of speed bumps that led me out of the compound, around and back to the attendant. He gave me an approving nod and added, 'It would have been easier in fourth.'

I looked for Dat but couldn't see him, so I returned to the place in the gallery where we had been standing. He emerged not long afterwards from the parking lot holding his night storm helmet and immediately joined a group of girls on the other side of the compound to take the test. Dat had taken off his jacket and his arms were out in front of him manipulating an imaginary motorbike, no doubt bragging to the girls about his racing career. He then strapped on his helmet and swaggered over to take command of the black motorbike. In case there was still someone who had not taken notice of him, Dat revved the bike with gusto. While I could not hear what the attendant said, firm words were clearly exchanged.

Dat traced the figure eights with all the grace and speed of an ice skater, relishing the opportunity to perform in front of a crowd again. As he emerged from the eights the attendant hollered at him to slow down, which he did, balancing the bike at a standstill before creeping slowly forward while ducking his head down as if he were going at great speed.

Everyone in the crowd roared with appreciation, everyone except the judges and me.

Dat negotiated the chicanes at high speed while standing up on his stirrups and then, as he turned around to complete the test, he waved at the group of whooping and cheering girls who had gathered around the finish line.

I will never know for sure, but I would like to think that there was an instant when Dat thought about what he was doing, when he considered that with some apologising he could still get his licence if he took the straight and uncomplicated path, that a lifetime of inconvenience was not worth a few seconds of glory, that he could do the right thing. I like to think that at some point he thought of me.

But there was no hesitation that I could see as Dat dropped back to first gear, revved the engine to its limit and raised the bike onto its rear wheel. He surged forward and hopped over the speed humps with one arm swinging in the air as if he was riding a bucking buffalo.

He then rode right out of the compound. I was worried that he wouldn't return and that on top of everything else he would be charged with stealing a motorbike from the motor registry. No doubt I would be found guilty as an accessory.

A few seconds later he re-entered the compound, still doing a wheelie, and completed the course again from back to front before parking the bike next to the fuming attendant.

Dat held out the key with his nose in the air, forcing the attendant to take it from him as if he were a valet at a fancy hotel.

The crowd was still hooting and cackling as I ran off, leaving my examination completion slip crumpled on the ground.

Maybe I should have been more firm and told him flat out that it was over instead of just refusing to speak to him. But I had never been in a relationship before and had never felt so betrayed.

He apologised profusely. 'I couldn't help myself. It was those girls. They dared me to do it.'

I said nothing.

'Look. How long do you think I was going to keep my licence anyway? They would have taken it from me soon enough. Why is it such a big deal to you? I'm the one who has to pay the fines.'

Two days later, he returned to my stall to tell me that he had made some enquiries and found a crooked instructor in another district who would let him sit the examination again and could print him 10 or more licences for the right fee. 'I'll sit it again. Just to make you happy!'

Still, I said nothing.

'Tell me what I have to do then!'

A few of my customers were gathered around us, enthralled by the drama.

'Give him a second chance. Let him make it up to you', a woman in an orange tracksuit urged.

'He seems nice enough', said another fellow in a business suit. 'Don't hold so much bile in your belly. It'll make you age prematurely.'

'The customer's always right', remarked Dat with that grin of his. This time I nodded.

We went out for dinner and then out to the bridge. I didn't initiate any conversation with him and hardly responded to Dat's questions. I sat with my back straight and proud on his motorbike, my hands behind me clasping the luggage rack.

On the bridge I could see Dat's teeth: he was almost snarling. 'It's not like I killed somebody.'

'I'm sorry, I'm trying but it's different between us now', I confessed. 'I wish we could go back to the way it was, but we just can't.'

I wanted to say more. I wanted him to know that he was a child and probably always would be. He would never learn how to take care of himself, let alone me. While a part of me still cared for him, I did not love him. And I did not want to be with him, not as a wife, not as a friend.

In retrospect, I should have made this clear, but I did not want to hurt him and never thought that he would really hurt me.

Dat suddenly grabbed my hands and looked straight at me. 'I almost don't want to tell you this while you're in such a foul mood, but you have to know, I have to tell you. Something amazing has happened. I can't believe how lucky I am!'

Apparently dozens of people had filmed him doing the driving test and posted the clips online, which had immediately gone viral. This was bad in a way because the gangsters had seen it and now knew he was still in town. They'd spread the word that he was a marked man, and he knew he should leave straight away if he knew what was good for him and his family.

But this did not matter because Dat was going anyway. The manager of an amusement park outside Saigon had also seen the video clip and had gone to great efforts to contact Dat and offer him a job as a stunt driver in one of his shows.

'It's not far from your home town, Mai. We can go south together. Make a fresh start. All the mung bean crepes and sweet sticky rice that you want. I've even thought of a stage name, 'Flaming Phoenix'. What do you think? I reckon there are probably doctors in Saigon who can help you with your face too, at least make that birthmark less noticeable. With the money I'll be making we can pay whatever it takes. What do you think?'

'When are you going?' I asked and I pulled my hands away from his.

'Three days. Less if we can pool our savings to buy the tickets. I know it's very sudden. I can go first and you can meet me there in a week if you need some time to tidy up and say your goodbyes.'

As gently but firmly as possible, I told him I was settled in Hanoi. My business was going well and I had plans to expand and start selling pork rolls in the afternoons.

'My father is getting old. I have to be here to help my mother look after him. I'm sorry. I can't go.'

'Don't be silly. You just need some time to think about it.' It was as if he did not hear a word of what I had said. 'Remember, you won't find anyone better than me.'

'You don't understand. I don't need time to think about it. If I have to be lonely for the rest of my life then I'll deal with that. But I don't want to be with you anymore.'

There was a flash of angst on Dat's face as if he had momentarily registered what I was saying, as if he had finally acknowledged that I was there but was not there for him.

I braced myself for his rage. But instead he smiled, only not in the brash and boyish way that I had become accustomed to. It was something closer to a grimace.

'Okay, if that's what you want. Maybe we can see one another when you visit your grandmother every year? You can come and see me in the show.'

'That would be nice.'

'At least celebrate with me tonight, Mai. It could be our last night together.' And he was grabbing my hands again.

'I'm not sure, Dat, it's late and I have to work tomorrow morning ...'

'Don't be like that. I've even booked a room at our favourite karaoke club. A deluxe room, not like the filthy little cupboard we usually sing in.'

I agreed because I like karaoke and, again, to be nice to Dat.

He had already called ahead to book the Mufasa room at Lion King Karaoke; it had two small stages and could easily accommodate 15 people. He had even arranged for some of the snack foods that I like: Choco Pies and spicy green mango. A bouquet of yellow roses sat beside the two microphones.

Dat performed his grungy angry songs and I worked on some Trinh Cong Son classics before singing pop tunes. We did a rendition of Lam Truong and Minh Thu's 'This Very Moment', with each of us standing on our own stage and singing to the other.

I must admit I enjoyed myself. It was a befitting way for Dat and me to part.

Resting after the duet, Dat put his arm around my shoulders. As he drew close to me I could smell the Da Lat red wine on his breath. I had drunk half a glass in the time it took him to finish the bottle.

'Mai, you know I've never asked much of you. But before we part, don't you think that we should give ourselves to one another – entirely, I mean? Just once: I know you want to. And it's not like I'm going to tell anyone. I don't want us to have any regrets. Who knows, you might like it so much that you'll change your mind about coming with me.'

And with that Dat pulled at my blouse. I slipped out of his headlock and without thinking, perhaps it was the wine, I slapped him in the face. 'We shouldn't, Dat. It's not right.'

His face glazed over. More than a small part of me felt guilty that I had hurt him. And for a second, even as I was so very frightened of Dat, I wanted to comfort him.

'Do you know how many girls have dreamed of being in your position? I've had much better-looking girls than you throw themselves at me. What makes you think anyone else would want you with that horrible smear on your face and that freaky ability of yours? I told the other motorbike boys about you feeling colours or whatever it is you do, and they said that was all the more reason to stay away from you. They said you were cursed and that they wouldn't fuck you if you paid them and offered to wear a bag over your head. And yet here I am. And here you are, in "This very fuckin' moment", saying that it's not right for you and acting as if Buddha and all your piss-ant ancestors are in the room with us. Do you know how much this room cost me?'

'It's nice. Very nice. I'm sorry. Let me pay you back.'

'Yes, you will', is all he said before swooping upon me and pinning me to the sofa. My slaps and punches did little to slow his advance.

I don't remember clearly what happened after that. At some point I fell from the sofa and hit my head against the coffee table leg.

I recall screaming 'No!', 'Stop!' and 'Please!' as loud as I could but the room was insulated: nothing could escape. I told him I was still a Catholic and that it meant something. I cried out to him that he was right – he could have other girls and that he didn't need to have me. I screamed that I was a prawn and that he deserved better.

All of this made no difference. And I wonder now if I did not struggle, plead or reason with him enough. And of course, I should never have gone out with him that night, not to the karaoke bar. Maybe I should have cried out for longer and into one of the microphones so that the attendants might hear me. When they finally came in, with our two hours up, they found me cowering in the corner, with a small stream of blood running down my face and another one running down my legs.

'Not again', was what one of them said.

Yesterday I had to close my stall early. I knew something was wrong when I was preparing the rice because a waft of steam caused great offence to my nostrils. And then, while serving some customers, I suddenly felt sick and had to run off and vomit into the gutter.

My mother inquired into my condition with her snake-like tongue. 'What have you done to yourself?'

'It's a touch of food poisoning', I told her. 'Give me a day or two. I'll be okay.'

So today I am not selling sticky rice.

My head is light and spinning as I make my way to the pharmacy – not the one near my house, but the one a few blocks away, where they do not recognise me or know my family.

The test is surprisingly cheap, the same price as a serving of sticky rice and a glass of soy milk. The young girl at the counter beams, 'With any luck, there'll be happy news for you and your husband.'

As I walk home I think about how this little wand will reveal my fate, perhaps more than any diviner or soul catcher ever could. The directions on the box make it clear that no trances, dances or séances are required for it to work. And it takes less than a minute.

In the first few seconds, I figure that if one line appears – a number 1, which is red and rough like gravel – my life will proceed as it has been; no fairy tale to be sure, but with genuine prospects for me to make it better through my choices and my efforts.

If I get the other result of two lines – a number 11, which is off-white and crumbly like limestone – this will only confirm what my mother knows already, that with heaven rests all choices and that fairness and free will are not meant for people like me.

In the final seconds, the earth turns and I have no idea where my feet will land next.

Then slowly the two lines take shape and I stare at them in disbelief. They are black, both on the paper and in my mind and do not feel like anything at all.

Chapter 2
The Ball Boy

There are, and I am sure of this, only two types of people in this world. The vast majority are zeros: nothings, spaces to be filled. You can find them cowering in corners, protecting their weaknesses. Zeros are rarely on the front foot or in control of the tempo; they are reactionaries in every sense of the word. For them, the game of life is carefully marked out by rules and routines according to which feats of strutting self-expression are repressed, with violence if need be.

'Fetch me that ball, boy. Quickly!'

I swagger across the court and, feigning clumsiness, toss the ball so that it falls well short of old man Ha's reach. 'Fetch it yourself', I mutter under my breath. 'You're the one who needs the exercise.' I take some satisfaction in seeing him move and moan like a porpoise stranded on the shore.

As he bends down to retrieve the ball I remind him, 'You really should have a spare ball before you serve, Mr Ha.'

He raises his voice to address not so much me but his buddies. 'I only ever hold on to one ball because I hit so many aces! Anyway, who are you to tell me what to do, ball boy? With that rose-coloured hair, you look like the sort of fellow who likes to clasp on to a pair of balls. That's how you keep your little boyfriends happy, isn't it?'

Guffaw. Guffaw. It doesn't take much to amuse them.

Ha practically underarms his second serve. The sluggish ball lands in the middle of the service square and sits up. His opponent should be able to hit a winner, but is overwhelmed by the simple awareness of this fact. The ill-timed return only makes it halfway up the net.

Fifteen-love to the zeros.

This morning, as usual, I am surrounded by nothings: old man Ha's partner, Madame Dao, only hits forehands and steers clear of the umpire's chair because dogs and cats sometimes piss there. Ha's opponent, Dr Anh, never approaches the net because he is petrified of lobs and volleys. The good doctor's wife and partner will only play on the shadiest end of the most sheltered court because the sun puts her off, but she refuses to wear sunglasses because they make her look like a blowfly.

All of them are draped in what they think are the latest sporting fashions. Their shoes are gaudy with dragons and yin–yang symbols where the proper logos should be. The women wear tiny skirts and halter tops that threaten to burst apart at the seams to reveal their swollen frames. The men favour polyester shirts from which it is not uncommon to see the labels and price tags swinging. I can tell straight away they are ill-tailored fakes; they might as well be wearing plastic bags.

No doubt, these people all have jobs and families to return to when their twice-weekly session of middle-class, middle-aged flirting is over. For their sake I can only hope that sport is not a microcosm of life.

But don't get me wrong, I don't loathe all of the zeros out there. It would be pointless and unhealthy for me to do so. Such bitterness is a primary cause of dark bags and crows' feet, which would be a ghastly offence against eyes as generous as mine.

Instead I have sincere appreciation and a sliver of pity for nothings. They are the raw material: blank canvases and unfilled score sheets that figures like me need to fashion our masterpieces and claim our titles.

I am a one: solitary, singular, erect. I'm always looking to move upwards and onwards, eager to expose my weaknesses so that I can turn them into weapons. But, and this is important, it is not my intention to be a complete player or to have every shot in the book. Such ambitions are admirable for most, but not for me, for the simple reason that I will never be bound by any book.

This is contrary to the purpose of being a one, which is – in both sport and life – continually to tell one's own story, to compose one's own symphony, to weave one's own tapestry, to be nothing less than exquisite and true.

Sometimes being a one is lonely, but it is surely better to be a tragic icon than another happy idiot in the crowd.

'Get the ball, boy! I've already lost my rhythm and I'm close to losing my patience. You only have one thing to do all day and you can't manage it. A stray dog has more tricks than you. How did you ever become a ball boy with that attitude? Who do you think you are?'

'Sorry sir. I'm not myself today.'

'And for God's sake, why's that cardboard box on your head? It's not even sunny. You look ridiculous, like a chopstick with a piece of deep-fried tofu on the end of it.'

More guffawing from the flat-footed sods.

I kick the ball in Ha's direction. My phone rings and I slide it under the box to answer. My box is ideal for protecting me from the sun's rays without inhibiting phone reception. It is Thanh, another ball boy, who needs me to confirm the price of some skin-care products he is purchasing for me. As I hang up I see Ha with his mouth agape, astonished and enraged. I am still in the middle of court, stalling his precious fun.

'You're unbelievable! And where the hell did you get that phone? I'm paying you one dollar an hour. That thing must be worth a thousand or more. It's newer and better than mine. Who do you think you are, boy?!'

I stand to mock-attention and offer Ha a kowtow that almost sends the box falling from my head. 'A thousand pardons, Mr Ha. Please be patient with me and I will attend to your needs.'

But let me first address your questions, old man, because you have only recently arrived at my club and so your impudence is understandable. You do not know that we could play set after set without you winning a single point. You do not know the Himalayan peaks that I have ascended only to return to these Mekong plains. You do not know that this phone is more chic and cutting-edge than yours because its owner is far more chic and cutting-edge. So let me go over that script I have transcribed in my mind, the one that tells of my life to date. Rest assured – soon, by word of mouth or media blitz, you will know exactly who I am.

My mother informs me that I entered the world in total silence and with hardly a wriggle so that the midwife had to smack me on the bottom to make sure I was alive. Even then I did not cry.

As far as I can remember, I have only cried twice. The last time was during William and Kate's wedding, which I witnessed streamed live onto my phone. On that historic day I was moved by a cascade of sensations brought about by the romantic drama, the wealth of finery dotted with comic fascinators, the bridal party's taut and unblemished skin, that ever so meek kiss before a doting global audience and the magical wand that marked a line of regal elegance – from the bride's train to the profile of Prince Charles' convertible in which the happy couple left the Palace. I was cheering and all of a sudden weeping with the masses lining the streets of London. But unlike all of them I was convinced that, like William and Kate, I was destined to be a beacon of pride and class, elevating the hopes of a dour nation.

So you can see that, although I am not one for crying, this is not because I am cold-hearted. It's normal for children to bawl and for adults to sob. I don't condemn others for being vulnerable, but have decided for myself never to be a victim, never again. This resilience against all forms of pain, evident at my birth, was triggered by my first bout of crying and a sorrow so great that it demands much fortitude and a little time to recount.

The event occurred at my birthplace, which is full of zeros and nothings. It calls itself a city, but is in no way bustling, cosmopolitan or forward-looking. It is a provincial capital, with the emphasis on provincial.

My house is situated near the old market on a street that not long ago was the horse and cart depot. There's even a framed picture of me as a two-year-old sitting in a cart holding on to the reins of a bony, whip-scarred horse. On the road and sidewalk there are piles of turds, some dry, others not so dry. My father liked to look at that picture in the display cabinet and contemplate, 'I have not seen a turd – horse or human – on our street for more than a decade. Such progress.'

Just before I left he was smitten by the proliferation of electric bikes in my home town. 'I hear that everyone in Beijing has an electric bike now. Surely this is the way of the future. Thu, my boy, look at all the joy and benefit your grandfather gets out of his electric bike. It's easy for him to drive and doesn't go too fast. He can take it down to the river to do tai chi in the mornings and then to his veterans' club in the afternoon. And in the evenings your cousin rides it to his extra mathematics and English classes. Charge the battery overnight, and it's ready to go again the next morning. Marvellous!'

That is how I remember my birthplace: a haven for brittle old fools and docile adolescents, buzzing slowly from nowhere to nowhere.

In recent years, Japanese and Korean investment has set off an industrial boom in my province so that it now boasts two department stores, a strip of car dealerships, a successful soccer team, and a university specialising in finance, IT and foreign languages. The province is so rich that the authorities are constructing an entirely new city 30 kilometres to the north of the old one. I've seen the primetime advertisements encouraging people to move up into the 'Shanghai Standard' sky rises and invest in 'New Leaf' villas that back onto the American-designed golf course. Everyone seems to rejoice in their lack of originality. No one seems to comprehend that money alone cannot buy style and that the mere absence of horses on the road and shit on the pavement does not indicate development or civility.

At times I have wondered whether there was some deeper significance to my name. Maybe by calling me 'Thu' (Autumn) my parents had a deep yearning for Paris, New York, Milan or St Petersburg, where the change of seasons ignites the landscape with colour and resets everyone's sensibilities. Maybe – and I know this is wishful thinking – there is something salvageable in my family history, something I can savour.

'It wasn't my choice', replied my father when I asked him. I preferred 'Manh' (strong) or 'Son' (mountain). Your mother liked the sound of 'Thu'. And since it was October I thought it made sense.'

At times my father can be ever so simple, which would not be so bad were he not also sadistic.

He never spoke to me about his mixed parentage. I suspect my father preferred to forget that his father was half Khmer and his mother part Cham. He has always been irked by his middle name, 'Che', which he shares with the dashing Vietnamese singer Che Linh, who Father considers a traitor for leaving the country after the War. Father does everything he can to repress difference. He's always eager to assimilate.

This is why he joined the army and was eager to follow orders and march in parades. He fought in Cambodia shortly before I was born. Going to battle against his fellow Khmer no doubt alleviated his sense of self-hate and made him feel like a winner. He eventually rose to the rank of colonel and took command of the army human resources office in the province. This suited him immensely because it involved meticulously inspecting each individual's personal history for lumps and impurities. He treated his fellow soldiers, indeed everyone, as if they were pieces in a giant jigsaw puzzle, and liked nothing more than consigning them to their proper place. When a piece didn't fit, then it needed to be jammed in with force.

Although my father never pressured me to join the army, he always insisted that I fit in, follow the throng and know my place. One of his favourite sayings was, 'Mess with ink and you'll be stained; bathe in the light and your future will be bright.'

That proverb makes the millipedes writhe inside my gut. Don't let anyone tell you that it merely advises youth to steer clear of trouble and make wholesome friends. What a load of shit! It forces free spirits into submission so that old tyrants can rule. It insists, as my father insisted, that we be chameleons; blending into the background in the hope of surviving for another day. But I refuse to camouflage myself or desert at the first sign of danger. I couldn't cower even if I wanted to because of what I am: a snarling, technicoloured beast with laser-beam vision, a disco ball welded to my thrashing tongue, manicured claws and an insatiable lust for flesh – beholden to no one.

My aim is to pulverise all of the puzzles that I come across into jagged pieces and catapult them into space where they can never be solved. I disdain the flat earth, this two-dimensional world, and prefer instead to live in a nebula of colliding particles: always fighting; fucking; shameless; sublime; unique; free.

But I wasn't always like this. Most of my young life I was an insipid photocopy of my cousin Thuan. Five months and seven days my senior, Thuan and his mother lived with us because his father, who was also a soldier, had been killed in a training exercise during the War.

Thuan and I slept, ate, studied, made mischief, showered in the rain and, above all, played badminton together. We began playing at the age of six, trained by my parents, who were once provincial mixed-doubles champions. At first I partnered with my father while Thuan, who was always stronger and more aggressive than me, played with my mother. By the time we were 12 we were playing against them. I occupied the front court, picking up and pulling off drop shots, trying my best to block attacks. Thuan leapt and darted across the rear court; he was the smasher, the saver, the commander, and to me seemed more man than boy. We did reasonably well in a number of regional competitions, but – and this is not false modesty speaking – I impeded us from going any further. I was a competent player, but lacked inspiration and grit. I was not playing for myself but rather for my parents and to be with Thuan. Both on and off the court, I was driven by that most insidious of desires: compliance.

Admittedly, if you had asked me whether I was content being Thuan's cousin, I would have responded with an emphatic 'yes'. But back then I did not know what true joy and success was because I had been conditioned to be subservient.

It was for this very reason that Thuan and I almost never played singles against one another. He was my superior in every way and I was his faithful stooge; it seemed dangerous to disturb this natural order. I remember one time when we were play-fighting with two long sticks of sugar cane. He was always the irrepressible Monkey from the *Journey to the West* TV series that we adored, while I was faltering Pigsy or the insipid Sandy. We duelled with great vigour until, according to the unwritten script, Thuan knocked the staff from my hands. I was almost ready to surrender. He lunged forward to finish me off, but this time I instinctively parried his attack and snuck around behind him. Then, again without thinking, I reached around and grabbed both ends of his cane and pulled it inwards so that Thuan's hands – still holding on to his weapon – were pinned against his chest. I squeezed as hard as I could, flexing the sugar cane to near breaking point, sandwiching us so tightly together that I could sense my cousin's panic at the prospect of unprecedented defeat. Thuan squirmed and whined to no avail. And it was then, on the precipice of triumph, that I capitulated, dropping the sugar cane and allowing Thuan to swivel and sweep my feet from under me. A second later he came crashing down, repaying my insolence with an elbow to the stomach, hollering with a victory known only to kings.

'I thought you had me there', Thuan said, puffing.

'Lucky bastard!' I feigned disappointment to feed his ego. 'The sugar cane juice made my hands slip.' At the time I did not know how to win.

My relationship with Thuan began to change with the onset of puberty. There was a night in particular when both of us could not sleep. We were restless with the uncertainty that comes with metamorphosis, our voices were mostly broken, our skin oily, our loins yearning to know the gratification reserved for adults. Thuan and I had recently started sleeping top-to-toe. I turned the right way up and switched on the bedside lamp before placing my face centimetres from his.

'What's the matter with you? Go back to sleep, we've got badminton training in the morning.'

'Not until you show me your pubic hair.'

'What?! Are you crazy? What for?'

'Go on. I've just started to get mine and I know you've had yours for a year. I want to know if mine is growing the right way. I've never seen anyone else's close up. Go on. Show me your hair and I'll show you mine. There's nothing to be shy about. It's natural to be curious about these things. I need to know.'

'I don't know what's gotten into you lately. You're really starting to worry your parents. Do you know that?'

But Thuan could see that my eyes were wild and insistent. He sluggishly got out from under the sheets and, mirroring me, perched himself on his knees. The light from the lamp was softened through the mosquito net, which also served to shield us from the world outside.

Together, and it was the last time I could use this term to describe us, we lowered our cotton boxer shorts. In a single motion, I pulled my pants down to the crook of my knees. Thuan paused to reveal his coal-black shrubbery, which served only to build up the tension before – witnessing my self-confidence – he unveiled his timid bird. And there we knelt, naked and equal before one another, still slightly aroused by the fantasies of teenage slumber.

With the intensity of a jeweller, I examined Thuan's manhood. His was longer to be sure, but far less beautiful. A bulbous vein meandered along the stem of his penis among hairs of varying length, whereas mine was gun-barrel smooth. His testicles hung low from the warmth of our blankets, the left one much more so than the right. I examined myself and was pleased with my coiffure, which I tended to every second night before showering. At the same time I could appreciate the untouched wilderness that Thuan had preserved, which had its own charm and allure.

With great tenderness and precision I moved my index finger, ever so slightly bent, towards my awaiting cousin. I was eager to test the integrity of his proboscis so that I might compare and contrast it with mine which, by that stage, I had become most familiar with. Now as I reflect upon that instant, I am reminded of the image of God's hand reaching down to connect with the beseeching finger of that naked fellow painted long ago on the roof of that Italian church, and which I've often seen printed on fancy shopping bags. But then, as I was about to make contact, Thuan's penis and his entire body seemed to hiccup and with the swiftness of a startled rat he retreated under the bed covers, his shorts still tangled around his knees.

The next day Thuan moved into his mother's room and announced over dinner that he had developed an 'allergy' to me. Naturally, I was wounded by this proclamation. Yet it did not take me long to realise that Thuan was right; he was drifting in one direction and I was charging towards another. I came to regard Thuan not as someone to be mourned, but rather as a skin that had to be discarded so that I might flourish and grow.

Soon afterwards Thuan gave up badminton for soccer, which provided me with an excuse to retire my racquet and shuttlecock. Oddly enough, as my cousin and I drifted apart, I grew closer to his mother. My aunt had always taken great care when it came to her clothes, physique and makeup, arguing that by preserving her appearance she was honouring her husband's memory. This was disingenuous because she was known to enjoy the attention of other men. But for someone who hardly left our district, Thuan's mother had an admirable appreciation of fashion and grooming – things for which I also demonstrated an uncommon aptitude. For hours at a time my aunt and I watched the fashion channel while snacking on watermelon seeds and dried longans. We flipped through piles of magazines rating the dress sense and shapeliness of celebrities such as Minh Hang, Jennifer Pham, Li Bing Bing, Kim Hee Soon, and Beyoncé. It was from her good example that I learnt the importance of skin care, and it was from her example that I learnt to embrace and manage change rather than resist it.

My camaraderie with Thuan's mother aggravated his resentment towards me. He made faces at me at home and either pretended not to know me or jeered at me with his troglodyte teammates when we crossed paths at school. It was from his perfidious mouth that I first heard the taunts pansy, queer, and *pe-de*. And I suspect it was Thuan who came up with the nasty nickname 'Huong Hoi', which evoked a putrid fragrance while alluding to the lampooned homosexual boss in the films *Fool for Love* and *Let Hoi Take Care of It*. Both the movies and my nickname were popular among my dim-witted classmates – which is to say the vast majority of them.

So, Mr Ha, I garnered an important lesson about how quickly love can grow into hate. And you should know that it was Thuan's final and most egregious betrayal that drove me out of my home town and eventually brought me here to be your ball boy.

But before we get to the most tragic scene in the fast-paced, self-directed movie that is my life, you must know about Ngoc and why, to this day, I still worship and long for him.

Ngoc came into my life via a measured misfortune. I was late for school – biology class if I remember correctly – and was riding at great speed. The silver and gold-coloured tassels I had attached to my handlebars were fluttering in the wind and tickling my elbows. A sudden flat tyre caused me to hit a pothole; I skidded over a layer of debris, collided with the gutter and fell onto the sidewalk. As I picked myself up, still ginger and confused, I saw up ahead a tall bicycle pump perched on the edge of the gutter with an electric-blue ribbon tied around it.

I approached the pump with a mix of adrenalin and self-pity and still remember the first words that he uttered to me: 'Need some help?'

Ngoc was astride his white Peugeot bicycle, propped up on the rear wheel stand, slowly pedalling backwards with a toothpick hanging casually from his lips. I was struck by his superb posture, his bulky thighs which were barely contained by his faded blue jeans, and the simple sophistication of his crisp white business shirt with the sleeves rolled up to his forearms. There were no logos visible on his person, and I later learnt that Ngoc even removed the washing instructions from the inside of his clothes out of a resolve not to be branded or dragged down by dead weight. There was a touch of grease in his hair and a few smudges on his hands – just enough to give him a gritty-but-not-dirty look.

In that very first instant it was apparent that Ngoc was no common tyre repairman, that he was an outsider, and that I needed to know him. He eventually revealed that he had sprinkled shards of glass on the road as a marketing strategy, and that the ribbon was a sign to interested passers-by that he was libertine in every way. Yet I am certain that if he had told me these truths then and there, I would still have given him my business and thanked him for coming to my rescue.

Without a word, Ngoc took my bike and set about patching the rear tyre.

His office was a picture of order and efficiency. Ngoc's tools were laid out in a long pouch, next to which was a red plastic bucket full of water. He used an adjacent concrete electricity pole with moulded square holes in it to store his wares: the bottom hole for tubes and glue; the middle for nuts and bolts; and the top one for his lubricant. Behind his bicycle there was a rolled up rattan mat propped up against a petite betel palm.

'I haven't seen you before', was all I could come up with.

'Just rode in', and he pointed his tube lever at the antique bicycle which I now noticed had a sculpted tan leather seat. 'I came to stay with my aunt and uncle a few weeks ago, but that didn't work out. So here I am, on the streets again.'

'Sucks, doesn't it? Being stuck in such a boring and awful place I mean.'

'I've been in worse', Ngoc said with intriguing nonchalance.

He patched the rear wheel so promptly that I was afraid our chance encounter was drawing to an end. Then Ngoc turned his face up to look at me and, for the first time, we made eye contact.

'Your rear spokes are loose and the front wheel looks a little buckled. I think you should let me take care of it now. It is dangerous for you to carry on in this state. The repairs will take some time, though. Are you in a hurry?'

'Yes, thank you. I mean no, I'm in no hurry. Whatever you think is best. I feel lucky to have found you.' I was dreadfully self-conscious standing before him in my school uniform.

Ngoc told me to fetch his rattan mat and I squatted down upon it. Over the next 40 minutes I gently prodded him to recount his story.

A few nights ago he had had a fight with his uncle, who owned a purse and wallet shop at the central market. It was over whether he could come and leave the house as he pleased and the hours that he had to work at the store. His uncle sought to impose a curfew; Ngoc insisted that there be none. As for work, at first his uncle demanded six days a week, conceded five, and then four with short lunch breaks, but this remained a long way from Ngoc's baseline of 'probably never'.

'I love to work', Ngoc explained, 'but I have to love my work. And for now that means bicycles.'

His father died when he was 11, struck down by liver and lung cancer. 'Eleven years and nine months too late', Ngoc said, spitting into the gutter.

After his father's death, Ngoc and his mother moved from one relative's house to another before deciding to make it on their own in the city. He had spent most of his school years collecting litter for recycling and selling chewing gum on a restaurant strip, but assured me that he knew more than enough words and numbers to do business. Shared hardship brought Ngoc and his mother together; that is, until a year or so ago when it became clear that he could not approve of any of her lovers, who were always replicas of his abusive father. They quarrelled with the worst words and some violence. Finally, she demanded he leave the city and go live with her youngest brother in the provinces.

Ngoc acquiesced, and as he departed received from his mother a tearful kiss on the cheek and three $US50 bills rolled up in a rubber band. He had, in any case, recently begun to yearn for country air and hoped to find some hills or even mountains to conquer. With his bicycle and little else, the young man caught a train to the city limits, where he began his long ride. Whenever possible he detoured along unsealed roads and bumpy tracks extending through the rice paddies and villages. Ngoc bathed, sang, slept and made love outside. 'I lived like we're meant to live', he proclaimed to me with a spoke spanner raised. There was one occasion when a prostitute insisted that he hire a room, and though he agreed, he did not spend a minute longer indoors than was necessary. After three weeks, Ngoc arrived in my home town with less than $4, which he used to buy himself a welcoming box of chocolates.

He had acquired his passion for bicycles by accident. Ngoc was on the back of a friend's motorbike swerving through the city late one night when a yellow Mercedes coupe ran a red light and cut them off. They hit the kerb and went sailing over the handlebars. Ngoc somehow escaped with only a broken toe; his friend shattered both wrists and suffered deep lacerations all over his legs. To her credit the driver stopped and, once assured that they were alive, shoved a solid gold bracelet into Ngoc's friend's bloody hands as compensation for her error and to help them forget they had ever seen her face and number plate.

That very night, Ngoc decided he would never again submit himself to the control of another human or the power of a machine. So on the day the bandage was removed from his toe, Ngoc purchased what he liked to call his 'snowy stallion'. He joined a group of young cycling enthusiasts who sought to reclaim the streets every Friday night. Their peloton was propelled by a range of desires: some of the cyclists were environmentalists seeking to reduce their carbon footprint; others were communists reconstructing the Viet Minh's iron horse cavalcades of the 1950s; a few casually paraded their expensive carbon-fibre frames; all were looking to engage in some well-mannered philandering. Of course, none of these incentives suited my Ngoc; so he left them after being given a set of unwanted panniers and learning some valuable lessons about bicycle maintenance, saddle position, and pedalling technique.

Thereafter, Ngoc set out to reclaim the city streets for and by himself. There were times when he rode in the midst of the traffic and felt like a fish in a mighty school, twisting and turning in unison with the commuters. At peak hour he would pass stationary motorbikes and cars, climbing onto the sidewalk, rushing the wrong way down one-way streets and zipping past traffic police in their peach coloured uniforms. As his legs swelled, he took to shaving them. At the same time the young man developed a lean strength in his upper body and core. According to Ngoc's ideal of human anatomy, 'Upstairs is for show, but downstairs is where all the work is done, and all the pleasure is had.'

More than anything, Ngoc liked riding at night. His favourite stretch of the city was a newly built tunnel which, due to shoddy planning and excessive compromise, was underused by day and empty at night. For Ngoc it was the perfect training facility. Upon entering he faced a powerful jet-stream that required him to press his head down, maintain an even cadence and listen intently to his body's rhythm. With an old stopwatch that he had affixed to his handlebars, Ngoc timed how long it took before he emerged totally exhausted at the other end. And then, as a reward, he made an about-turn and re-entered the tunnel. But, not being one to take it easy, Ngoc accelerated until he was moving at precisely the same speed as the wind on his tail. And for priceless seconds he felt neither resistance nor compulsion; no friction upon his tread, no strain in his legs. It was then, in the small hours of the morning, that he would shut his eyes and let go of the handlebars.

Another U-turn and click of his stopwatch, and the young cyclist would do it over again, only faster.

After our first encounter I did not know his name, nor did he know mine. We were then, and always have been, more comfortable referring to each other in nameless, intimate terms: *anh* and *em*. Once my tyre was fixed, I rode around town in a daze. I did not bother with school, reasoning that I was incapable of learning while my heart threatened to lunge out of my ribs.

I looked for him each morning and afternoon, slowing down as soon as that electric-blue ribbon came into vision. He never seemed to change his clothes, nor was he ever filthy or dishevelled like other labourers. With an irregular flow of customers, Ngoc seemed to spend as much time tuning his own bike as he did fixing others. At every opportunity I waved to him and said hello – 'Xin chao Anh'. He nodded. Sometimes he would give me a demure wink or hoist whatever tool he had at hand. If he was sitting on his propped-up bicycle cycling through its gears I would try to ascertain the pace of his pedalling as if it was a measure of his mood. I sensed that his cadence was picking up in anticipation of another rendezvous. That was the first month of our relationship.

When we made contact for the second time, it was I who sabotaged my bicycle. This involved a series of pin pricks to the wall of the rear tyre. I reasoned that a slow release flat would be difficult for him to detect and increase our time together, while also making it easy for him to deduce that I sought more than a repair. Again we conversed as he worked, but this time in a more easy-going way. I recounted the little there was to recount about my life: my nothing parents, my zero cousin and my defunct badminton career. I offered my name and he in turn revealed his. 'Ngoc' suited him. I savoured its androgynous chime; my ever so precious jade: smooth, hard, statuesque.

And then he extended the invitation I yearned for. 'Maybe we can go for a ride sometime? That is, if I can ever fix this puncture. I can show you around your home town.'

'When? When do you want to go?'

'Sunday mornings are quiet – meet you here at five.'

'Excellent. Just give me a whole new tube then. Wouldn't want this to happen again. What's your number and facebook name? Just in case. Don't worry though. I'm not going to pull out.'

'No phone. No keys. No wallet. No obligations.'

He was so streamlined, like the raw food eating hipsters I had seen profiled on the fashion channel. Looking back, the fact that he didn't have a phone made our relationship splendidly inconvenient. We met the way people used to meet: by pure chance or preordination. It has also meant that I do not have the slightest electronic evidence that Ngoc was ever part of my life.

For the rest of that week, I was like a small child awaiting *Tet*. I went to bed and woke up early as if this would help bring forth the gifts, frivolity and fireworks one associates with New Year. When Sunday eventually arrived, I was out the door before my parents had left for badminton. They were astounded by my enthusiasm. I was candid with them: I had a new friend, a bike rider; it was a bromance brimming with promise and adventure. Mother and Father were relieved to know I had a male comrade after having confined myself to a small group of dour emo girl classmates. Ngoc's presence in my life calmed them just as it kindled every nerve in my 17-year-old body.

We rode for almost six hours, with only two brief intermissions for breakfast and green tea. I had never been so far from my home town without my parents. Ngoc showed me streams I did not know existed, and unveiled rows of limestone karsts that I'd paid little attention to before. We listened for birds, looked out for monkeys, and were chased by stray dogs. On returning home, I was at once enlivened and exhausted. My thighs and calves had reached a state of numbness beyond pain and I was certain that no rider of bike or beast had ever known saddle soreness like mine. I would have collapsed had it not been for Ngoc's proposition.

'Come back to my place for a drink and massage. Otherwise you won't be able to walk for a month.'

Ngoc was living in an abandoned weather shelter for train crossing attendants, barely long enough to contain the plastic collapsible beach chair that was his only piece of furniture. Yet, except for the graffiti on the walls, it was clean and tidy. All of his possessions were arranged along one wall and his books and magazines were stacked under the beach chair, which lay open and waiting for me.

'Take off your pants and lie down on your stomach', he said with a casual confidence. I did as he commanded. With my face to the ground I peered between the chair's plastic strips and made out the titles of his reading material: *The Mekong on Two Wheels*; *Cooking for Carbohydrates*; the popular Chinese novel *The Name of the Devil*; a couple of wuxia novellas by Jin Yong, and Vu Dinh Giang's celebration of sex and violence, *Parallel*. Then I turned my head to the side to watch him work.

Ngoc wet his hands from the water in his drink bottle and squirted some on my legs, making me tremble. He added three droplets of bike lubricant to each hand and rubbed them together for warmth. Clearly, this was not the first massage he had given. He began to stroke my calves and hamstrings with fluidity and precision, as if he was searching my inner tube for tiny pinpricks. He kneaded the lactic acid out of my legs, which felt painful and therapeutic. Warm blood gushed back into my lower body. As the back of my legs relaxed, my manhood hardened, pressing down against the beach chair straps. No longer weary and defeated by the morning's exertions, I was eager for more adventure. Then, with the knife-edge of each hand, Ngoc applied a rhythmical tapotement to my raw buttocks. Because I could not help it, I moaned. And that is when Ngoc kissed me on the back of my neck with an erotic motion far beyond anything my dreams could conjure. 'You can turn over if you like.'

Again, I did as he asked. 'I'm sorry. I'm sweaty and stink a little. I'm sorry.'

I looked down to see my member protruding from the top of my cotton underpants like a mouse poking out from its hole. 'I'm sorry' seemed to be the only thing I could say.

With his index finger and thumb he tenderly clasped my bell end, pausing for a few seconds at the very tip, a technique that he called micro-effleurage. Each deliberate stroke of his fingertips sent a tsunami of pleasure through my body. Although my eyes were closed, I suspect Ngoc was startled by the hastiness and fury of my climax.

'I'm sorry. I haven't done this before. And I'm so terribly sore from the ride. I don't know if …'

'That's okay, *em*. That's okay. Today was an introduction. We don't have to do anything more or go anywhere else. Move aside though, I wouldn't mind lying down for a little while.'

Ngoc helped me remove my splattered shirt. I wondered how I was going to explain it to my parents. He asked if he could remove his shirt and pants, which he said he found chafing. I agreed and stroked his bare chest a few times before sheepishly rolling to my side so that he could spoon me. And for the first time I felt his enchanted branch, straight but not stiff, snuggled in the crack between my cheeks. Before drifting off to sleep, I thought about how the two of us were a perfect fit.

The next day my legs were so stiff and sore that my mother had to bring my meals up to my room because I couldn't make it down the stairs. Even standing up was a challenge. The following day I could maintain a vertical position but not for long, so Mother had to drive me to school on her scooter. As I was driven past Ngoc I retracted my head into my shirt so that he would not see me feeble and dependent. It was not until the end of the week that I could walk with ease. By the next Sunday I proved that love can soothe any perineal pain because it was with only the slightest hesitation that I hopped back on my bike and returned to my precious jewel.

So Mr Ha, know that it was with glee that I pedalled towards the perdition awaiting me.

Ngoc was, as before, a perfect gentleman and did not impose himself on me. He was somewhat startled and most certainly titillated when I took the initiative, tearing off my clothes and then his, clawing at his tanned neck and back like a cat in the night, kissing him in any place that I could, professing that I was his without fear or compunction. Ngoc absorbed my passionate eruptions and then held me as if to say that even the most eager and talented student needs a firm teacher. So again we were spooning on that deck chair and, millimetre by careful millimetre, Ngoc completed me. It was, I admit, an awkward and even painful sensation at first, but such is the nature of progress.

And progress is exactly what ensued. Sometimes he advanced, at other times it was me; there were adjustments and even corrections, but never once did we stall or retreat.

Over the next two months I was immersed in the pleasure that was Ngoc, a pleasure that was all-consuming, but also enormous fun. That tiny concrete booth was a sacred temple and an amusement park. Once we had mastered the conventional positions, Ngoc showed me how to do 'The Buffalo Boy's Flute', and 'The Vietnamese-Vitruvian'; I twisted my ankle in the process of achieving 'Uncle Ho's Joyous Victory'. The equally satisfying contortions that I devised were named after food cravings brought on by our exertions: 'The Extra Chilli Baguette', 'The Bursting Duck Embryo' and 'Pappa Roti's Yeasty Buns'. We were as young men should be: inventive, wanton, implacable.

Our lovemaking took place before and after school. We revelled under the pretext that we were riding in the countryside. My parents were relieved that I was out of the house and had a healthy hobby. As my father pointed out, I had never been fitter and I radiated cheer. Sometimes we did go for a ride, although never again for six hours. On occasion we left the snowy stallion locked up and set out on my bicycle. I sat on the rear-wheel rack as Ngoc pedalled and steered. With my feet on either side of his and my hands grasping his hips, we moved in complete harmony. For me it was never a strain because Ngoc insisted that he needed to keep in shape and that I should therefore relax. So he took charge while I sat back. When we whooshed down an incline I threw my arms up as if I was perched on the bow of the Titanic hollering to the world that we two were comrades, compatriots, companions.

Allow me to point out for your benefit, Mr Ha – because I know that you are inclined to abhor man-to-*nam* love – that, at the very least, we did no evil, we caused no harm. Evaluate us, for instance, against all those sobbing concubines and faithless arranged marriages. And it should go without saying that my and Ngoc's lovemaking outshines the sundry ways that men use prostitutes and rubber love dolls to avoid their lifeless wives.

Of course what I and Ngoc shared far surpasses any cloistered fornication that you, Mr Ha, have indulged in. So know that I accept neither condemnation nor pity for what I have enjoyed, especially from a perverted fuckwit such as you.

Indeed I have become convinced that if queer love is ever wrong it is because we have lived down to straight expectations, when in truth our love is right and natural. It is the love of our forefathers who ruled over great civilizations. It is worthy of celebration and esteem, something that's meant to be.

One weekend afternoon, after another blessed encounter with Ngoc, we were basking on his beach chair when, more out of necessity than design, I professed my love to him. 'When we are together I feel like I can do anything, break buffalo horns if I want to. It's as if the heavens are a saucepan lid about to burst open.'

He was silent. And his face, as usual, was inscrutable.

'I remember, *em*, the first, last and only time I uttered those words. I was a little younger than you and was screwing a guy much older than me. At the time I thought his response was callous, but I have come to understand the wisdom in his words. That's why I'm repeating them to you now.'

'This is not the time for love. Maybe there never was such an era. But the terrible mistake that pups like you make is to devote yourself to someone today in the hope that – perhaps even because of that devotion – things will get easier and better in the future. Let me make it clear: no matter how hard we try or how much we believe in ourselves and one another, tomorrow will not be brighter than today. Why do you think our gay community refers to itself as living in the Third World? It is because we are destined to be abused, excluded, discarded. This is no place and no time for love – not for us.'

'If you don't love me then say so. But don't say that. I don't believe it. Not when you've brought this much to my life. You've given me everything to look forward to. You've completed me, *anh*.'

'If you don't believe me, then consider that those like us lived freer and happier lives before, when our camaraderie was beyond the comprehension of the masses. Segregation of the sexes allowed us to be out and about: men walked the streets hand-in-hand; we comforted and kept one another warm; unabashed, we slapped and tickled our buddies. We were in the clear because we were unknown. Back then, other than their spouses, men did not mix with women. We could take wives for propriety's sake, close our eyes and screw them while dreaming of our true loves just enough times to produce a few children. It was a lie, but one that was simple to maintain. What you call "progress" has made these lies more complex and costly for us.'

'But I have never felt as free as I do now, *anh* Ngoc. Here with you.'

'Remember this: sexual freedom for others is our oppression. Their "can" is our "must not". They can embrace in public, which means we must not. They can have many partners before settling down with one, which means that we must not have any. Their light casts us into the shadows. Now they know about us, they can brand us as different. Now that we're on the map, we're targets.'

This is what my Ngoc said when I told him I loved him. And although I reject the defeatism in his words outright, it is nonetheless a message I take very seriously and have kept close to me at all times, like a memento.

And I must acknowledge to you Mr Ha that, in the short term, he was right.

Because even as we enjoyed what Ngoc refused to acknowledge as love, my grave mistake during those months of ecstasy was to think that my parents, teachers, and society were too backward and uninformed to concern themselves with us. Perhaps a part of me wanted to believe that with the proper instruction and a dose of empathy, they might become enlightened and accept that I was happy and free. But, adopting Ngoc's perspective, they were already far more modern than I had assumed, which is to say that they were malevolent, devious and vile.

Only a few days after I professed my love, modern reality formally announced itself with a mighty thump. I awoke immediately from my post-passion nap as a forceful hip and shoulder against the door of Ngoc's shelter pushed the latch screws right out of the wall; it was clear that with another light push the door would fly open. We had dedicated that week of lovemaking to the *Star Wars* movies and had reached *Episode V: The Empire Strikes Back*. I was completely naked and while there was probably time for me to cover up, I was too much of a braggart to bother. Ngoc was in his underpants, which he always put back on as soon as possible so as to 'keep it all warm and in the right place'. It could have been anyone: the head of the local commune, vagrants, the police, or train crossing guards. But, when the door burst open I was not surprised to see my cousin Thuan. And there too was my father's new digital camera held up above Thuan's wide, debasing grin.

'*May la gay!*' he howled, referring to me using the pronoun '*may*' more commonly reserved for dogs and servants. I felt the clenching force of every molar in his jaw as he enunciated that awful import from the English language – '*gay*' – that is so often used to defame us. Thuan's horrid shriek swathed us in a cloud of wilful ignorance, so thick with scorn that, while today thoughts of my being 'bent' or 'queer' evoke pride, the word '*gay*' still sets me ablaze as if it were a Molotov cocktail.

Just as Thuan took the photograph, beams of sunlight from around his silhouette merged with the subtle glow of the shelter's grimy window. The combination of sunshine and shadow was a tribute to our supple bodies, highlighting our velveteen muscles in their patina of sweat. No flash was necessary and so, one artificial 'click' later, Thuan was out the door.

As I lay embracing my love, I heard my cousin running back up the gravel road. I surmised that after following me from home he had parked his motorbike some distance away so that we wouldn't hear him approach. This was the last picture ever taken of me in my home town. I have not seen it, although suspect it would not be difficult to find on the internet, and wonder how many litres of sperm have been spilt in joyous praise of it. I suppose I have never sought it out because I prefer the picture that I took in my mind's eye. Yet I like the idea of placing that final image alongside the one of me as an infant on the horse-drawn cart. For all the changes to me and my surrounds, a thread runs through my life and those images – one that holds profound lessons for humanity. When I am famous, scholars will debate the significance of these pictures over countless hours and pages:

> In picture one we see the concluding days of four-legged transport in Vietnam. The faded circa 1985 image is treasured because of its capture on celluloid of the changing of worlds in a moment. The second picture, set in an abandoned train conductor's shelter, serves in one regard as a micro-museum of the industrial era. This famous picture, known as 'the True LENS' ('Love, Erotica and Neo-Sexuality'), was transmitted to the universe in a fraction of a millisecond and thus also marks the timeless and spaceless revolution of the early digital age. Most striking, in both images is the naked innocence inscribed on the face and sublime body of the subject. This innocence contrasts the hardship and debauchery that would follow in Master Thu's life, as has been recorded in several books and an HBO drama.

It was almost amusing to see my demure mother hysterical.

'What have you done to yourself? What have you done to our family? Let me see your arms. No don't show me. I don't want to see the wings of my angel scarred by needles. I've booked you into the clinic tomorrow. I can only hope to heaven that you haven't got AIDS. Of course the doctor's wife will tell everyone in town. But what does it matter? You are ruined. Everything's ruined. How will we ever purge ourselves of this sin? How are we going to cure you of this disease?'

Father was predictable and calculating, but I could see the veins on his head and arms pulsating with passive aggression.

'This depravity is a passing stage brought about by all of that foreign television and music you've consumed with your aunt. We should've seen it coming. I've read that many youth regard what you have been doing with that criminal as modern and hot – '*mot*' as you young people like to say. It is not hot or modern – it is evil. I'll be looking into the appropriate re-education measures to salvage you from this social wreckage. Know that I've informed the security police about your assailant; they'll deal with him and no doubt they'll investigate his relatives. There's no hope for him, but you can still be reformed, someday have a wife and children, be normal. The rectification process – it'll take time, but as Uncle Ho said, "It takes 10 years to grow a tree, and 100 years to cultivate a person."'

You can see, Mr Ha, why the very next morning I had to wake and leave home before my parents prepared for badminton. And perhaps you can also see why it was without hesitation or guilt that I took the money from their wallets and the tin box they kept in a ceramic urn in the courtyard. I viewed this not as stealing, but as cashing in my inheritance – early to be sure, but also at a substantial discount to my parents. My decision to leave was not driven by fear so much as an allergic reaction; I simply could not stand those people and that place anymore. So before the sun had risen, I set off from the house full of zeros on my finely tuned bicycle, leaving nothing behind.

Of course I made a detour along the train tracks. And though I knew he would not be there, I stopped at the shelter to pay homage to my Ngoc. The door was hanging open and the inside swept clean. However, in the corner of the room there was a piece of paper folded over and weighed down by a handful of gravel. The note was bordered with smudges of bike oil and what I feared was blood. I had never seen his writing before. Each word was pressed into the paper with mental and emotional strain. The simple prose was full of rage, self-learnt grammar infused with artistry.

Em,
Know that I have tasted
Your father's friends' batons.
And am no longer handsome.
I have been meaning to tell you
How bored I have become
With our furtive affair.
And that when you pedal
Your toes stick out
Too much.

Reading each line felt like a fingernail being torn from my hand, and the motif of violent rejection was a knife in my innards. It was then, for the first time in my life, that I cried. And if I never cried again, that single occasion would more than fill my quota such that if my life was captured in an epic poem the refrain would be:

With the autumn came a monsoon of tears.
With the autumn came a monsoon of tears.

Since then I have discovered a speck of reprieve from concluding that Ngoc quite possibly left unstated his love for me in order to lighten my guilt. And the evidence I have for this is that enclosed with Ngoc's note, which I have long discarded, was his electric-blue ribbon, which I still keep.

I arrived in the city as a refugee, and was willing to take shelter anywhere I could. It is lucky for you, Mr Ha, that I happened to come across An Duong Tennis Club, with its sloping, dog shit-stained courts. Lucky for you and for everyone here that my standards were so sunken from my ordeal that I agreed to become a ball boy. But in truth I don't believe in luck, dumb or otherwise. In contrast to you, Mr Ha, and just about everyone else, I believe in the fate one makes for oneself and then manipulates and betrays.

In the first months of my arrival I reverted to living as a chameleon. And, not surprisingly, my timidity was a magnet for mockery and abuse. The menopausal monster I called 'chief' refused to recompense me for the first month because I was on probation. At the same time, I was given the worst and most arduous jobs, none of which offered the prospect of tips: cleaning the toilets and showers, scrubbing the shoe marks off the baselines, and drying the courts with two broken pieces of squeegee, knowing that in a few minutes it would rain again. Often she reminded me that I was a no-good out-of-towner without any prospect of obtaining a residency permit and therefore lucky to get whatever work came my way. The players called me everything from 'darling' to 'dickhead' and only really acknowledged my existence when directing their anger at me. People castigated me because I had not delivered to them their lucky ball, because I was standing in a distracting pose, and because the water I brought out was too cold and the energy drinks too fizzy. Because of me, players lost points, games and entire matches that were critical to their self-esteem. And when they did not play well, they did not work or live well. So, as was the case back home, I was a bad omen. I ruined lives.

Mostly, I was ostracised and abused by the other ball boys and the coach. It was the coach who revived that inane nickname 'Huong Hoi' that somehow followed me across provinces. As I swept up sunflower seed husks and cigarette butts, he wet old tennis balls and smashed them at me to improve his aim and my agility. And he stirred up the usually docile guard dogs with a pair of my underpants so that they pursued me without relent.

The six other ball boys and I slept in a room above the shower block. But 'slept' is not the right word because the others had boundless energy when it came to harassing me at night. A rumour was concocted that I had a taste for waste, such that even now when I open a used water bottle I sniff it for traces of urine. In the morning it was common for me to find a dog turd at the foot of my mat or chicken manure sprinkled over my sheets and in my shoes. One evening I awoke to see, an inch from my nose, a steaming coil of human shit on a piece of toilet paper. The other boys barked and roared as I vomited into my blanket.

All of this I endured without hope of amnesty or retribution. No punishment was too cruel for me and no excrement too foul. Always, I believed I deserved worse.

Tennis thus served up my penance, but it would also allow me to make a most miraculous comeback.

One sleepless night I decided to go down to the clubhouse and take my chances with the mosquitoes and guard dogs (some of whom I had managed to befriend with games of fetch using old tennis balls and sweatbands). As I was tiptoeing down the stairs, I noticed that the clubhouse light was still on and a handful of people were frolicking inside.

It was Mr Diep's group, which played on Sunday, Tuesday and Thursday nights. They had played until midnight and then hired the clubhouse for the entire evening, bringing along a television and copious amounts of boiled chicken, duck's blood pudding and corn liquor. The men welcomed me with their faces a joyous crimson.

'You're the one with the girl's name right? Thao? Thu? That's it. Come here Thu my boy and watch Wimbledon with us.'

One of Mr Diep's friends flicked a 100,000 VND note at me and said that I should make myself useful by pouring their drinks and giving them massages. I was happy to oblige, in part because there were only four of them, but mostly because it was the closest I had come to kindness in a very long time. As I massaged their necks and shoulders, I listened to them complain about how their wives did not understand their passion for tennis: how the action on court allowed them to endure the tedium of domestic life; how the rules ensured a measure of justice now extinct in the streets and at work; and how the most profound friendships could only be forged in wartime and during tiebreaks. Only weeks earlier, someone had the idea of taking advantage of their seclusion and hired a team of whores to watch the French Open with them. But the girls' fake nails scratched their backs raw, they asked too many questions about the purpose of sport and prattled to one another during important points. Thereafter, Mr Diep and his friends concluded that the watching and playing of tennis is properly reserved for men, and that I was a gift from the grand slam gods because I was silent, willing, and understanding.

I garnered this information over the next four hours but, as with millions of others who had joined us to watch the Wimbledon final that year, was only partly conscious of my surroundings. That match – the first and best I have ever seen – was so engrossing and inspiring that it changed my attitude to tennis: from revulsion when the coin was tossed, to indifference by the start of the second set, to mild interest minutes later. By the time the final set began, I was addicted. And all of this was because of one remarkable man.

I did not need to see other professionals to realise that Roger Federer was the best. He moved around the court with the poise and fleet-footedness of a ballroom dancer. Bolts of lightning flew from Roger's racquet to smite his opponents. He did not require a coach, properly regarding all forms of guidance as stifling.

From the start it was also clear to me that Roger was more than a tennis player. He was a symbol of style and civility. The cardigan and pants he donned as he entered the court could just as easily have turned heads at a Monaco casino. The traces of gold on his bag, headband and shorts were delicate and debonair. His personal logo was etched on his shoes in the shape of Icarus's wings. I was enraptured by how the front side of the 'R' moulded perfectly into the spine of the 'F'. 'RF' represented for me a new element on the periodic table – the rarest and most valuable substance known to humankind.

Because you are old and senile, Mr Ha, I should perhaps remind you that RF lost that day. It was as if he had met his kryptonite – a new force that I know you adore because you think Rafael Nadal is tough and inexhaustible, so very Vietnamese. But, as is the case with many men, his hyper-masculinity is a fragile mask for his repressed homoeroticism. Of course, it is not the eroticism I condemn, but rather his efforts to repress it. So too, I condemn the twisting mishits that he brings to each rally, as instructed by his uncle Toni. I condemn his lopsided arms and snarl, and his brash, ill-tailored attire – his shorts are too long and his shirts unforgivably sleeveless. And I condemn the tribal manner in which he zigzags across the court and snaps at his underpants before each point.

Roger's historic defeat confirmed what I knew only too well: that life is not meant to be just or charming. So I did *not* cry then. But Roger did, and as I watched him hold up his consolation plate – with Mr Diep and his friends cheering for the underdog and hacking away at the tall poppy – I was overwhelmed with a desire to comfort him. Roger needed my strength in the face of newfound uncertainty. What was necessary at that moment was for him to rest his head in my lap and for me to run the back of my fingers along his gossamer soft locks. 'Don't fret. Everything will be alright, Roger', I would swear to him. 'You are still number one. Still number one.'

'Give me one of your racquets', I said to the coach with a mad man's conviction, 'and before summer's end I'll give you a lesson that you'll never forget.' It was another humid morning, a lull before the after-breakfast players arrived to humiliate me.

The pack of ball boys squatting around the coach cackled and snorted like hyenas. But when the laughing subsided, my challenge remained. The coach knew he could not refuse me without damaging his alpha-male status. And so he nodded, took from his basket one of his oldest racquets and passed it to me. I suspect that it was once purple, but there were so many chips and scratches on it that I couldn't tell for sure. The towelling grip was ragged and sweaty, like the ones I had used on badminton racquets. The diminutive head size also reminded me of my badminton days, but this racquet was far heavier.

'Remember to hold the pointy end and make sure you keep it out of your arse. I want it back after I've given you a thrashing!' The cackling resumed, and I walked away.

That lunchtime, with no one else daring to face the noon-time glare and heat, I began my training. I stalked across the road to the water treatment plant where there was an expanse of bitumen and a wall along which a wonky line had been painted at net height. The space was rarely used because the bitumen was breaking up and wet, but within the week I could play around every crack, bump and puddle. The sound of the rushing water helped to purify my thoughts and focus upon all that mattered: the ball. With each groundstroke, I concentrated on willing the ball to collide with the very centre of my racquet; I imagined the next shot being even more precisely struck, and then played that imagined shot. After a few weeks of this regimen I drew spots on the wall and tried to hit them twice in a row, then five and ten times, with alternating forehands and backhands, topspin and slice. As I improved, my drives threatened to knock bricks out of their mortar, while my drop shots were butterfly kisses from the ball to the wall. I practised in every spare moment. And when I was so tired that I could no longer run, I worked on my serve; not focusing on generating brute power, but rather on my fluidity and form, which made for speed and accuracy while also preserving my shoulder so that I could practice for yet another hour. At first, I did it for Roger and to be more like him; but before long I was preoccupied with bettering him by becoming me, a superman untroubled by kryptonite.

Feel free, Mr Ha, to learn what you can from my training. I have no secrets and encourage spectators to record me with their cameras so they might review my technique in slow motion as many times as they please. Indeed, as people at my club and others began to do this, I came to the realisation that no one – regardless of their admiration and desire – could be like me. I was a natural talent to be sure, but my meteoric rise was also the outcome of an individual history and work ethic that simply could not be emulated by others. The badminton with which I had been well-drilled was a wellspring of hand-eye coordination. My limber upper body was able to strike with the speed and ferocity of a cobra. In line with Ngoc's cycling and anatomical philosophy, I developed powerful and fastidiously shaven thighs. Our sustained lovemaking fostered stamina and imbued me with the improvisation skills of a silver leaf monkey darting through the treetops. Superimposed on all of this was an intense anger and craving for justice, such that in every ball I saw the mangled and mashed faces of my father, cousin Thuan, and the cops who had hammered Ngoc with their batons. And then finally there was the coach who was the culmination of all these patriarchs and scoundrels. The only way to deal with him was by repeated slaps across the face until he came to his senses and accepted me, indeed revered me, for who I am.

I began challenging the other ball boys to matches. The weakest boy was no opposition, nor was his immediate superior, nor the one after that. It was as if I was playing a computer game in which each level involved new traps, dangers and henchmen with special powers. Shot by shot, I not only defeated my ball boy foes, but won them over as well. Often I played to their strengths and deliberately exposed the chinks in my armour so that I could improve and they could feel as if they had some chance of winning. And because tennis is a gentleman's game and humility is essential to greatness, I always congratulated my opponents when they took points from me or came close to doing so.

Given the dramatic rise of my tennis prowess and my reputation, it was no surprise in the last week of summer when the coach informed me that a wrist injury prevented him from playing. With a cold, steely gaze, I informed him that any time in the autumn was good for me.

It was not until the moon festival had well and truly passed and the coach had endured persistent taunting from his ball boys that he finally acquiesced and stood across the net from me. Our match was, after all that build-up, a non-event. The coach was not bad, but he was a predictable ball feeder, a textbook follower, a counterpuncher with a safe but uninspiring double-handed backhand. He grunted, shrieked and scurried like so many female Russian players with neither art nor flair. He was not a true player.

The result was preordained, but not the ending. For as I approached the coach to clink our racquet heads as a sign of appreciation, he leapt over the net to my side of the court and grabbed my battle-scarred racquet.

'Don't ever lay your hands on this again!' he announced before flinging it over the back fence so that it smashed against the gutter of a house. The coach then reversed his brand-new, top-of-the-line, freshly strung racquet, and presented the handle to me.

'This is yours. Take it. Just tell everyone that I'm your coach.'

Would you believe he even knelt down and lowered his head, displaying all the chivalry of a samurai surrendering his sword?

And as I clenched that yielding blade, the crowd of onlookers burst into applause. They cheered for me with a gusto untainted by envy because I had reached heights that they could not possibly dream of reaching themselves, and because with all of their tiny hearts they wanted me to soar higher. And in that instant it was as if we had all been transported back to that fateful Wimbledon final, only this time grace had triumphed.

During the previous season I could not find anyone to play tennis with me, and now they queued, pleaded and even paid to do so. Players asked me to warm up with them and I was regularly challenged to games. My fee was 100,000 dong and I insisted on giving all contenders a 15-point head start in each game just to make it interesting. I would have made far more money had I agreed to play doubles, but always felt as if my side of the court was already cramped with just me in it.

On occasions when an audience gathered to watch me play, I would instruct them in good etiquette. If I was to play for them it seemed only proper that they show me the courtesy of not speaking on their phones and, better yet, switching them off. I demanded that spectators only applaud when I struck a clean winner, not when I forced my opponent into error. People in neighbouring houses with small balconies overlooking the courts were firmly advised that they should not eat hot food or cradle babies while enjoying my play because of the inherent hazards and in memory of Michael Jackson. After becoming convinced that none of the people around me could develop into supreme tennis players, I set my goals much higher; seeking through example and instruction to cultivate them into better, more civilised people.

To be sure, most of them were stubbornly barbarous, but not all of them all of the time. And certainly not Thanh, the ball boy who arrived from the highlands not long after me and who was hard-working, loyal, decent, and as loveable as a hound. Thanh had a mighty mop of hair, which he always tried to tame with a headband. He also had a reasonably good swinging left-handed serve. He was slightly older than me but was, by all significant measures, my inferior. This he knew well, so that of all the praise I have received for my tennis and demeanour, Thanh's was the most heartfelt.

'I like to watch you play, Mr Thu. But, you know, I like to *listen* to you play even more.' Thanh closed his eyes as if he was savouring a boiled sweet. 'I listen to the thunderous crack of your serve and how you snap your wrist at the very last instant to add pace and spin; I listen intently to your feet as they slide like river stones over the court; the frightening whoosh of your topspin forehand, the engulfing silence that comes with each slice backhand, and your drop shots, which fall on crackling banyan leaves and stay there. Often I try to hear you puff, grunt or swear. But you never have, not once, because you are not like the rest of us. I hope you do not find my praise irksome, Mr Thu.'

I told Thanh that I appreciated his attention and honesty and informed him that I had been looking for a reliable man to act as my lackey.

'That is all that I could ever hope for', he replied.

His first responsibility involved helping me to undertake a metamorphosis that I had been considering for some time. Having been blessed with a gentle wave through my hair, I wanted to distinguish myself further from my surrounds while drawing closer to Roger by introducing a few brown streaks. In my home town I had on many occasions helped my aunt dye her hair, so I knew exactly what had to be done, and that I could not do it myself. I sent Thanh to get the dye and directed him in how to apply it. He performed all that was asked of him without fault, but I suspect that either the dye company or shop assistant betrayed me because I emerged from my frothy chrysalis with a red bouffant that blazed brighter than the Swiss flag. Thanh was taken aback and deeply apologetic for playing a part in this unintended result. I assured him it was not his fault and that I had a knack for righting egregious wrongs. Regardless of this, I quickly came to like my new look and so did the other ball boys; by the end of the month the heads of all the ball boys displayed the full range of piquant colour that can be found in fire and chilli.

This was one of many salubrious effects I had on those who once taunted me with faeces. My leadership also brought cleanliness and order to our cramped little studio. The ball boys began to fold their clothes and place them in boxes, or hang them on hooks behind the door. Shoes and sandals were lined up on one side of the stairs and knick-knacks secured in old tennis ball cans. I drafted a roster for sweeping and dusting, always allocating myself extra shifts so that no one could accuse me of being imperious. To my astonishment, someone even hung up a picture. It is a gaudy scene of carp leaping out of a waterfall with 'Buon Ma Thuot' emblazoned across the bottom and rectangular cut-outs that would have displayed the temperature, time and date were the contraption still working. Despite not appreciating the picture, I found the effort and the thought of it most uplifting.

Although not the most senior of the ball boys in terms of years, I came to be regarded as the wisest, and so the others would look to me for guidance. Most importantly, by exerting the softest and surest power, I taught the ball boys that masculinity does not mean brutality, but rather being confident enough to embrace the demure. Following my statements regarding the value of oral health and self-restraint, two of them made valiant attempts to quit smoking cheap cigarettes. Others had success establishing relationships with girls, thanks to my advice to 'honour them as you honour me, and buy them flowers on alternate Tuesdays'. I taught them how to dress with panache and to recognise the importance of accessories and the even greater importance of not over-accessorising. Those ball boys who previously never washed made a habit of doing so, and one even developed an appreciation for cologne.

I was insistent about skin care and how it is never too early to safeguard the elasticity of one's face. This was particularly important for those of us who toiled day after day in the sun, but who also aspired towards office or studio work in the future. And so, while I have never belonged to the 'whiter-the-better' camp – and never could, given the swarthiness I inherited from my Khmer ancestors – I saw very early on the common sense in covering up. To this end I harnessed the potential of the water bottle boxes that were regularly discarded. I took to several of them with a knife and came up with a design that would make an experienced haberdasher envious: the sides folded to sit evenly on each shoulder; the back section extended to provide full UV coverage; a series of vents in the top could be closed on cool mornings; and an adjustable visor at the front shaded the wearer's eyes.

This has, as you can see, Mr Ha, become standard issue for the ball boys at this club and is also donned by many of the players as they rest on the sidelines.

So try, Mr Ha, to come to grips with the fact that the 'ibox', as it has come to be known and which you scorn, represents the epitome of resourcefulness – the skilful integration of functionality and form.

Now that you are done playing, old man Ha, and have removed your shoes and shirt, reclining with your hands resting on your slimy belly, you may be ready to find out how I came to own this smartphone and why I deserve it.

You are, of course, too old and dim to know exactly what I achieve with this phone. But simply put, I use it to keep in touch with all the other number ones out there, digitally tethering myself to them so that none of us are set adrift in an ocean of zeros. Roger tweets me about his latest victory and how his twin daughters and sons are doing at home. There are vast networks of men from Binh Duong to Brussels who I also connect with for comfort, adventure, titillation, or to pass the time. I ask my phone what the weather is like in Rio and the price of sea cucumbers in Taipei – and it tells me. There are podcasts on Da Vinci's inventions to listen to, collections of poems by the Xuan Dieu to contemplate, Big Toe hip-hop videos to watch, and articles to digest on the hidden palaces of Emperor Khai Dinh and Angora rabbit farming in Dachau. Everything from my deepest yearning to my most fleeting desire is satisfied. It is the closest thing that I have to a home and is, in every way, superior to the one into which I was born. On occasion I even use it to call someone.

Because you asked, you should know that this modern-day lifeline was an indirect and unforeseen result of my decision to come out to the other ball boys. I told Thanh first and he reacted with trademark frankness and fidelity.

'I am not totally sure what "homosexual" means, Mr Thu. Given that I am not as far travelled and learned as you, would you mind if I asked you a few questions?'

'Feel free to inquire. I'm a curious man myself.'

'Thank you. Will you grow breasts?'

'No.'

'Do you wish to marry me? And that's not a proposal.'

'Never. You're not my type. Even if you were, the state would not permit it. And if I were the Party General Secretary, a prospect that I have not ruled out, no one – homosexual or otherwise – would be allowed to marry because I see no benefit and much harm in yoking two humans together as if they were beasts of burden and then rejoicing with excessive amounts of cognac and seafood.'

'Have you ever slept with a woman?'

'Many times', I lied, but had certainly had opportunities to do so.

'What was wrong with those women that you would reject all others?'

'Your question should really be "What's right about the men who I've made love to that I could not possibly return to women?"'

'Will I catch this homosexuality from you?'

'You were not born so blessed and would struggle to be anyone other than who you are.'

Thanh had a habit of rubbing the cleft of his chin with his index finger when he was deep in thought.

'I do not pretend to understand you, Mr Thu, and never have. But I see no reason to respect you less today than I did yesterday as our club champion and moral exemplar.'

Thereafter, it was easier and less time-consuming than I had thought to come out to the ball boys because Thanh took it upon himself to do the explaining and, where necessary, the arm-twisting. I thanked Thanh sincerely, which made him blush, and assured him that his loyalty and liberal-mindedness would soon be rewarded with a most spectacular gift.

Mr Vui played six times a week in two different groups, and on the face of it was an upstanding club man and citizen. He had the angled jaw of a Hong Kong soap star and a sprinkling of distinguished grey hair around his temples. Vui played with the latest racquets and wore designer tracksuits, which he imported from Singapore to avoid fakes. All of this was paid for by a multi-level *World of Fones* store that was owned and managed by his wife. By Vui's own account, she paid him a stipend to stay away, arguing that he and his family had only ever known bankruptcy and indigence. Mr Vui's two daughters attended an international primary school and were looked after by his mother-in-law and an *au pair* after hours, which also suited him because, by his reckoning, one of his daughters was a twerp and the other was a bitch. So while he was a man of leisure and means, there was a futility in Mr Vui's life, which he articulated to me one day during a change of ends as an inability to hit a topspin backhand.

'Not being able to hit a topspin backhand didn't stop Steffi Graf from winning a grand slam', he reasoned to me, 'but it still causes me woe.'

Apparently the coach had tried to help him to no avail. And so now his problems were mine to fix. We met at lunchtime and I drilled him with one backhand after another, insisting that he grip his racquet fiercely and drive with his legs, holding the racquet head up high, swinging down low and then rising up again and over the ball. After half an hour of drills, about four-fifths of his backhands landed in the net, while the remainder flew over the baseline.

He asked to rest and as we sat beside one another Mr Vui took out his state-of-the-art phone from his tan leather *World of Fones* holster. We played a few online games, zoomed in on ourselves from a satellite, and I swiped quickly from picture to picture of his wife and children in taffeta dresses at birthday parties and death anniversaries. Throughout all of this Mr Vui's hand was on my thigh, hunched like a cat about to leap on its prey.

'There's a European clay court tournament on the television right now, *em* Thu', he said, finally breaking the silence. 'My house is a little too far away, but I know a hotel near here with satellite television. Let's go and watch it and you can give me a few more pointers.'

Mr Vui paid for two hours. We sat on the end of the bed and I was startled when he turned on the television to see that there actually was a tennis tournament on. 'Switch it off, *anh* Vui', I said to him with an endearing whine.

I pushed him back upon the mattress and explained that he could relax in the knowledge that I had my hand on the rudder. In a matter of seconds his shorts were around his ankles and I was in control of Mr Vui. He was tall but tender at first, and was then obliging for a while before becoming stubborn to please at the very end, so that it took all of my ambidextrous attention to relieve what may well have been years of tension pent-up in his haunches. With his discharge came a carnal roar that set the sparrows flying from the hotel rooftop.

Immediately afterwards, Mr Vui dashed into the bathroom and returned with towels and toilet paper as if he was going to erase the evidence from a crime scene. I sat calm and bemused on the bed as he crouched on his knees trying to scrub away his shame – still with no pants on. And then Mr Vui began to sob, saying that he was not ashamed of me, but rather of himself.

'I'm not a gay *pe-de* and neither are you', he proclaimed. 'You are confused and just a boy. I'm oppressed. Both of us innocent. That fuckin' woman. She made me do this.'

He wept as he told me how their marriage looked good only on paper, how it was a union of families and interests but never of hearts and loins, and how their household was as fabricated as the photo album of them that they kept on the coffee table with fake backdrops of Hawaii, Sydney and Phu Quoc. His wife was more interested in money than people and so they had only had sex three times in the past two years, on days that were designated as auspicious by a fortune teller. Even then his wife insisted that she would only ride him while she was clenching fistfuls of US dollars and wearing a necklace of jangling gold taels. Despite barely touching him, she had screwed all the love and passion out of his life. Mr Vui offered further excuses and tears, concluding with a promise that he would never again use me like that and, in turn, that I should not speak to anyone about what we had shared. As a goodwill gift, Mr Vui offered me a 200,000 dong note.

I swore that our secret was safely buried and refused his money, asking only that he let me stay in the room for the remaining hour so that I could savour the air conditioning. Mr Vui thanked me profusely. As soon as he left, I turned the fan speed up and the temperature right down. As the icy wind hit the sweat on my face, I closed my eyes and wondered how long it would be before Mr Vui returned for another lesson.

He showed more restraint than I expected, staying away from the courts altogether for four days and then avoiding my gaze for two. But exactly a week after our first encounter he requested another session, professing that even though his backhand had not substantially improved, he sensed he was on the brink of progress. We practised and then, as we sat resting, he fondled me. This time, Mr Vui had a much better idea of what he wanted. He said he abhorred judgemental hotel receptionists and was wary of their security cameras. Since his life had become unbearably sterile, again the fault of his half-android wife, Mr Vui wanted a love that was impure, like the videos he had seen on the internet, filthy but not unhygienic.

I knew just the place: a public toilet block on the road to the CBD that was much cleaner and far less frequented than the surrounding gutters and trees. 'If we leave right now the cleaners will be on their lunch break and won't disturb us. We can even avoid paying the 4,000 dong fee if we get out before their siesta ends.' Mr Vui was more than happy with my choice of cubicle and technique – 'The Colgate Clinch' as Ngoc had christened it. Afterwards, I sat on Vui's lap with my arms around his neck as he giggled and snivelled simultaneously. This time, however, he did not apologise or offer me money. Instead, Mr Vui intimated that they were clearing out some superseded phones at his wife's shop and that he could try to get his hands on one for me if I liked.

'That would make it easier for us to keep in contact', I exclaimed with wholesome enthusiasm.

To which he replied: 'I don't know what the future holds, *em* Thu, but I know I really care for you.'

'I feel exactly the same way', I professed, lying in every respect.

Our third liaison, again in that public toilet block, was foreshadowed by an assurance from me that Mr Vui would discover the delights of both giving and receiving. We began as we did before, but when Vui reached the apex of his pleasure parabola, I pulled him up, turned him around and pressed his head down upon the toilet seat before applying a few brisk slaps to his behind and proclaiming with my best Japanese accent that his passive and yielding *uke* was about to become acquainted with my most assertive *seme*. I untied my shorts and was glad to find myself excited, not so much by the ivory backside in front of me, but rather by the prospect of a game plan perfectly executed. And then I entered Mr Vui, eliciting in him an invigorating mix of pain, shame and bliss. When he yelped for the third time, I deftly flicked his phone holster under the bathroom door with my foot and then crept around in front of him, perching myself upon the cistern. I tried to look into his eyes, which were darting. I brushed his hair, tickled his ears, and then guided his mouth upon me. Mr Vui deserves some credit for his zest, but he had no idea what he was doing and was obviously inept at giving anything to anyone. So much so that in that instant I conceived of the name 'Ebenezer's Chomp' for his actions and began to see why his wife needed supplementary stimulation. Of course there was no use at this stage instructing Mr Vui, so I closed my eyes and thought of Ngoc powering through that city tunnel, of Roger in his dainty cardigan and of how close I was to a constellation of killer apps. It worked, and as I approached match point, I flushed the toilet with my heel, which was the sign for Thanh to make his entrance.

He did not let me down, slamming the door open at just the right time, but with a little too much force given that it was unlocked. There was my Sancho Panza, holding up Mr Vui's phone exactly as I had instructed him. Mr Vui turned around and it was in this instant that he made a decision. The red-eye reduction flash went off first, giving him an instant to recognise that our tryst had been a farce and that the line between abuser and abused was not clear-cut. Then the main flash took another second or so to warm up, which gave him even more time to cover his face or turn away, if he so desired. But he did not and, as much as he might deny this, I believe this was because deep down Mr Vui wanted to be unveiled; he wanted to live in truth and screw the consequences. And it is a tribute to the refinement of my reflexes that at the precise time that those tiny LED beacons unleashed their celestial beam, I made the choice to expel my sweetened soy milk all over him.

An instant later, Thanh was out of the toilet block and running down the street, pursued only by the sound of the returning attendant, who swore at him for not paying his money.

My lover and student of topspin backhands grabbed me by the collar and lifted me up with surprising force so that my bare buttocks were pressed against the wall. His right hand grabbed my throat and I would have had to kick him had I not been able to croak, 'I have your phone.'

And with that, he was Mr Vui again. Crying and apologising, this time with even more sincerity. 'What do you want? What can I give you?'

I gave Mr Vui some sheets of toilet paper to clean my man jam off his face before informing him, 'I am neither a bandit nor an extortionist and ask from you only what you can give with ease: three phones just like yours; one for me; one for our photographer; and one for a friend who you will never know and who is, as we speak, preparing to upload all of your contacts and that picture of us into the cloud for safekeeping.'

Once the phones were delivered to me along with three sim cards with propitious numbers, I went on to explain, I would return Mr Vui's phone to him. He could even have another free lesson in backhands if he so desired.

'Give me two days', agreed Mr Vui, because he knew he had no choice. 'You can keep your tennis lesson.'

After that Mr Vui was a little surly towards me, but this diminished in time. Indeed, it is an indication of my charisma and his newfound generosity of spirit that, every week since then and of his own volition, Vui has presented me with three recharge cards to top up my call and data credit. I give one to Thanh, who does not know what to do with his phone anyway, and use two myself, as our third friend was a necessary figment of my imagination.

So that is how I came upon this miraculous machine now tightly moulded to my senses. And if, Mr Ha, you still do not understand or accept me, you should at least know by now not to underestimate me.

Mr Ha, there is one more thing that you must know before you depart in your Korean sports car: I have revealed to you only a preview of the action-packed, pathos-free movie that is my life. You asked, Mr Ha, who I think I am and I have told you. But you know nothing about the more engrossing story of who I will become.

Know then that you need not ask for a practice session because I recently retired from tennis and am considering selling my racquet. Given that there has been some conjecture, let me make it clear that I did not sheath my sword because of injury or the arrival of a new upstart ball boy. I have never harboured anxieties about protecting my record or getting out while I was on top. My best days are always ahead of me and my legacy never complete. If I am a champion at anything it is not because I have won, but rather because I am one. It is because my adventures in life and love are the full expression of me alone.

And so recently I concluded that I had achieved as much as I could in tennis, overcoming the forces of conformity and raising the standards of play and civility at my club in one swift chip-and-charge motion. Now the baseline is a border, the net is a barrier, and being on court is like being in a cage. I suppose I grew bored – which, as far as I'm concerned, is the most compelling reason to give something up.

But if my smartphone has taught me anything, it is that there are an infinite number of worlds, people and gadgets out there for me to master. And so, with the shifting of seasons I have decided to save for a laptop and a camera and answer my true calling as a photographer. Of course, I will not be just a photographer, but rather the photographer: the photographer who can capture an entire epoch in a single frame; the photographer who straddles and unites the worlds of sport and fashion; the photographer who manipulates his images so as to reveal their innermost truth; who evokes both the objectivity of the umpire and complete empathy with the contestant; the photographer whose exhibitions challenge us to be who we are and – vitally – to live as if. As if the past is no anchor. As if the future is without sacrifice. As if there is always the possibility of new beginnings.

Chapter 3
The Professional

SMS (Samsung) from Thao:
Boss just left something on my desk. Urgent.
Sorry darling =(
Be there asap <3 <3

Thao's always running late. Obviously out of her depth. Was never cut out for big business. Too sweet. Too homely. Unprofessional.

'Waiter! Boy! Bring me a cappuccino and a glass of mineral water.'

'Yes madam. Straight away.'

'Hold on. Don't go running off just yet. Listen carefully. Last time I was here I didn't get what I asked for. There are four things you need to remember. One, I need skim milk, not full cream and certainly not UHT. Two, it must be a weak coffee, half strength. Three, I want extra chocolate sprinkled on the top. And four, I need two of those durian wafers on the side. Write it down. Four things. Can you manage that?'

'Yes madam, but please know that our hot beverages only come with one complimentary wafer, so if you don't mind you will have to pay extra for the second ...'

'I wouldn't be here if I cared about the price of wafers. Just make sure you get it right. Four things. And the mineral water.'

Email (iPhone) from Dzung of KPMG: Hi Kieu, Heard your company won the big PIV Oil tender. Dinner on Friday to celebrate your victory and commiserate my defeat?

Poor darling. He's probably being punished for losing that contract. He'll get over it. Dzung's a decent guy. It was harder than I thought to get the details of KPMG's bid out of him. Took five dates. I even had to let him feel me up. For a while there I thought I was going to have to meet his parents. But he caved in, just like they all do. Now I've got him by the balls, but I won't twist them off. I'll keep it to myself that he was the one who scuttled their bid. After all, Dzung might be useful to me later.

Email (iPhone) to Dzung of KPMG: Busy.

Incoming Call (iPhone) from Quynh in Human Resources:

'Good morning Ms Kieu. I've got two applicants who would be suitable personal assistants for you. They can both start next week. Do you want me to arrange for you to meet them?'

'No, just send me their CVs. Make sure to include their pictures and birth dates. And you've double checked their qualifications, work history and medical reports, yes? My previous PA claimed to have a TOEFL score of 110, but I'm sure it was about 50, which was also probably her IQ. The last thing she did before I fired her was to farewell a client with, "We love you from your bottom to your heart". There's no way that she graduated from the Foreign Trade University, at least not without cheating. We have to be scrupulous when it comes to recruiting. We can't be the best without the best people.'

'Yes, Miss Kieu.'

'Good, make it so.'

Facebook (Samsung): Harry Nguyen has checked in at Singapore Bird Park.

Facebook (Samsung): Super Junior Promotion! Post a mashup of the members of your favourite band on facebook for the chance to win one of 50 backstage passes to SuJu's upcoming concert tour of Vietnam!

Twitter (Samsung): @Prada. See the new Roman Polanski short film, Ravishing, *made by and for Prada www.prada.com/en/ravishing*

I look up and see Thao coming through the door. She speaks to the maître d' and then sees me waving my phone in the air and rushes over. Her clothes are tidy enough, but she has a fake bag and wears a cheap belt. Worst of all, Thao still has long hair, which she ties back like a country bumpkin. She says her husband likes it that way. I'd shave my head before submitting to that bygone hairdo.

'Hello my dear. It's soooo good to see you. You look extraordinary. It's like you're getting younger with each day.' I stand up and kiss Thao on both cheeks.

'I'm awfully sorry for being late. My boss has been tormenting me nonstop.'

'Is that the boss with the fake tits? The one who hired a numerologist to calculate the circumference she'd want for her new boobs?'

'Yes, that's the one. I wish I never told you that. You keep bringing it up. You haven't told anyone, have you?'

'No, never. You know you can trust me with anything.'

How can Thao expect me to keep that to myself? She must realise that I've told everyone in the industry by now.

'Yes, of course. Sorry. And sorry again for being late, Kieu darling. The traffic today is worse than usual. I almost got hit by a taxi as I turned into this street. The driver stopped and yelled at me even though it was his fault. I know I always keep you waiting. A thousand pardons, a thousand pardons.' Thao bows like a Japanese housewife.

'No problem, dear. No problem at all. I just keep working, doesn't matter where I am.' I show her my phones. 'You know me. Always connected.'

I put my iPhone on the table and tuck my Samsung away in my Hermes purse: personal correspondence can wait. I half smile and half smirk at Thao. Who does she think she is? We may be from the same village, but that doesn't mean she can hold me up all the time. We're not like most people in Vietnam. Time is not elastic for us. It's rigid. It's worth more than money: it's respect.

'You're punctual as usual, Kieu my darling. I bet you're always early to your appointments.'

'It's not easy to fit everything in. But it helps that I've started to walk everywhere and never leave District 1 if I can avoid it.'

'But walking's so filthy, so crude.' Thao makes a face like she's holding up dirty socks.

'Just a minute, the waiter's coming. Another cappuccino for this dear woman. And a plate of French fries. Tell the chef to cook them for a little longer than usual – I like them crispy. And make sure you bring out ketchup, chilli and soy sauce, and mayonnaise, each in separate dishes, not spread out on the plate. Understand? French fries; extra crispy; four separate sauces.'

'Yes madam.'

'You watch. He'll screw it up. Probably on purpose. Haughty little shit. Doesn't know his place. We should've gone to a different restaurant. Honestly, this establishment has been backsliding ever since the cute French manager returned home. Figured he'd completed his slum service no doubt. It's in Vietnamese hands now. A couple of managers from the sob story school that picks up street kids, feeds them with false love and then trains them to be two-star servants. Most of the waiters are from the same school. That fellow over there struggling with the armful of entrées was probably selling cigarette lighters by the highway last year. I don't know why they bother. You can't change people like that, not with all the bleeding heart goodwill in the world.'

'I agree, totally.'

'Where was I?'

'Walking, dear Kieu, you were going to explain your walking.'

'Yes, there are a few things worth holding onto from the countryside, and walking is one of them: keeps us lean, strong, alert. And it means I don't depend on drivers.'

'But the sun will burn you black. Haven't you seen those anti-aging cream advertisements? That one for *Xinh Xuat Xac* lotion says that for every hour you spend in the sun your skin ages 30 days.'

'What do Vietnamese know about skin? Anyone who's spent time in the West knows that white people will do anything for a tan. They sunbake, go to solariums – I've seen them spray themselves with cans of orange paint so they can look more like us. All the while we're trying our best to look like pale and sickly versions of them. Can you believe that model Phi Thanh Van becoming famous for her swarthiness and then going to all that trouble to turn white? Perhaps it's a publicity stunt. Maybe she was sponsored by a skin clinic to do it? Bad decision, regardless of what she was paid. Before she looked like an Amazonian queen. Now she's as pasty and wide-eyed as every other Hello Kitty idiot. Me, I take pride in my brown skin. There's no way I'm covering up like a Muslim woman every time I step outside.'

'But Kieu dear, it's not safe to be walking in the streets, even in the daytime. Last week a colleague of mine had her purse stolen while she was crossing …'

I reach down and pull out my capsicum spray from my handbag to show her. She shuts up. While I'm down there I also reveal my new Dr Headlock Executive Edition headphones.

'Darling, do you know about these? They're a blessing for people on the go. Plug them into your phone and the world outside just fades away. Sometimes I don't even have any music on and just use the noise cancelling function. They kill the buzz, the banter, everything and everyone is cancelled out. Forget those in-ear things. For headphones to work properly everyone has to see you with them. Motorbike taxi drivers, hawkers, beggars and young men see me walking with these on and know to back right off. It's as if I have a "do not disturb" sign over my head.'

Thao's cappuccino arrives.

'Make sure you bring those French fries, waiter!' I remind him. 'With the sauces.'

'So no plans to get your motorbike license then?' Thao asks. 'I can give you some lessons if you like. I'm sure you'll get the hang of it this time.'

I sense the ridicule in her voice. Snide bitch. She's always trying to find fault with me.

'You know I can't. It's not for me, never will be. My palm reader told me as much. The swirls on my right pinkie fingerprints mean that I'm destined never to ride a motorcycle. And see this crease on my left hand? It means I'll never cook an edible meal. It's not like I care though. Not anymore.'

And with that I reach into my Louis Vuitton purse and retrieve the little card that will muzzle Thao once and for all about my not being able to ride a motorbike.

'Is that what I think it is? How did you get it? You never told me you were learning to drive a car!'

'I only started practising last month. A driver at my office offered to teach me.'

'Doesn't the course take six months?'

'I was speaking to one of our consultants, a Belgian guy, and he said that Human Resources got him a car license without him having to sit the exam. And so I called them up and asked them to get one for me too. I had to pay, of course, but only 700 US. Next time we go back to the village I'll drive us. I've got my eye on a BMW X6.'

'Wow! I can see us now motoring through the main street. Get something with a sun roof. No, no, get a convertible. You're so brave, a real twenty-first-century pioneer. You'll be driving racing cars soon.'

Sarcastic little vixen – can't finish a sentence without taking a swipe at me.

'How much is it to buy a car nowadays? Expensive, isn't it?'

'Absolutely. We drivers are terribly persecuted. And the taxes make me wonder if Vietnam is more communist than ever. In the West, people pay less than half of what we have to dish out. When I was studying in Australia I could have bought a cute little hatch for $15,000. The same one here is double that price. Government vultures. You know, car buyers like me are the only hope for Vietnam to be a middle-income country like Malaysia or Thailand. The fact that we have to pay so much for cars shows how far we are behind the rest of the world. It's as if Vietnamese are not good enough to drive cars. As if success isn't its own reward. It's a penalty. Already the roads are congested and potholed, covered in swarms of people and filth. Car registration is on the up and every month another road in the CBD is blocked off to cars. Blood-sucking bureaucrats always bringing down giants so that everyone else doesn't feel like a midget.'

'But isn't it dangerous, Kieu? My husband says he's never going to drive a car, at least in Vietnam. He says going more than 30 kilometres an hour on our roads is a death wish. It's not like Germany with their autobahns and rules. One of my bosses is from Stuttgart and he says Germany is 110 per cent different to Vietnam. He says in Germany even the criminals follow the rules.'

'The speed suits me just fine. I've never felt more certain of myself than when I'm rocketing along in two tonnes of climate controlled comfort. I'll admit I was a little nervous at first. But then I reasoned that it is better for me to kill a motorcyclist than for someone to kill me. I can at least pay off the family with a thousand dollars or so. They would probably thank me. I wouldn't be like all those Chinese hit-and-run drivers. Remember that clip on the web of the van colliding with that child in the market?'

'How could anyone forget?'

'The driver seemed to aim for her. Afterwards he stopped, thought about it, and ran over her again before driving off. As I watched all those people stepping around her crumpled little body I almost wept. But, you know, that shocking affair confirmed an important lesson for me. The common people, they just don't value life like we do. Life's cheap for them. They can take it or leave it. When I think of what makes the world go round, I think of that delivery van crashing into that toddler over and over again.'

Reminder 1 hour (iPhone): 14:00 meeting with Minh Thanh. Remember to adjust the HSBC financial modelling tools.

Email (iPhone) from Sam of AB Bank: There's serious money to be made from the Vinashine restructure. Let's meet next week for a drink.

I put my phone back on the table just as Thao picks hers up. She probably doesn't even have any messages. Just wants to show off. No doubt writing an SMS to herself or her husband to keep me waiting. Again. So very pathetic. I glare at her and finally she places it back on the table.

'Careful with your phone, darling', I tell her. 'Keep it close to hand and away from the edge of the table. I wouldn't even have mine out except that I'm expecting some calls. Also, make sure you hook the strap of your purse around the leg of your chair like I have. You can't be too careful.'

'But we're in a good establishment, Kieu …'

'That doesn't mean a thing. It's not like they can frisk everyone who comes in here. That guy over there's been sitting on his coffee for an hour waiting for just the right moment to strike. The waiter's no better. He'd happily give up his job in exchange for one of our phones or wallets. Shameless. Shameless crooks.'

'You can be a little heartless sometimes, my dear.'

'My heart's got nothing to do with it. Think about it. If you were making one US dollar a day and saw this one thousand dollar phone just centimetres away, what would you do? Would you worry about what would happen to you if – and that's a big "if" – you were caught? Would you stop to consider what your parents or teachers or Uncle Ho told you about what's wrong and what isn't? Maybe, for a millisecond, just before you grabbed it and ran. I'll tell you what's heartless. Heartless is tempting them by leaving your phone out like that.'

'But we were poor not so long ago, remember? And some of our family and friends back home are still needy, even if it's not as bad as it was before.'

'I remember all right. It's because I remember what it's like to be poor that I don't trust poor people. It's because I know them so well that I despise them so much. I remember after my father left us, how my mother had to beg for food and clothes. I'm pretty sure she had to screw at least one of our landlords. And at primary school I remember how the other kids snubbed and mocked me because I was skinny and ragged.'

'We weren't exactly popular, were we? Still, I'm fond of our old school. I was so sad when I found out that it was knocked down to make room for a new shopping centre. It was like all those childhood memories of ours were being cleared away.'

'You know what I recall from that time? After the New Year holidays when our chubby friend Nhung – the one whose family owned the stationery shop – came to class with her brand-new Backstreet Boys pencil case full of felt-tip markers. I've never told anyone this, but on the same day that she showed off those pens to us, I stole one, a purple one. She probably didn't even notice it was missing. But I treasured it, kept it hidden at home. I was forever frightened I would be caught. So I only ever used it once a week or so. Not to write anything, but to draw – a pair of tiny lilac shoes, a dress, a television, a house.'

'Thanks for sharing, Kieu darling. That's terribly sad. Sad, but also cute. I wish it had been easier for you. On the bright side, now you can buy as many purple things as you like.'

'Haven't you noticed that nowadays I don't own anything lilac or purple. Clothes, makeup, nothing. For me it's the colour of desperation. I detest it. The only exception is my Montblanc fountain pen – I sign contracts with it – here.'

I withdraw the lustrous, cigar-sized pen from the side pocket of my Hermes handbag and hold it in front of Thao's face.

'May I?' Thao holds the pen and pretends to scribble on a napkin, then places it on the table near her phone so that I have to snatch it back.

'It's white gold', I explain, 'filled with the most exquisite purple ink. Every time I use it I remember where I came from and how I'll never go back there again.'

'Kieu darling, I know it was tough back then, especially for you. But maybe it's best to forget about all that. Everyone's better off now. And we're better off than just about everyone. Let it go.'

'How could I? How could I let go of the rage I harboured in high school knowing that our classmates were paying for extra lessons and higher grades? And yet every time I got the top mark in an exam, I was the one who was accused of cheating.'

'Yes, I know darling. But we left our home town a long time ago. It's better to leave some of the unpleasantness behind too.'

'I remember leaving all right Thao. How could I forget us coming to the city for our university exams and discovering how expensive everything was and how nasty people were? I recall very clearly us, freezing and exhausted, studying into the early morning under the street lights. Even now, when I withdraw money I'm reminded of the time our landlady evicted us because she found some students who could pay more, and how we huddled together in that ATM booth. I remember how everyone in this city looked at us as if we were dirt that had blown under their doors or mould that had suddenly appeared in their bathrooms. And, you know, I don't blame them. Because if the Kieu of back then saw the Kieu of today, I have no doubt she would bash me over the head and run off with everything that I own. Well, this Kieu has worked too hard to let that Kieu get away with it.'

'Okay, okay, I'm moving my phone. I'm putting it away from the guy in the corner with the cup of cold coffee, away from the waiter, all the common people and the Kieu who's just arrived from the countryside. Let's not talk about the past anymore. It's so depressing. Let's talk about the future. Are you getting the new iPhone?'

'I was tempted to, but I'm tired of iPhones. You?'

'I'll stand in line all day if I have to, or I'll pay someone to stand for me. Your company pays for your phones. Why not get a new one?'

'I used to love Apple. Now I'm not so sure. I still like the sleek lines and how they take a razor to everything: one button, right in the middle, no need to fiddle about. I call it the "Make It So" button. Don't you wish people were like that? Wouldn't it be great if people's noses were buttons and all we had to do was press them and command, "Make It So"?'

'I know exactly what you're talking about.'

'Anyone who's not exactly to our liking could be swiped, pinched or flicked into shape. And once we're done with them, they just go into standby. I must remember to tell this to my new PA – this is what I'll expect of her, and she of others.'

'You can thank the venerable Steve Jobs for that. He demanded that people work for him in the same way that machines did: intuitively, efficiently, obediently.'

Which is by far the smartest thing Thao has said all morning.

'Exactly. And the fact that he's gone is one of the reasons I don't have Apple cravings anymore. You can't just roll another visionary like that off the production line. Look at how he lived, doing his own thing, never afraid of failure. How he refused to pander to his underlings. He told people exactly how it is and how they should be. It was all about self-expression for him. His jeans and black skivvy were iconic, just like Audrey Hepburn's black dress.

He even wore his cancer in an avant-garde sort of way – with authority and poise. You know, I almost didn't go to work the day he died. I grieved for all of the gadgets that we'll never know.'

'Me too. Me too. I burnt incense to him on the 49th and 100th day after his passing.'

'But he would have wanted us to move on. To be honest, I was growing tired of all those iShadows and spaghetti white earphones. And Apple stuff is so common now.'

'You're right you know. I swear I saw a street sweeper using an iPhone, or at least it was a good fake.'

'Yeah, so last month I replaced my second iPhone with a Samsung. In fact, I'll probably get another one for work and ditch Apple for good – I hardly use my iPad nowadays. And I've sworn never to own an Apple watch, unless that is they join forces with Longines, Tissot or Rolex and come up with something that's actually stylish.'

'Wow. I never thought I'd hear you or anyone say that Apple was unstylish. Uncool.'

'I'm a Samsung girl now. My only reservation is that Samsung is sourcing so many of its components from here. You just watch the quality and sales fall. Vietnamese can't be relied upon to make top-quality products. The workers don't have the discipline and the managers aren't strict or smart enough – totally unprofessional. And let's not even talk about the Vietnamese Bphone. Honestly, my advice to Vietnamese companies would be to not bother trying to keep up with others. It's embarrassing.'

'I'm not sure about that, Kieu. My father-in-law always says that if Vietnamese can be disciplined and effective soldiers, then they can be disciplined and effective workers. And you know, I hear that Samsung shares are up on the back of increased productivity from Vietnam and global demand for Korean goods.'

Thao likes to pretend she knows something about share markets.

'Well, I agree with you when it comes to the demand for everything Korean. Don't you just love Korean TV and K-Pop? It's totally fake and manufactured, which is what's so authentic about it! You know, it's better than real. It's "unreal". Do you know that English word? There's nothing unreal about all those Vietnamese rip-offs of Korean shows and music videos though. It's soooo embarrassing. We just can't match their production values. You know Thiem, the director of communications who I introduced you to last year? He says that production values are the only values that count.'

'I see what you mean.'

Email (iPhone) from Dzung, Deloittes: Can we meet next week? Most nights are doable. Let me know and I will move some other appointments around to fit you in.

The French fries arrive and Thao invites me to start eating. I pull out a small crispy chip and dip it in the ketchup, chilli and mayonnaise.

Thao follows, but favours the soy sauce.

'Remember how we used to share sheets of rice paper with dried shrimp rolled into them at school?' she says. 'How we counted the tiny shrimp and tried to tear the sheet so that we each got the same number?'

It's as if she's guilty about how far we've come and everything that we've left behind. Or should I say how far *I've* come and everything *I've* left behind?

With that idiotic wistful look on her face she states the obvious. 'For the price of this one dish, we could have bought a month's worth of rice paper rolls.'

'That's something to celebrate, not mourn. Sounds like you would prefer to eat those filthy little rolls?'

'I know this sounds crazy, but sometimes I do. Sure, we didn't have any money in the village. But we didn't have so much to worry about either. Maybe I expected less back then so I wasn't as disappointed when things didn't work out. I'm not sure. But I know sometimes I want nothing more than to dip one of those rice paper rolls in some Tay Ninh salt and munch away. When my son starts school, I'm going to find someone who sells them. And I'll get one for him and me to share, just like we used to.'

'You're hopeless, Thao. Let me put it this way. Do you want your son to eat French fries in a restaurant or rice paper rolls off the street? He wouldn't last long on the latter I can assure you. He'd be as thin and frail as a chopstick splinter. And do you really think your son's school is going to allow hawkers to sell rice paper at the front gate? It will have a proper canteen selling proper food like beef steak and French fries.'

'I suppose you're right. You're almost never wrong are you?'

'What do you mean "almost"? How's Hieu anyway? Almost old enough for school, eh?'

'Yes, he's off to pre-school next month. He's wonderful. I just adore him. You should come around to see him. I'm sure he'd love to play with his Auntie Kieu.'

'Yes, I will, of course. I'll diarise it. Are his grandparents still looking after him? You said they were causing you grief. What did you call them? The tyrant and the terrorist …'

'No, it's not like that. I was upset when I said that. Please don't remind me. I admire them, really I do. I've come to understand that it was hard for them to accept a humble country girl for a daughter-in-law. Dai's their only son after all. You know that for a while they suspected I was a gold digger. So I tried to impress them by working hard and being successful, making just as much money as Dai. But that only made things worse because the real problem was that I didn't have the good graces and charms that they expected from their daughter-in-law. I'm just not dainty and genteel enough.'

'It's like the twentieth and twenty-first centuries never happened for them. They'll insist that Dai take on a concubine if you're not careful.'

'And you know, it's not like I haven't tried. I never once complained when we lived with them. Three years. Three years I suffered in their house even though we could have rented our own apartment. I did chores – washed the dishes every night and our clothes on the weekends – even when I had to work late and even though we had hired help. All of this so they could see I was a virtuous daughter-in-law and wife. Now we've finally moved out and they act as if I've deeply wounded them. They say they love me and miss me even more than their son. They've offered to buy a newer and bigger villa for all of us to live in. But of course it has nothing to do with me. It's all about their precious grandson and their vision of having three generations under one roof. To make it up to them we have to go back with Hieu for dinner three times a week, and then there's the lunches and family events on the weekend. You know, I'm starting to think it was a mistake to move out. I've hardly seen my new place. And all the commuting isn't good for my relationship with Dai, it puts a lot of stress on us.'

'Don't do it. Tell them to get lost. Get your husband to tell them where to go. You shouldn't have to spend another second with them.'

'I can't do that. And I can't ask Dai to do it either. He actually agrees with me about most things. And he loves me and Hieu no end. Dai would do anything for us. But he can't stand up to his parents. Dai says that everything he knows about love and caring for others, he learnt from them. There's this line of his that makes me clench my fists every time I hear it: "If I am a good husband to you and a good father to Hieu it's because of them; it's because I'm following their example of how to look after my family." I told him that if his devotion to us is based on his devotion to them, then *our* family doesn't really come first – *his* does.'

'Spineless. I'm sorry, but your husband's spineless as a jellyfish.'

'But Dai assures me it won't be like this for long – that it's just a transition period. I'm not so sure. We enrolled Hieu in the school near our house. It's an excellent school, set up by a Dutch couple who use the best of Eastern and Western methods. They have compulsory English and Chinese classes from Grade Two, and they teach five types of chess. It has a strong community, regular fairs, sports, fundraisers. I've met some lovely mothers there.'

'Sounds a lot better than our school. What's the problem?'

'Dai's parents said we should've run it past them. The thing is, we *did* mention it, but as usual they weren't listening. Then last week when we came for dinner they were waiting for us, sitting at the table like directors of a board addressing an underperforming CEO. It's as if Hieu is being raised by a committee and I'm not a member. They asked why we didn't enrol him in the American School they'd recommended, the most exclusive school in the city. Apparently they'd already paid a deposit to guarantee a place for Hieu, all without saying anything to us. It was supposed to be a surprise.

'"We know you didn't want to hurt our feelings and that's why you didn't say anything before you enrolled our grandson in that school", Dai's father said. "That's very commendable of you. But you have to think of what is best for Hieu. Trust us. We love him more than anything, even more than we love the both of you. You two are young. You think you know what you are doing, but you've never raised children before, how could you possibly know?"

'Dai's mother became more and more frantic. She insisted that we were sending him to the Dutch School because we didn't have enough money for the American one. She accused Dai of losing his job and keeping it from her because he was ashamed. She'd heard from one of her friends that the Vietnamese financial markets had recently taken a turn for the worse and that big companies were firing people by the hundreds. Apparently she hadn't slept a wink for days. Also, she had seen stories on the news of daycare workers beating and strangling children and threatening to drown them, and was petrified that this was going to be her grandson's fate.'

'Sounds like emotional blackmail to me.'

Thao nodded. 'Throughout all of this I stayed quiet, not a sound. And you know I was so … so angry, I wanted to pick up my son and storm out. Dai was holding my hand under the table and I was squeezing so hard I thought I was going to crush every little bone. I'll give it to him though, he calmly explained to his mother that he still had his job, and in fact he was thinking of going for promotion. He explained that we had researched many schools for Hieu and that the Dutch one suited us very well because it was near our house and excellent value.

'"If it's an issue of money then let me pay", Dai's father told us. He said that if we were pressed for time, then he would drive Hieu personally to and from school and that Hieu's grandmother would take care of him until we came over for dinner.

'"Doesn't that sound like the best option for everyone?" Dai's father said. "Isn't that the best thing for Hieu? Nothing is too good for my grandson, especially if he's going to be a world famous maths professor like Ngo Bao Chau. But if he's going to make the most of his gifts he needs the best education. That means sending him to the very best school; not the second best: the very best. Your Dutch school might save you some time and money now, but in the long run it will prevent him going to Harvard or Oxford."'

'Our parents would never have had the gall to treat us like that. That's one thing I like about our parents, they know their place and they stay there. They don't have a clue about what we do or what's best for us. How could they? They've hardly gone to school; they're petrified by the city. They're grateful for the money we send back every month and pleased we come home once in a while to light incense at the family altar. That's what I call "respect". Not your interfering in-laws.'

'No, it's not like that. They really do love Dai, Hieu and me. They've done so much for us. You know, when I need them to look after Hieu they drop everything to do it, straight away, even when it's inconvenient for them. And Dai's parents have given us so much: small things like flowers and fruits from their garden; and other things like the laptop that they bought Hieu for his fourth birthday and the diamond necklace they gave to me on my wedding day.'

'Yes, I remember that necklace.'

'But, you know, I often think I would happily never receive another gift from them and cook for them every week if they just listened to us once in a while. For heaven's sake, Dai and I are successful financial planners and risk analysts. How can we be so in charge at work and so powerless at home? I'm tempted to let them have their way on this school thing. It's just easier and they have a point about Hieu deserving the very best. But promise me this, Kieu. In 30 years, when we're grandmothers, promise me you'll never let me treat my son and daughter-in-law in the same way.'

Email (iPhone) from Matt of Techbank: Erica, Will, Carrie and I off to Da Lat on the 25th for canyoning and wine tasting. Love it if you can join us. We're staying in the Emperor's palace. My company will take care of everything. Say 'yes'.

Email (iPhone) from Maria Pham: Kieu, can you get me the FVT investment figures in Cambodian forestry before noon tomorrow? And please remember to rework those ANZ calculations.

Facebook: Cathy Nguyen likes One Summer Night, *by Chelsia Chan and Kenny Bee:*

> One summer night, the stars were shining bright
> One summer dream, made with fancy whims
> That summer night, my whole world tumbled down.

'Let's not talk about my family, it's all too complicated. Tell me about your work, Kieu. If half of the rumours I've heard are true, you're quite the business magnate – winning big tenders. And your financial models are selling like fresh prawns. Your bosses must be delighted. What's next for you, my darling? New York? Hong Kong?'

'It's going well enough. I've nothing to complain about.'

I'm careful not to reveal anything to Thao. Beneath the bubble tea sweetness, she's as jealous and calculating as they come.

'And how are you getting on with your bosses?'

'I'm still reporting to Wim Conlon and Maria Pham – did you see the "Power Couple" profile of them in *Asia Business Weekly*?'

'No, but I heard about it. They sound amazing. In their mid-30s and already millionaires. Gave up their careers in the US to be trailblazers on the Ho Chi Minh S-Ex. I remember you saying that Wim was inspirational, but Maria was harder to deal with, that she had some Viet Kieu adjustment issues.'

'I used to think Wim was fantastic. His father was a preacher and he has this amazing way of speaking to you as if he knows your deepest secrets and has all of the answers. Wim's an ultra-distance runner and has these dragon-green eyes that flare up whenever he's talking about hedge funds and hydration packs. And he makes an upturned claw with his hand when he's deep in conversation, like he's a conjurer or something. I've started doing it myself.'

'Sounds impressive to me.'

'He's okay. He calls himself an aggressive ethical investor. Wim gave me all these self-help books to read. He said they were compasses in his quest for wholeness. *Outsourcing Your Business to Buddha* and *Karmic Mergers and Takeovers*. Claptrap really, all this stuff about mindfulness, webs of life, transcendent thinking. The Orient for round-eyes. I knew I'd outgrown Wim when he told me with a straight face that he was spiritually rooted to a pack of bonobos in Central Africa.'

'How intriguing.'

'And you know Thao, while on the surface he's all new age, easy-going and in love with everything Vietnamese, in reality Wim looks down on us. I think they all do.'

'What do you mean?'

'Well, he's always talking about the need for a dynamic, horizontal work structure and acts like the best-friend boss, but watch out if you bring your lunch back to your desk in Styrofoam. Once he screamed at one of the IT guys for dumping a wad of paper in the waste bin instead of the recycling bin. It was like the poor guy had committed a mass atrocity or strangled an endangered Mekong catfish.'

'How are you supposed to eat?' asks Thao. 'Out of your hands?'

'If we want to bring food back to the office we have to use stainless steel tiffins and wash them afterwards like we're housemaids. He bought a collection of them embossed with the company logo. He says it's how Asians have transported their food for a century and carries his with pride. I've seen him leave the building at lunchtime wearing a conical hat, swinging his little meal containers, grinning like a village idiot.'

'I think that's cute.'

'Wim's all for Vietnamese traditions. He thinks he knows Vietnamese better than we know ourselves. Every time he and Maria go on a trip they come back with a box of traditional goodies for all of us in the office: lavender honey from the Meo Vac highlands; five-year fermented fish sauce from Phu Quoc; rice wine from Tay Nguyen. Everyone in the office knows you can buy that stuff from the local market, probably for half of the price he paid, but no one wants to tell him. And you should see their house. Wim's got these display cabinets in the living room in which he's collecting at least one artefact from each of the 54 ethnicities in Vietnam. He's up to 23. It looks like a pile of junk to me. I'd set a match to all those knick-knacks before they put a curse on me or attracted a cockroach infestation.'

'Sounds to me like he loves Vietnam. I still think he's sweet.'

'Well, I used to think that too. But when we went to Hanoi for a work trip last month and he saw roasted dogs stacked up in the shopfronts, suddenly Vietnam wanted to make him vomit. He actually stopped and protested. 'Friends not food! Friends not food!' he chanted to this butcher with his Lonely Planet Vietnamese. Luckily the store owner had no idea what he was saying. But then Wim made me translate for him. I was so embarrassed. I told the butcher I was a tour guide for terminally ill tourists and that Wim was deranged because he was in the late stages of pancreatic cancer.'

'Nice work. Maybe you should go work for the UN?' Thao giggled like a squirrel nibbling on a nut.

'That's not such a bad idea. Anything to get away from Wim for a while. You know, sometimes when I look at him I don't know whether to laugh or retch, sitting there in shorts on his Swiss ball, the underarms of his shirt raining sweat. He's blocked the air conditioner vents in his office because he says he doesn't want to be responsible for some extreme climate event that will kill millions of people in the Delta.'

'That's bizarre.'

'He's harmless enough, though. I've pretty much figured him out. To Wim I'm the industrious little lady with thick-rimmed glasses who looks to him for advice. As long as he thinks he's the one guiding me, I can do whatever I want.'

'Is his wife Maria the same? How do you get on with her? I heard she looks like a younger version of Nguyen Cao Ky Duyen. I've never worked with overseas Vietnamese. It must be weird – them being the same as us and different at the same time. Does she speak Vietnamese?'

'Her Vietnamese is all right. It's a bit stuttering and old-fashioned. She uses old words for places like *Uc Dai Loi* rather than *Oxtraylia* and substitutes English words for Vietnamese ones she doesn't know. Strangely enough, as I've moved further away from Wim, I've grown closer to Maria. I'd even go so far as saying she's a mentor to me now.'

'Wow. Last time we had coffee you said she was a stuck-up bitch.'

'Yes, I did say that. She struggled returning to Saigon. She revealed this to me after work and a few glasses of cabernet. She's been back to Vietnam before, but just a couple of times and only to see relatives. She said it was Wim's idea for them to move here and that she hated it at first. She couldn't deal with the heat, dirt, rats and rain. The poor people, beggars and cripples infesting the city before New Year also disturbed her. And after she arrived someone tried to rip her necklace off when she was driving her scooter through Tan Binh.'

'Pretty standard welcome to Vietnam.'

'But after a year or so she came to like it here. We even went to Ba Chua Xu temple together – we prayed for a profitable year and for the bankruptcy of our competitors. Wim was there and seemed to think everything was sacred and amazing. Maria was more focused; it was all about praying for money. She's far more genuine than him. She lives, eats and shits here while he treats the country like it's an open-air museum.'

'Sounds like they see things very differently, how did they ever get married?'

'Who knows? I don't think it will last. Lately they've been spending a lot of time apart. I've had something to do with that. A couple of months ago Wim went off to Tay Ninh by himself and so Maria and I started hitting the town after work. Been going out every Friday since then. Last weekend we went out twice. She loves flirting with men and she's a pro at getting them to buy us expensive cocktails.'

'Be careful, Kieu. You don't know the sorts of drugs they can slip in your drinks.'

'I know, I know. But it's Maria I'd worry about when it comes to potions. I crashed at her place last weekend and we woke up in the afternoon with awful hangovers. She went to her medicine cabinet and mixed some powder with mineral water for me and in a few minutes I was a new soldier.'

'What was it?'

'It took some coaxing – she admitted it was white rhino horn. She got it from a traditional medicine shop in Cholon.'

'That must've cost a fortune. Aren't they extinct?'

'She didn't tell me the price. She did say that when she and Wim bought it she told him it was a traditional herbal pick-me-up that had been blessed by a Cham matriarch, which is why it was so expensive. He would have whinged for days if he knew the truth. Maria said she had no problem with killing animals for human needs. Survival of the fittest, you know. That's exactly why she's come to adore Vietnam. It suits her entrepreneurialism. She says America's too liberal for her now. Companies can count on being bailed out and citizens are forced to buy health care.'

'Wow. I thought all Viet-Americans loved the USA and hated it here.'

'Maria does love America, but she hates the liberal disease that's infected it. She thinks its terminal. She wants to be here in the new New World. You know, she told me her grandfather never returned to Vietnam because he didn't want to support the communist regime. Maria says she steps out onto the street every day and has never seen a hint of communism. She thinks Vietnam is the land of opportunity.'

'I can see why you admire her. You must introduce me.'

'She's so right isn't she? Look at us, look what we've made for ourselves out of nothing. If you can't make it in Vietnam today, there's no one to blame but yourself. You can't blame the war, the Americans or the Chinese. It's just you. Either you're ambitious and talented or you're not. Maria has these great labels for people: makers and takers. Either you make something of yourself and contribute to the economic prosperity of the nation or you take from it and from everyone else. Simple as that.'

'Such insight. Inspiring. I'll remember that next time I feel sorry for myself or for others.'

'You know, Maria met the Prime Minister's daughter at a party a few weeks ago. She just loved Madame Phuong and was impressed by how in Vietnam today a 30-year-old woman can lead multi-billion dollar investment companies. It was a revelation for her. Seeing this tenacious young businesswoman claw her way to the top made her realise that the country has come of age — we've left the past where it should be. "I don't know what market socialism is. But whatever 'ism' applies here", she said to me, "I'm for it."'

'Sounds like a true patriot, your boss. It's so good to know we can welcome our brothers and sisters back to Vietnam, back home.'

'You know, last week after dining with some clients Maria and I were drinking cosmopolitans at the Renaissance Riverside and she revealed to me that she never felt like she belonged in America. Sure, she did well at school and in business. She had American boyfriends and married a white man. But she never felt fully accepted. She said she suspected that even if she strived all her life she could never break through the "bamboo ceiling". It was a really touching moment. Maria told me that although she left Vietnam when she was a baby and found it difficult living here at times, she felt she was where she belonged. "Drink the water, remember the stream", Maria said to me with a tear in her eye. She got that idiom wrong — it's not "stream" but "source" of course — but I didn't correct her.'

SMS (Samsung) from Chi Ba: Little sister, can you spare 10 million dong? It's a long story. I'll pay you back. Promise.

The waiter brings our bill and we make our way to the door to pay it.

'Allow me.' I say to Thao.

'No, no, my dear, I will pay', she says. 'I was the one who asked you out, remember?'

'But I was the one who chose this restaurant. Let me pay. It's nothing, really. Use your money to buy Hieu a new outfit.'

'But it's nothing for me either. OK, let's not fight. Let's be like Westerners and split the bill. How does that sound?'

'Okay, but I'm paying next time.'

Thao's such a stingy bitch. I paid last time and now she wants me to dish out again. She's never going to change.

'Don't work too hard – send my regards to your parents next time you speak to them,' Thao says. 'We'll do lunch again soon.'

'Yes, we must. Big hugs and lots of kisses to you and to little Hieu. Take care. Wait, wait. Hold on. Where's my iPhone?'

Chapter 4
The Goalkeeper

Usually I fall asleep in an instant and wake up just as quickly without an alarm. I see no good reason to be restless and don't care to dream.

But tonight I'm not myself. And this was no ordinary day. Today I suffered three grave disappointments, the memory of which traumatises me. So that, as much as I crave slumber, I find myself lying awake, hypersensitive to my surroundings.

The night air sits wet and heavy on my neck. Grime from this afternoon's soccer match clings to my chest and legs. I stare up into a void.

Although I pledged to shun air conditioning in solidarity with my peasant compatriots who have no desire for such luxuries, I fumble for the remote control in my bedside drawer and turn on the fan function in the hope that the hum will calm my mind.

Indulgence begets indulgence. Suddenly, I'm painfully aware of the grey river stone that I started using as a pillow a few months ago after hearing that Ho Chi Minh had rested his head on just such a stone while leading the anti-French resistance from Pac Bo Cave. When I first used my revolutionary cushion, I was amazed at how perfectly it moulded to my skull, as if my physical development had somehow been in step with the forces of nature that had contoured this unbecoming stone over the ages. I slept even more soundly than usual, at least until tonight. Tonight, the pillow pounds against my temple as I try to rest on my side. I push the stone away and lie flat on my back.

At the base of the bed is the coriander-coloured body pillow, embroidered with daisies, part of a set my mother bought to tempt me away from what she called 'that savage rock'. After thanking my mother for the gift, I informed her that I would never use it because it embodied the comfort-seeking pursuits of the bourgeoisie. Further, it was from China and so contributed to Vietnam's dependency on our foes to the north. I likened her present to the toxic apples and carcinogenic bras that had been 'Made in China' for Vietnamese to consume.

'The Chinks would like nothing more than for us to nestle our heads in their fluffy pillows', I told her, 'so we don't hear them marching across the border to smother us in our sleep.'

Now I reach over, grab the pillow and hug it with all my might. No one will know.

It occurs to me that maybe I fell asleep and that it is almost daylight. But I cannot hear any vendors or motorbikes outside my window. Nor can I make out the sound of my father's snoring upstairs. He's still out at an official function. The morning remains a long way away.

Unable to bury the disappointments, I turn my full attention to them and to those who have betrayed me. I try to put the three treacheries of the day into some manageable order, puzzling over which is most wrenching. Perhaps I should tackle the greatest disappointment first so that I can then confidently face the lesser instances. But, then again, maybe I should begin by confronting the smallest betrayal and then work my way up, conditioning myself like a professional athlete.

There's no use measuring them against one other. These disappointments have cascaded from one into the next to form a morass of confusion and anger. Together they challenge everything I know and treasure. How many of my 17 years as a nominal child of Uncle Ho have been a lie? What does it mean to be loyal to my beloved Vietnam? In what can I believe? Who can I trust? Perhaps it's not so much falling asleep that I fear, but rather the choices to be made when I wake.

I leap out of bed and log on to my computer. If I cannot rest then I will work. Work to turn this night into day. There is a long chain of unread emails in my inbox; some of them are flagged important. They can wait. I compose a message adding to the recipient list the general secretary of the local People's Committee along with the head of the Public Security Office. I cc the presidents of the Hue City Youth Union, Women's Union and Ho Chi Minh Scouts. All of them must know.

> Dear comrades,
>
> I write to you as a citizen and true believer in the Socialist Republic of Vietnam to report three egregious crimes against the state. They have all, I am ashamed to say, been committed by Party members. The crimes include but are not limited to corruption and treason, prolonged consumption of a noxious foreign culture and behaviour unbefitting of a Party member. My objective in reporting these crimes is to assist the Communist Party of Vietnam in its constant mission to manage, serve and lead the people of Vietnam. A detailed account of the offences and profiles of the perpetrators will be forwarded to you by the end of the week. Rest assured that my assessments have been carried out with diligence and impartiality, especially because the offences were committed by my father, my ex-boyfriend and me.
>
> For independence, freedom and happiness,
> Comrade Vo Thi Kim Lien.

Just as I am about to click 'send', I feel a surge of doubt; not so much over whether this is the right thing to do, but whether it is the right way and time to do it. No one is working at the moment anyway. Better to wait until the morning when my head is clear. It will give me a chance to proofread my message. Moreover, experience tells me that such emails need to be accompanied by a phone call or meeting. Too often the authorities – for all their conscientious efforts – have informed me that they have lost or failed to receive my correspondence.

Logic prevails and I make my way back to bed. Once again, I find myself recalling the events of the day, wondering how I could have been so wrong and whether – with the guidance of the Party – I can rectify my life.

My father's betrayal of the state is the only crime that I could have anticipated. Therefore I rebuke myself because, looking back, I should have examined him more critically and reported his errant behaviour when I first grew suspicious two years ago. Some might say I was right to give him the benefit of the doubt or that I was too young and naïve to do anything until now. But this strikes me as false reasoning. A revolutionary has an acute awareness of injustice and wrongdoing and is ready for combat as soon as she is 87 centimetres tall; that is, the length of an AK-47. The truth is that my misplaced loyalty to my father blinded me to his infidelities against the fatherland. Upon sorrowful reflection, I can now see how this once courageous and patriotic man became so decadent and corrupt.

I seize my green body pillow and picture the sitting room of my home where I witnessed my father's criminal activity this morning.

The wall behind the wooden settee is covered with commendations and prizes. In the very middle is placed the first one we received as a family. It is one of several certificates acknowledging us as a culturally progressive family. I remember my father holding me up under my arms so that I could hang it on the nail, and how we stood back and gazed at it together with delight. I was five years old then and our house had only three rooms, with the squat toilet outside. Now four additional storeys have been added and there's a bed of sunflowers standing shoulder-high growing on the roof along with a small strip of grass where my father practices his putting. All of this success has been built on that humble commendation. The plastic gold frame and the emblem of the Socialist Republic of Vietnam have faded. Nonetheless I treasure it now more than ever because, under the layers of false consciousness that have settled upon my household, it represents a time when we were at one with communism and in step with Marx, Lenin and Ho Chi Minh.

As the commendations amassed, the number of employees and petitioners queuing outside our sitting room grew, particularly in the weeks before New Year. At first they brought small gifts: a half tray of premium mandarins wrapped in red cellophane; green glutinous rice cakes purchased on a business trip to Hanoi; calendars with pictures of orchid arrangements, football stars and cityscapes. Father always received them graciously, but we could only eat so many mandarins and rice cakes, and a room only ever needs one calendar. My parents began passing the gifts on to relatives; even then some of the fruit went rotten and the cakes were left stacked up and stale in the corner. The exception was the fermented pork – *tre* – that my father's office cleaner always made for him; it never made it to the second day of the year.

Last year I stopped eating the *tre* because I could no longer ignore the feudal bitterness that flavoured it. On several occasions I reminded my father that Uncle Ho was not one for extravagance, particularly when it came at the cost of his underlings and the nation. 'As President he lived as simply as when he was a guerrilla warrior, ship hand, pastry chef. Remember when we went to Hanoi and saw the splendid austerity of his hut? And the rubber tyre sandals he wore for 20 years until the day he died. Remember what he said about benevolence being a pillar of a revolutionary's morality? A benevolent Party member is the first to endure hardship and the last to enjoy happiness. Surely your employees and their families need these gifts more than we do, Father.'

Father replied that because of the Party's sound economic management, the needy did not need as much as they used to.

'My meetings often run late into the night and over weekends. Everyone at the Public Works Department knows that I am one of the hardest working people in Hue. And just like Uncle Ho, I nurture my employees like saplings so that they grow straight and tall. Sometimes they want to thank me for my efforts and guidance with these gifts. It would be rude for me not to accept them.'

But his subordinates at the Public Works Department are not the only gift givers. The companies Father deals with bestow on him far more lavish offerings. Three months ago, we received an electric recliner in which he likes to sit and read weekend editions of *The Worker*, *Security Police*, and *Vietnam Golfer*. The chair is still wrapped in plastic because Father doesn't want to stain the suede, which is too warm for Hue anyway. Only a week after the chair arrived he received a small box made of walnut in which there was a delicate bundle of sparrow saliva that must have been worth at least US$1,000. His personal assistant had to find a Chinese chef to prepare it for him and his associates as an entrée of bird's nest soup.

When I interrogated Father about these gifts, he said that he was overseeing the development of an apartment complex and the chair was from one of the furniture suppliers. 'It's from a foreign company, my daughter. Consider it a transfer of private wealth to public goods since I am a devoted servant of the people. And don't start lecturing me about foreign account deficits or how a Vietnamese chair is twice as good as any foreign one. You just can't get chairs like this in Vietnam. These companies pay import taxes on everything they bring into the country. They're contributing to Vietnam's development, not its dependency. As for the sparrow saliva, it was not even related to my work. He's a friend in the industry who I play golf with. I gave him some tips to improve his putting. What do you want me to do? Sell these things and give the money to the poor? If you're worried about corruption, why don't you turn your attention to those international charities rather than harass your hard-working father?'

'What about all of those bottles of cognac and whisky, Father? You used to be happy with a small gourd of rice or corn wine. Now you have a cabinet full of crystal bottles with fancy labels on them.'

Father's salt and pepper moustache curled whenever he was angry. 'Trust me, my daughter. I have been a Party member and cadre since before you were born. I know what is right and wrong and how to serve my country. Everything I have done I have done for the Socialist Republic. Everything I have earned, I have earned for you. I am a civilised man who does not like to strong-arm anyone, especially my own child. You're welcome to sit in the armchair if you want to. In fact, if I was sitting in it and you told me to move, then I would defer to your precious behind. But if you want to sit on the ground, if that makes you comfortable, then that's your choice. I won't tell you how to sit or what to eat and drink. You're old enough to decide those things for yourself. In return please don't tell me how to do my job and serve my country. Is that understood, comrade Kim Lien?'

'Yes, Father. Can I ask just one more thing of you? I notice that you have been playing a lot of golf lately. Not just in Hue and Danang, but also in Thailand and Hong Kong. I have thought about this a great deal and even done some research. I have come to some very strong views about golf that I need to discuss with you.'

'Quickly, Daughter, get it off your chest.'

'My first concern is for the nation's natural resources. These golf courses are taking up prime land and vast amounts of water that should be dedicated to our food security and economic advancement. Even though Vietnam is a lower-middle income country and developing rapidly, we cannot afford to squander our resources. The needs of the many must take precedence over the leisure of the few.'

'Yes. And number two?'

'The caddies. You'll remember our last family holiday to that resort in Nha Trang. I saw them lugging your bag full of golf sticks and running to fetch you iced tea between holes. They'd bow to the golfers and respond using "*thua*" like servants. Allow me to be straightforward with you, Father. I am in total solidarity with the caddies, and totally opposed to you as a golfer. No fee or tip can compensate these coolies for the exploitation and indignity that they suffer. Every muscle, bone and organ in me wants to take up their proletarian burden and lead them to rise up against the golfers who seem more like feudal lords to me than sportsmen.'

I was happy with myself when I modified the title of Lenin's famous essay to assert, 'Father, the imperialism of the golf course is surely a most advanced and sordid form of capitalism.'

My father was not so happy. I could hear the sole of one of his Italian shoes tapping under the table. Father did not ask me to articulate my third concern, but I forged ahead, convinced that I would win him over with the might and urgency of my reasoning.

'Thirdly, there are significant costs and risks for *you*, Father. I note that you put aside a full day for each game of golf. And then there's all the practising that you do at the range and on the strip of synthetic grass on our rooftop. Imagine how much you could achieve if you spent more time focusing on the development of the city and less on that little white ball? No doubt you are aware that golf's gaining a bad reputation in some Party circles. No doubt the people you play with are beyond reproach, but there are also many unscrupulous characters on the fairways. And then there are all the pricey restaurants, karaoke bars and hotels that are frequented afterwards. That's exactly why the Transportation Minister banned all of his employees from playing golf. And when people criticised his initiative as an infringement against their rights he correctly pointed out that no one has the right to be corrupt and misuse our resources. Therefore no one has the right to play golf. It is only a matter of time until the Party in all its wisdom implements the Minister's ban more broadly. This is why you have to be careful, Father. Is your golf worth being officially censured? Imagine how ashamed, as a culturally progressive family, we would be.'

With this my father stood up, or perhaps it is more accurate to say that he leapt up because his chair fell backwards onto the ground. And as he glared down at me, for the first time since I was very small, I felt afraid of him.

'What did you say? Me? Ashamed? I am not going to listen to this anymore. But you will listen to me, Kim Lien. Listen to me carefully. Every game of golf that I play is for the nation and the Party. If I am not discussing business and forging profitable relationships on the golf course, then I'm resting and recuperating so that I can better serve Vietnam. Our leaders know this, and so should you. You have no place judging me. Look at how many golf courses there are in China, Thailand and Singapore. There are even decent courses in Cambodia and Laos. And you want to deny us our place in the sun? You want to deny me my place on the fairway? I should not have to justify myself to my own daughter, but know this, I am proud of myself today teeing off on the tenth as I was launching missiles into columns of Chinese troops 35 years ago. And know that I'm ashamed, but not of me. I'm ashamed of you, Kim Lien, for treating me with such disrespect, with so little filial piety.'

I did not sleep much that night. It was wrong, I thought, for me to doubt and question him. Father was a highly decorated soldier and cadre. He had served with honour as an artillery man in the 1979 war against the Chinese. When I was young I used to always ask him to recount his death-defying adventures. 'The Chink aggressors like to say that they taught us a lesson in that war, but from what I saw on the frontline it was us Vietnamese who were dishing out the punishment. The only people the Chinese regime knows how to massacre are their own!' Somewhere along the way either he stopped wanting to tell me those stories or I stopped wanting to hear them.

The morning after that argument, which took place seven months ago, I apologised to Father for lacking filial piety. Since that time I have not raised my concerns with him, despite the fact that more largesse has arrived at our door.

So I had good reason to be suspicious last night when Father informed me that I had to be out of the house in the morning because an overseas associate was coming to discuss important business. And I had good reason to tell my father at breakfast this morning that I had to rest at home because I had been up late at a Woman's Union meeting and also because my period was due. All of this was true, but my queasiness and fatigue were feigned. Indeed, I had no intention of fulfilling my promise to stay in my room and, upon reflection, do not regret deceiving my father because it was the only way to learn the truth.

'Fine', he relented. 'But these negotiations are very sensitive, business in confidence. You have to let me work in private, Kim Lien. No interruptions. It's good that you want to learn how the public sector functions so that you can help run the country in the future. That time will come, but not yet. Do you understand?'

'Yes Father, absolutely.' And it was like he was inviting me to eavesdrop.

My mission was made easy by the fact that there was no one in the house to catch me. Mother, who was also at the Public Works Department (my father found her a job in accounts), left after breakfast. Then our two maids departed for the market. When the doorbell rang, I was seated at my desk with the Women's Union documents neatly stacked in front of me. As anxious as I was to know what was going on downstairs, I waited for the opportune moment. If it was a formal meeting they would be busy bowing to one another for some time and there was no use in me risking being discovered before anything of substance transpired.

At that stage I can honestly say that I did not know what I would discover. Of course, there was clearly something suspicious going on. Perhaps my father was receiving an especially indulgent gift. I even considered whether he was bringing home a mistress. Part of me was simply eager to catch my father out, to get one up on him. It was an impish but innocent game. Maybe I cannot help but snoop.

I emerged from my bedroom with my socks still on which allowed me to glide over the hallway tiles like a ghost. As I sat at the top of our spiral staircase, 95 per cent of me still believed that my father was a righteous man who loved his country and was committed to socialist revolution, but who on occasion lost his way. After all, Father and Uncle Ho were the most influential role models in my life. In fact it was Father who introduced me to Uncle Ho and who encouraged me to learn about his life and ideology. Father told me all about how Uncle Ho was one of the greatest figures not only in Vietnam's 5,000-year history, but in all of human history. He had taught the Vietnamese to read, reclaimed our pride and independence against France, repelled the neocolonial Yankees and authored timeless texts that adapted Marxism-Leninism for the Vietnamese and oppressed people all over the world. If Chairman Mao had spurred the Chinese to stand up then Uncle Ho had inspired the Vietnamese to fly.

Father taught me that, 'Whenever you don't know what to do just ask yourself: "What would Uncle Ho do?"' The answer was simple. 'Uncle Ho would do what is right, emphatically so!'

For an instant, as I was perched on that step, I considered whether it was wrong to deceive my father. But all of my doubts dissipated, as they had at other crossroads in my life, with the conviction that Uncle Ho would have approved of my actions. Indeed, it was as if his spirit had possessed me and was propelling me forward.

At first all I could hear was my father talking about how Hue had a rich cultural heritage but was also seeking to become a twenty-first-century city. He offered his associates green tea and mung bean cakes. And then I heard the most frightening and outrageous response. Not so much because of the content, which I understood as simply 'Thank you, thank you very much', but rather the language in which it was conveyed: Chinese. I heard it again and then again in another voice. There was no mistake. Chinese men had infiltrated my house; not the variety who had lived in Vietnam for generations, but Mandarin-speaking outsiders.

Then there was a pause before I heard a Vietnamese voice that was not my father's. And I realised that one of the Mandarin speakers was a Vietnamese interpreter.

'Mr Kuang asks you to forgive him for being so direct', the interpreter explained. 'But he knows that you're a very busy man and does not want to waste your time. He appreciates that the relationship between our central governments at the moment is delicate. But Mr Kuang is convinced that the best way to improve relations between the People's Republic of China and the Annamese is to put politics aside wherever possible and to build stronger business ties. Such mutually profitable relationships will facilitate greater peace and understanding across our borders, which are historically meaningless anyway. The Chinese and Vietnamese are one family. And the best thing for the family is for the Vietnamese prodigal son to return home. With this in mind,

Mr Kuang wants to, as far as possible, avoid the red tape and obstacles put up by Beijing and Hanoi and focus on strengthening the bond between Dragon Lord Enterprises and the good people of Hue.'

'I am glad to say that your views are also mine Mr Kuang, 100 per cent.' And the deference in Father's voice was so pronounced that I imagined him kowtowing as he spoke.

Then the Chinese started again. Of course I did not know what he was saying, but my toes clenched with revulsion at the sound of it. It was not tonal in the sense that it undulated gently like Vietnamese, but rather sunk to guttural lows, rose to raspy heights and levelled out with long drawn whines. It was the language of invasion and pillage. And so I imagined the Chinese man's tongue flapping like an obscene cow's tongue, a replica of the U-shaped line they had slung over Vietnam's Eastern Ocean, what they shamelessly referred to as the South China Sea.

'Commander Quoc, you understand far better than me the need for world class urban developments in your city', the interpreter explained on Kuang's behalf. 'I appreciate that you have approached my company, Dragon Lord Enterprises, for its expertise. We are very keen to extend our business ventures into Vietnam and view this development as a natural fit and perfect opportunity. Rest assured, our projects are renowned all over the world for finishing on time and within budget. But to achieve this level of certainty and cost effectiveness, we simply cannot employ any Vietnamese workers, at least not right now. Our Chinese workforce has a wealth of experience with these buildings. They know exactly what to do and when to do it. In time, with proper training and acculturation, Vietnamese will take over from them. But not right now, not for this project. It's just too important, too important for both of us.'

'I understand Mr Kuang and once again I am with you 100 per cent. Admittedly, I was uncertain before, but now I fully appreciate the need to import your skilled personnel and give your company various concessions. And while they're here, I know your employees will contribute to the economy and it will be a wholly positive move for Chinese–Vietnamese relations. But, as you know, there are forces both at the highest levels of my administration and out in the streets and rice fields that oppose these measures. These people refuse to see the big picture and plan for the long term.'

'Mr Kuang says that he is confident that those in the halls of power have come to understand the situation, but is far from confident about the peasants. In his last correspondence with you he made it clear that the peasants could not be reasoned with, that they did not know the value of money and could not see beyond their tiny horizons. He stressed that they had to be made to bend, as Confucius said, like reeds in the wind.'

My father's response was nothing less than treasonous. 'Your patience with respect to the farmers is most appreciated, Mr Kuang. A thousand more pardons for the delay. We failed to factor in the extent of their backwardness and the impact of anti-patriotic forces outside of Vietnam who spread lies and incite revolt via the internet. Why else would the peasants challenge the government's ownership and wise use of the land? Where else would the farmers get these misguided notions of human rights and democracy? What do they know of such things? In any case, my people have made the remaining peasants a final offer, more than fair compensation. We will ensure that they leave without further disruption.'

After a pause for the interpreting, Chinese words again spewed into my house.

'We routinely encounter similar obstructions in China and regard them as frustrating but manageable. One cannot move up and forward without others trying to keep one down and drag one back. Perhaps you know of that English story about the man Gulliver and how he is tied down by those tiny people who he wants only to help and educate. Often I think that story is also the story of Dragon Lord Enterprises. Of course, it is never pleasant for anyone to leave the land of their ancestors. But the past cannot put a brake on the future. And those at the bottom cannot anchor those at the top. My company is not in the business of treating anyone unfairly. We do not take without compensating and in this case, as you say, we have been generous. But our good will is not as vast as the South China Sea. As we speak, our engineers and construction workers are kissing their wives and children goodbye. We cannot have them sitting idle. Any delay on this project would mean delaying others in Uruguay and Uganda. We have extremely tight deadlines. The line between profit and loss is, I'm sure you understand Commander, precariously thin.'

By this stage I had removed my phone from my pocket and started the voice recording app, pointing the microphone down into the stairwell, trusting that the incriminating statements would waft upwards like toxic fumes.

'Yes, yes. I know exactly what you're saying', my father replied. 'Once again, please accept my apologies for any uncertainty and stress that you have had to endure. I will urge everyone in the Public Works Office to strive with greater purpose and use my connections in the Party and the government to ensure that we move resolutely on this matter. I am entirely attuned to your needs and know what is at stake for Hue, for Vietnam and for all of us.'

Again the Chinese man spoke, this time at a slower pace and in a more formal manner such that there was no pause between what he said and the interpreting.

'Your efforts on this matter are appreciated by everyone at Dragon Lord Enterprises. Please, Commander Quoc, accept this honorarium in recognition of everything you have done to date and know that, as agreed, you will be compensated as each milestone is reached. I want to thank you for serving my company and your country.'

Again my toes clenched with antipathy as I envisioned the waxy red envelope sliding from one man's clammy palm into the other's. No doubt that envelope was crammed full of American bills or perhaps even taels of gold. The man who had introduced me to revolutionary morality was taking a bribe. I could not deny it. And this was surely not the first time Father had betrayed Vietnam and everything I stood for.

All of a sudden I found myself hurtling down the stairs, driven by a potent mixture of rage and righteousness. Thinking back, I like to imagine that I acted with the boldness of martyrs like Kim Dong who at the age of 14 chose to give up his life rather than give up on his cause. I like to imagine that I was doing what Uncle Ho would have done, emphatically so.

'Halt! Halt!' I commanded. And I was moving so fast that when I hollered 'Halt' for a third time at the base of the stairwell my feet almost slipped out from under me. 'As leader of the K45 cell of the Ho Chi Minh scouts, youth traffic control officer for Phu Hoi Ward and incoming deputy secretary of the students' union at Hue University, I command you to stand down.'

My father did not look at me. He was staring into his tea and rubbing his forehead.

'I have reason to believe that both of you have conspired to siphon wealth from the workers of the Socialist Republic of Vietnam, that you, Commander Quoc, have contravened the cadre code of conduct and you, Mr Chink, have violated the conditions of your visa.'

With this final accusation I turned directly to my Chinese foe. He was younger than I had thought, only in his early 30s. I was struck by how unstriking he was. His face was long and his cheeks angular and slightly sunken. There was no facial hair, no pockmarks, dimples or distinguishing features. The Chink's hair was neatly trimmed on the back and sides. He did not wear glasses. His suit was navy blue and his shoes were plain black. His government had no doubt trained him to go about his business in an inconspicuous fashion. In fact, I would have mistaken Mr Kuang for the interpreter had he not been sitting directly across from my father. For some reason I was drawn to the Chinese man's sleeves, bejewelled with white gold cufflinks in the shape of dragons. I envisaged him sweeping the hard-earned wealth of my compatriots into those sleeves as if he was performing a dastardly magic trick.

The interpreter conversed with the businessman. Then the Chinese goon turned directly to my father and revealed his limited grasp of Vietnamese.

'Your daughter?'

My father nodded solemnly. 'I cannot apologise enough, Mr Kuang. She doesn't know what she's talking about. Kim Lien hasn't started university yet. And she is at home this morning, sick, obviously delusional.'

Mr Kuang calmly offered his hand and my father clasped it with both of his. Kuang spoke at some length to the interpreter who grinned as he said, 'Mr Kuang understands that families can be complicated. He wishes your daughter well in her studies. He thinks your daughter is nice … cute.'

And then they made their way out the door. I stepped in front of him and proclaimed, 'Halt! Halt! I cannot allow you to leave Mr Kuang. I am hereby detaining you until such a time that the authorities arrive. Rest assured, if you are innocent, then you need not fear Vietnamese justice. While for the past 2,000 years China has never been fair to Vietnam, we will be fair to you. If you are innocent then you will be set free to continue with your business. If you're guilty then your punishment will be well-measured and your re-education thorough.'

With that I removed my phone from the front pocket of my pyjama top and held down the speed dial for the local security police.

That's when my father hit me. It was the first time he has ever done so, my mother and grandparents being far more hands-on in my upbringing than my father ever was. The blow came from his hand to mine and sent my phone flying across the room where it ploughed into our commendations wall. As I turned to face my father, he struck me again, this time across my face and with such force that I fell across one of our wooden recliners and then on to the floor. With the piercing pain came a jolt of adrenalin. And time seemed to slow so that as I landed I felt every shudder of the display cabinet and all those crystal goblets and bottles of liquor.

'Kim Lien! I made it absolutely clear! You were to stay in your room. This is not the time or place for your games. A thousand pardons. A thousand pardons Mr Kuang. My daughter doesn't know what she is doing. She is young and does not know her place. She's sick and is not thinking properly. I trust this incident won't get in the way of our business? Be assured that I will reprimand her and she will be sorry, *duì-bu-qǐ, duì-bu-qǐ*. Please forgive me.'

'Commander Quoc, do not be concerned.' Kuang was composed and spoke even slower and more assuredly than before so that the interpreter worked almost instantaneously. 'This is of no consequence. No one need lose face. We are both family men. I know that even when a father's efforts stand as tall as Thai Son Mountain, he receives but a pebble of respect from his children. Children do not always, as Confucius said, love what their parents love and respect what their parents respect.'

'Yes, that's very gracious of you Mr Kuang. We Vietnamese are also familiar with those proverbs.'

As I lay dazed more from shock than pain, Mr Kuang and his interpreter bowed again and departed, the interpreter quietly shutting the door behind them.

There was a tense silence as I crouched on the floor with my father standing over me. I could sense him breathing, slowly and deeply, using the tai chi techniques that he had started practising in the early mornings to address his high blood pressure. Father sat down again on the dark wood salon, his head leaning back upon the mother of pearl inlay depicting cherry blossoms.

'Get up and sit here with me, my daughter.'

But I insisted on standing tall and defiant, as if I was Thai Son Mountain.

'This could take some time. It's easier if you sit.'

'No, Father.'

'As you please. Is there anything I could say that would make a difference? That would help you feel better about this whole affair?'

'Can I speak? Without you striking me?'

'I'm not going to hit you again. Don't worry. But don't expect me to apologise either.' He leaned forward with his elbows on his knees and his head in his cupped hands.

'I feel like King An Duong Vuong', I said.

'What's that?'

'You know from the legend of Princess My Chau that you told me when I was small. We analysed it in my political history reading group. The Vietnamese King An Duong Vuong is betrayed by his beloved Princess My Chau after she is courted by the Chinese Prince Trong Thuy. The Prince tricks his bride into revealing her father's military secret, a crossbow that shoots 10,000 arrows made from a magical turtle claw. Maybe, like My Chau, you think that you are doing the right thing, Father, but you have betrayed us: me and the Socialist Republic of Vietnam.'

'What? Of course I know that story, Kim Lien. I taught it to you. It's just a fairy tale, my daughter. It's for children. And the message that you have to take from it is that children and daughters in particular have to honour their fathers; in doing so they protect the family and the nation. It is you Kim Lien who are Princess My Chau, not me. You have been courted by politics. Your head is shrouded in a cloud of ideology. You can't see what's real anymore. Me, our family, the Party and the country do not exist in a fable. The real world is much more complicated. In this world we have to make choices, choices that involve many variables and unknowns, where the outcomes are not black and white. So now you have a choice between me and your principles. I trust you will make the right choice, Kim Lien.'

'Father, I *am* a respectful daughter and a loyal Party member. As far as I'm concerned, there's no conflict in these duties. You can confess to me as a Party member. Tell me what you have done, everything, every dollar that you have pilfered. Consider it the start of a purging process. And I will dutifully report it in the knowledge that if you are contrite, the Party will show you clemency, especially given your service to the defence of the country. And as your daughter I will support you during your re-education, however long it takes.'

'Listen to yourself, my daughter. Do you have any idea what you're saying? I wish I was filming this conversation. You know what I would do? I would play it back to you in 10 or 20 years, after you have your own children and established your career. You would surely realise how foolish you were today, how wrong you were to judge your father so harshly.'

Father paused and then looked up at me still standing.

'Maybe this is my fault. Your mother and grandparents have always said that I have been too liberal with you. I never hit you, even when you were small and mischievous. I have always listened to you and taken your wishes into account, even when they were outlandish.'

Then he spoke intimately, as if he was letting me in on a secret that everyone else knew but me.

'Listen, please listen, my precious daughter. It is important that you forsake these childish ways and grow up. I should have burst the bubble in which you live a long time ago. But something stopped me. Maybe I wanted to live in that bubble with you and all those slogans, pamphlets, text books, philosophies and fairy tales. Where you pull a lever, press the right buttons or wave a wand and people act accordingly.'

'I *do* live in the real world, Father, the dialectical world in which capitalism will collapse under the weight of its contradictions and bring forth a proletarian dictatorship and then a classless communist society. Look at what's going on around us. Look at the global financial crisis, the demise of the European colonists and the American neocolonialists. Look at the pink tide sweeping across Latin America. And all those young backpackers who visit Hue, wearing t-shirts printed with Che Guevara or our radiant flag. Capitalism is unravelling and communism is blossoming! Marx and Engels saw this! The death of imperialism may be drawn out and no doubt capitalists will cling onto the means of production. We have to be wary, but we must also be assertive. We are on the winning side, Father; it's just as you taught me.'

'What you say is right, Kim Lien, but is it real? Does it matter? You see historical epochs, abstract ideas and global dynamics, but you're blind to what is going on around you. Go out to Dong Ba market or down to the river and look at your compatriots eagerly competing against one another without the slightest concern for class oppression. Go ahead and ask them what they think about the profit motive, surplus labour or commodity fetishism. They won't have any idea what you're talking about. No one cares about the contradictions of capitalism anymore. What the hell do you think a socialist-oriented market economy is if it's not a contradiction? More and more I have become convinced that being Vietnamese is all about living with contradictions: between the mountains and the sea; the East and the West; life and death – all are mixed together. Contradictions are the most consistent thing in our culture and our politics. That's why you're different, Kim Lien. There's no one like you, except for maybe that boyfriend of yours, but even he's not as dogmatic. That's why you're unique and special, but also why you never fit in. Everything's straightforward for you. You're so unyielding.'

'I've only ever done what you said you wanted me to do, Father – what Uncle Ho would do.'

'I know, I know, it is my fault. I was the one who introduced you to the Party's teachings at a young age. Your mother was always against it. She said it was unnatural for a young girl to be obsessed with politics and war. She wanted to take down your pictures of General Giap and replace them with flowers and ballerinas. She wanted you to embroider rather than study the regulation of state-owned enterprises. But you were enthusiastic and I was glad there was something to bring us closer together. However I always knew it was odd. Do you remember how you never cared for children's songs like

"Twinkle, Twinkle Little Star" but instead sang the Communist Internationale and recited "The Beautiful Bulgarian Rose"? And how you always insisted on hanging up the flag outside our house at least a week before national days? I certainly do. And I remember the glee on your face when we went to those tedious military parades and your eagerness to listen to Party proclamations on the loudspeakers in the street. My point is, you're still like that, nothing's changed. You still go to parades and listen to proclamations as if they were soap operas. I assured your mother that this was just a stage, but if anything your fervour has intensified.'

'I only do what any loyal citizen would do. Exactly what the Party dictates.'

'That's what I'm trying to get at, my child. There's no need to be so faithful. It's hard to explain, but everyone else in Vietnam seems to understand. What I mean to say is that I know the Party says you should obey its commands at all times, but in truth it only hopes you will comply with most of what it asks and probably expects far less than that. Your problem is that you not only follow what the Party commands, you exceed compliance. To make matters worse, you expect the same from everyone else, especially me. But non-compliance is factored into the Party's equations. The Party expects it but cannot admit it. In most cases it doesn't have to. Without a little fence-wrecking there can be no true independence, freedom or happiness; there would only be the Party, the Party, the Party. Basically, the Party wants you to get on with whatever you're doing and let it get on with whatever it's doing. The only thing it really demands is that you don't rock the boat. It's like my marriage to your mother. Our relationship was once full of passion and promise, but at some stage – I'm not sure when and don't care to think why – all of that faded. You're old enough to know we're not in love anymore. Of course this is not ideal; but nor is it a problem because there's no prospect of us separating. We stay together to maintain appearances, which are important to both of us and because there's no easy or better alternative. The message for you, Kim Lien, is to lower your expectations of both yourself and others. Otherwise you'll only ever be disappointed.'

'You underestimate me, Father. You're not telling me anything I'm not already aware of. I have no desire to be like other young people. I want to be part of a vanguard. I want to push others to become what they should be, what they want to be without always knowing it. And I *have* made concessions for your infidelities before, far too many. But this is different, this is corruption of the highest order. I can't look in the other direction. Not this time. So I'm asking you, as your devoted daughter and comrade, if you truly love me and are committed to the Party, then confess. Turn yourself and Mr Kuang in to the authorities. That would make all of this easier and would go a long way to relieving my disappointment in you. Take the decision and responsibility out of my hands as a good father should. The thought of having to report your corruption, and of having to face mother and all our family afterwards is most disturbing. But I'll do it if I have to. You know what Uncle Ho said: "Nothing is too hard; just set your mind to it, and it will surely be done."'

For a moment I thought he had come to a fuller realisation of himself and taken the first step towards becoming a new person. But as he spoke it was clear that he remained fixed to his old ways of thinking.

'Kim Lien, please, I am not corrupt, at least not compared to others who have the sort of opportunities that I have. Take a look at even the official news. It's all about scandals and rip-offs: Vinashin; Texaco; Securency; Vinalines; bauxite mines in the Central Highlands; plans to chop down Hanoi's ancient trees; corruption and misuse of public money in the order of hundreds of millions of dollars. Compared to other officials I'm as pure and innocent as a Buddhist monk. You probably don't believe me, but that's exactly what some of my colleagues have called me ever since I wore an orange shirt to golf one day: "the saffron-robed commander." And I can assure you that it's not a compliment. How many times have you seen me come home drunk? Hardly ever. I avoid massage parlours and have never been unfaithful to your mother, never. This is despite frequent goading from my associates to join them. It's a critical part of sealing the deal and building trust. You're old enough to know that these things go on all of the time. It's a routine part of business and government.'

'Go ahead and fool yourself, Father. But I won't be misled. What I heard this morning was no ordinary business deal.'

'And yet that is what it was. I'm not sure what you think you heard, but you should know that my dealings with Mr Kuang are harmless and in many ways constructive. The protesting peasants, they will be compensated, probably with more money than they deserve or ever dreamt of. They were never going to keep their land, Kim Lien. It's not even theirs to keep. The development is going ahead. It's for the good of the city and the country. Mr Kuang's company is good for the city and the country.'

I sat down, not next to Father, but in the seat the Chinese man had occupied, tilting my head so that he could see the crimson mark that he had left on my face, the sting of which evoked in me righteous satisfaction.

'And what about that?' I asked, pointing to the envelope that was so thick that it bulged out of Father's trouser pocket.

'Sometimes, my daughter, I don't have a choice.'

'What do you mean? You're one of the most powerful people in Hue! If you can't live according to revolutionary morals then who can? In fact, if you repent and stand up against corruption then that will encourage others to follow. You must be like Uncle Ho, who made it clear in his life and teachings that private interests are subordinate to party interests, group interests to collective interests, and temporary interests to long term ones.'

'My daughter, I wish I could always live up to your and Uncle Ho's morals. I really do. But life does not unravel in a simple dialectical process, with opposing forces evolving into better syntheses. I'm not saying that Marx was wrong; only that even if that is how the history of the world progresses, it doesn't work that way in the life of one man. There are many more factors and forces to take into account. And there are situations, like the one you have just witnessed, that are grey and murky. In such situations I cannot afford to be as pure as you want to me to be; no one can. Maybe you're too young to know what I'm talking about. Perhaps I have sheltered you for too long.'

'I don't accept that I am too young for anything, Father. By my age Uncle Ho was agitating for the peasants of this region to rise up against the French; he was engaged with the plight of workers and the oppressed, those he saw in his travels around the globe. But I don't need to travel overseas to know that stealing from the people is wrong. They place their trust in you, Father, and you have betrayed them. That's far more important than your betrayal of me and why I cannot let you continue like this.'

'Maybe that is the case. But this is much bigger than me. I wish the system was otherwise, but it's not and I can't change it. Let me put it this way. Imagine what would happen if I did not accept this envelope. If I rejected Mr Kuang's honorarium do you think he would leave it at that? No, he would get what he needs for his company some other way. He would have no problem finding someone else to help him. And, then, Mr Kuang, whoever is working with him, and all of their associates, would know that I am not a team player, that I do not know what is good for myself and for business. Moreover, I would have nothing to share with my comrades, both above and below me. And soon they would turn on me. Do you really think that anyone would admire me for rejecting a bribe and follow my example? This system of patronage engulfs us all. Resisting the system wouldn't make me a hero; it'd mark me as a threat. Everyone would suspect that I was keeping everything for myself. Or they would think that I was going to blow the whistle on them. And I can assure you they wouldn't take any chances; there would be severe consequences, for me and for our family.'

Father sat straight in his chair and stared unflinchingly into my eyes. 'Look at me and listen carefully, Kim Lien', he said.

And for the first time this morning, I did.

'Try to appreciate how much is at stake here and why my situation is difficult. I can't shield you from this any longer. If you want to be successful in the Party and in the public service, you have to know how things work in Vietnam, the real Vietnam, not the one in your fairy tales and philosophy books.'

'But what about communism and revolution? What about Marx, Lenin, Truong Chinh and Ho Chi Minh? What about the red dawn that you always told me was rising?'

'Vietnam is red, my daughter, but it's the red of this envelope in my pocket, an envelope in which all of us are trapped. Of course our family's trappings are better than others. Look around you. Has it ever occurred to you how we can afford any of this on my official salary of 5 million dong a month? That's not enough to pay one of the maids, for heaven's sake. This house, your food, your allowance, our vacations to Dien Bien Phu, Con Dao Island, the Cu Chi tunnels, and to Hanoi to see Ho Chi Minh's body, have in one way or another come out of those envelopes.'

Father was right, I had been willingly blind, not only to his corruption but to my complicity as his dependant. 'Are you saying that I'm no better than all the brats who get everything they want because of their family connections and power?' And that's when it occurred to me. 'Did I earn my offer to the Political Academy, or did you buy it for me?'

'It's not like that, my dear. You earned your place as much as anyone. And this money, this house, our other houses that will be yours someday, you will have earned them too. As I said, I have shown great restraint and virtue compared to others, and I have always worked hard. But I don't want you or my grandchildren to have to go through what I have gone through. That's what drives me to do what I'm doing; not greed or status, but my love for you.'

'I will not have it, Father. We should not have any of this. We should give it back to the people. Everything belongs to them. I'm sure you know the saying: "The Party leads, the state governs, the people own." We can live simply like Uncle Ho did in his hut, with a rattan mat for a bed and a single desk from which we can work and dine. We can eat rice flavoured with salt and maybe a bit of fish sauce. Otherwise we're no better than the comprador capitalists and puppets who repressed and stole from our own people during French and American Wars. I don't know how you can live with yourself, Father. Don't you feel guilty at all?'

'You would sit there, in this house, and talk of guilt and compare me to them? I deserve everything that we have. I didn't think I would ever have to remind you of this, but I was the one who went north to fight the Chinese in 1979, my parents' only son. And while I was away my father died without me at his side. If that wasn't bad enough I wasn't there to support your mother through her first pregnancy and then after her miscarriage. Where was I? I was on the battlefield. And it was there that I witnessed the death of my friends. For what? A lesson? What lesson? What can you teach a corpse? Maybe we fought for land or Vietnam's honour? A dead man doesn't care where he's buried. And as for honour, how many bodies have you seen, Kim Lien? How many people have you seen with a chunk of their head blown off and the skin on their back melting? How many comrades have you carried as they cried out for you to save them, and then pleaded for you to kill them? Men do not cry with valour as you have read in your books. They are hysterical children who have soiled themselves with fear. It's the sort of sound that returns to you in quiet moments and seeps into your dreams. It teaches you there's no honour, emphatically so. My father never told me what it was like fighting against the Americans. And I suspect his father never told him what it was to fight the French and the Japanese. They did me a great disservice. So now I'm telling you. I'm telling you that the most compromised peace is a thousand times better than the most glorious war. So even if you want nothing that I have earned over the years, take this message. We have sacrificed enough blood for this country, for the Party. The only way that I would give more is if somehow I could reverse time and make it so that I didn't see what I have seen or do what I have done. But that's not going to happen. Is it? So I'll take what little remains. If I don't, someone less deserving and more crooked will.'

It was like he had struck me again, this time with far greater force.

'Let me be clear, my child. If you are going to be disappointed and angry at me for the rest of your life, then so be it. But you will not report me, Kim Lien. I won't let you do that to our family and, most importantly, I'm not going to let you throw away your future.

'Remember, we named you Kim Lien not just because that's the name of Ho Chi Minh's childhood village. It means golden lotus. You, Kim Lien, are the flower, pure white and dazzling gold, that rises from the soil which, while no doubt putrid, feeds and secures you.'

With that Father left for work. Not long afterwards I left the house after retrieving my phone from the floor. Dejected and confused as I was, I was grateful that it was undamaged and that the voice recorder was still running.

Staggering through the streets towards Comrade Tuan's villa estate, I felt as if I was in one of those inflatable jumping castles with the wobbling floor, collapsing walls, and other people all conspiring to knock me off balance. I was so out of sorts that I marched right past Comrade Tuan's most unusual house and had to double back.

His house is a perfect cube with nine windows on each face and two orange marble pillars at the entrance. A frosted glass balcony runs around the upper two storeys, and in the middle of the structure is an atrium in which Comrade Tuan's father maintains his succulent collection. The architect's intention was to reinvent the 200-year-old Hue Citadel for the twenty-first century. Inside every room there is a control panel that lets off a gentle amber glow as you approach it, inviting you to adjust the temperature, lighting and music. Comrade Tuan's father is an information security expert who returned to Hue after retiring from the Ministry of Public Security in Hanoi. I have only met him a handful of times though because he spends most of the year travelling as a consultant.

After a fingerprint swipe I was able to pass through the outer gate and proceed to the front door. No one responded to the doorbell, so I knocked. Because my phone had run out of batteries I couldn't call Comrade Tuan, but we had shared our calendars, so I knew that he would be at home working on an assignment. I tried to turn the doorknob. It was locked, and so I knocked again, louder. Still, no one answered.

More than ever I needed Comrade Tuan to remind me of what is right and real. As I waited, I thought of how, from the day we first met almost a year ago, we were perfectly matched.

We were brought together by traffic duty. Of all their responsibilities, my fellow Ho Chi Minh scouts dreaded traffic duty the most. Many questioned whether it is even necessary given that the roads are rarely congested in Hue. They grumbled about having to wake up early and about being exposed to the pollution, dust and sun.

So as to be a positive example, I committed to extra shifts and to doing traffic duty even after I was technically too old to be a Ho Chi Minh scout. The problem however was that I was never good at it. In fact, until Tuan came along, I didn't know anyone who was. This was because road users refused to respect the authority of scouts who could not impose fines or penalties. But, as I explained to my fellow troop members, the greater the non-compliance, the sterner the enforcement. Excusing small transgressions will only encourage people to commit greater ones and, before long, society will be ruined.

Comrade Tuan shared my zero tolerance outlook; or at least I thought he did. The first time I saw him it was not long after I had returned from a vacation to Phu Quoc Island with my parents. The stint away had invigorated my spirit of volunteerism. So I was particularly eager to take on the stampede of motorbikes that morning. On the way, I saw him at an intersection not far from mine, already at work despite the fact that our shifts did not begin for another 20 minutes. He had a baby face and pudgy cheeks, but was obviously older than the average red scarf-wearing Ho Chi Minh scout, perhaps even older than me. The more I scrutinised him the more impressed I became. Comrade Tuan had no trouble stopping motorbike and bicycle riders from going down the wrong side of the street and deftly shepherded pedestrians towards designated crossing zones. He performed flag and arm gestures with a maestro's vigour and precision. And he employed not only the standard issue flag, but also a stainless steel whistle. Once I even witnessed him grab the back of a scooter that was about to make an illegal turn and direct it towards the righteous path. During rain storms, Comrade Tuan donned a thick tan poncho such that when he put his two arms out, he appeared to be a brick wall. As a result of his vigilance and dedication, Comrade Tuan's intersection was a pocket of blissful order. I suspected that many road users went out of their way just to be directed by his steadfast will. I know that I did.

'My name is Comrade Vo Thi Kim Lien, long-serving member of the Ho Chi Minh Scouts, student 392001 of Nguyen Ai Quoc Secondary School graduating in last year's K45 class, and youth representative on the Standing Committee of Thua Thien-Hue Province's Women's Union.' I put my fist up in air as a gesture of solidarity.

He did likewise, but in a more perfunctory manner. 'Comrade Pham Minh Tuan, Student 353256, Chu Van An High School in Hanoi, founding President of the Function over Form Architecture Club of Hue Polytechnic. I have just transferred to this city. What do you want? Can't you see that I'm in the middle of something?'

'Yes, I'm sorry. It's just that I couldn't help but be impressed by your directing. Despite my dedication, I'm ashamed to say that the traffic often defeats me.'

'Try directing our comrades in the Capital's Ba Dinh District during peak hour. This is a breeze compared to that; in fact I'm sure I could do it with my eyes shut and my ears blocked.'

'I have no doubt about that, none at all. If I could achieve but 60 per cent of your proficiency, I would be satisfied.' All along my intention was to tell him exactly what he wanted to hear so that he would say to me what I wanted to hear. And he did.

'If you are willing to learn then I am willing to teach you.'

'That's generous of you Comrade Tuan. Thank you very much.'

'No thanks necessary Comrade Lien. Any citizen would do the same.'

'"Kim Lien". Call me "Kim Lien". You know, like Uncle Ho's childhood village. But there are so few good citizens nowadays, Comrade Tuan, especially among our fellow youth.'

'Be wary of defeatism, Comrade Kim Lien. We must never lose faith in our fellow Vietnamese. Uncle Ho never did, even when the French had ruled over the country with an iron fist for more than a century, and even when the Yankees invested their vast resources into corrupting the hearts and minds of Southerners. The Vietnamese people are proud and irrepressible. It's in our genes. Perhaps a small minority of our compatriots have lost their way, but with benevolent leadership and firm re-education, they will surely join us on the revolutionary path.'

As it turned out, there was some space in his schedule that morning. And so I stayed on at my intersection well after my shift had finished in order for Comrade Tuan to watch me work. He scrutinised my intersection from afar as a surveyor gauges the land and then stood by my side examining my gestures with the attention to detail of a carpenter assessing the grain of a piece of timber. Throughout this time I was both nervous and reassured by his presence.

Afterwards we retired to a nearby tea house to discuss my performance. Comrade Tuan liked the bitterness of Vietnamese green tea. He flatly refused to drink coffee, soft drinks or bubble tea, regarding them as toxins that were as destructive to Vietnamese tastebuds as Agent Orange was to the natural environment.

He gave my traffic directing a score of 4.5 out of 10 but assured me that I could improve with some guidance and much effort. Apparently, my enthusiasm was commendable, but my directions were wild and imprecise, which fostered confusion and dissent among road users.

'It becomes easier and more effective when you realise that pedestrians, cyclists, bikers, all road users, are no different to ducks or sheep. It's easier to control many of them than it is to control an individual. Once they become part of the herd, they cannot bear to leave it.'

For him, speeding, not wearing helmets, riding a motorbike with more than one passenger and rule breaking in general, contravened the compliant instinct of Vietnamese. Such illegal practices grew out of phantom desires that were conjured up by foreign forces.

Even at that early stage, I felt as if we were so synchronised in our thinking that I could finish some of his sentences for him: 'The true will of each Vietnamese is to advance the collective will of Vietnam as expressed and championed by the Party.'

On more technical matters, according to Comrade Tuan, my flag work was flaccid. 'The flag is an extension of your hand. However, you don't so much wave but salute with it, taking the longest arc down with your elbow tucked into your side and then the shortest path up, resting the top of the handle near the bridge of your nose.' And, of course, I needed to get a whistle.

We refilled the tiny teapot with hot water no less than five times until it was hard for me to detect any flavour or colour in the final brew. When I called for a new pot, Comrade Tuan promptly cancelled my order and instead requested more hot water. This was not just to be frugal. As far as Comrade Tuan was concerned, each new pouring had its own character that had to be appraised in all its subtlety and complexity.

Having just arrived from Hanoi, Comrade Tuan missed being close to the seat of power, but had not left behind a close circle of friends or significant other. In moving to Hue, he was eager to help liberate the city from the last vestiges of its feudal and Diemist past. Comrade Tuan had no interest in sport, regarding the playing of it as 'the enslavement of the body' and the viewing of it as 'the annulment of the mind'. He was studying architecture at the Technical College and venerated the vision and grandeur of Le Corbusier who, he said, not only planned buildings but entire cities and worlds.

Comrade Tuan's vision for urban planning in Hue was to keep the Ancient Citadel, but to level just about everything else and replace it with a grid of high rise buildings. 'The past is a launch pad for the future,' he said with his nose pointed in the air, 'the present is what gets in the way.'

That morning we recited a few memorable stanzas from the work of Party laureate poet To Huu, considered how the strategies devised by Vo Nguyen Giap to defeat the French could be applied in the war against rampant inflation, and questioned the virtue of joining ASEAN given that its founding members had disdained Vietnam for so many years.

The sun was high in the sky when we were finally compelled to leave one another. I was impressed when Comrade Tuan produced a small plastic container into which he transferred the tea leaves for further consumption. And although our expenses were minimal, Comrade Tuan insisted that we split the bill out of recognition that as a woman I held up half the sky.

'Thank you, Comrade Tuan, for your time and insight. I am glad that fate has brought us together this morning.'

'There is no such thing as fate, Comrade Kim Lien. For true revolutionaries there is only individual will, human reason and the Party, all of which must be tightly integrated.'

In the following weeks we crossed paths at Party and community gatherings, and he gave me additional traffic directing lessons over tea. Our relationship developed progressively so that we met twice in the second week, three times in the third week, four times in the fourth week and then every weekday. On the Friday of that fifth week, with our tea delicate and pale, Comrade Tuan said that he had something significant to tell me and something important to ask.

He hesitated, only for a second or two, but long enough for me to identify it as a peculiar hiccup in the otherwise steady cadence of our conversations. My entire body was tingling with anticipation, much like I had felt leading up to the National Assembly elections.

'Well, the good news is that I've been selected by the People's Committee to attend the Vietnam–Laos Amity and Development Conference in Vientiane. It will be a valuable opportunity for me to connect with our comrades beyond the Western Border.'

'Congratulations Comrade Tuan!' I said shaking his hand. In so doing I suppressed my disappointment, firstly because I thought I was the best candidate for the honour, and secondly because I was hoping he was going to reveal something more heartfelt. 'The People's Committee has made a wise decision. When is the Convention Comrade?'

'Not for another six weeks, but the thing is, I'll be leaving next Thursday. The Committee has decided that the younger members of the Vietnamese delegation should trek to the Convention. On the way we will be touring parts of Interzones IV and V with veterans of the American War and staying with highland tribes to assist them with their literacy and civility. After a historic rendezvous with youth from the Laos delegation on the Truong Son range, we'll retrace sections of the Ho Chi Minh Trail, re-enacting manoeuvres that were pivotal to the defeat of the American neocolonists and their Vietnamese puppets. 'It will be an enlightening and uplifting experience and, just as importantly,

I intend to lose all of this fat that I have gained since I completed military service. I promise to return taught and true, more akin in appearance to Lenin and Trotsky than Stalin and Mao.'

The thought of not seeing him for six weeks was like a savage blow to my gut. To my credit, I was able to hide my pain and sentimentalism.

'Excellent, Comrade Tuan. I wish you all the best on your adventure and have every confidence that you will represent our province and people with distinction.'

'Thank you. Thank you Comrade Kim Lien. Your support means a great a deal to me. However, I want you to know that while this trip has many positives, there is one significant drawback.'

'What do you mean Comrade? There is surely no downside to such an honour?'

'No, you don't understand. I am most honoured. The trip itself has no downsides to speak of. I am referring to a drawback of being so far away for such a long time, away from you, Comrade Kim Lien.'

And with this he hesitated again, but this time for longer, scanning me for a reaction. I was sure he could sense the tingling which had once again come over me, this time with greater intensity.

'This brings me to my request. It occurs to me that I would be aided in my marching over the coming weeks if I knew I had someone to return to, someone to whom I could sing a song to lighten the burden of my pack, someone I could think about when not immersed in my duties, someone whose heart I could always connect with though we might be beyond cellular networks. I was wondering if you would be that person Comrade Kim Lien? What I mean to say is that I was hoping we could be more than comrades, which is not to say that we would not still be comrades. In fact, I'm sure our dedication to the Party would, if anything, be strengthened if we committed to one another in a more intimate fashion. Please accept my apologies. I know I should be more direct, less wishy-washy. But, you can probably tell that I have no experience in matters of the heart. What I mean to say is ...'

'You need not search for words, Comrade Tuan. I have for some time deemed us to be compatible. So my answer to your proposition is "yes". Emphatically, "yes".'

Comrade Tuan's beaming face displayed a mixture of joy and relief. And when he grinned I saw a tiny dimple on his left cheek that I had not noticed before and found most endearing.

Along with a small band of supporters, I walked the first 5 kilometres with Tuan's expedition, keeping my distance from him at first because I did not want to advertise our relationship just yet. But when it came time for him to finally go, I threw myself into his arms and nestled my head in his chest. It was our first-ever embrace and as much as I wanted to hold on, after a few seconds I pulled back from his portly frame and threw my fist up into the air. He did likewise, and with our arms like bolts of lightning piercing through a stormy sky, I am sure that everyone around us was in awe of our righteousness.

As I walked home and on countless occasions over the weeks that followed, I hummed the classic song that tells of two guerrilla soldiers on the Ho Chi Minh Trail making their way down either side of the Truong Son range. The lovers are separated by mountain peaks yet in total harmony when it comes to ridding the country of American invaders and laying the foundation for global communism.

> Truong Son East, Truong Son West
> Together consigned to the Truong Son jungle,
> Together yet so far apart,
> The road to battle exquisite this season,
> From Truong Son East to Truong Son West.
> From Truong Son East, I love you West,
> Descend from the alps into the light,
> From that mysterious land that intoxicates the soul,
> And those roads littered with enemy bombs.
> From where I am to where you are,
> As our forces unite on the frontline,
> We are united by unflagging love,
> Truong Son East with Truong Son West.

The delegation leaders had determined that the re-enactment should be as faithful as possible, which meant that the young trekkers had to live off what they could forage from the jungle and the generosity of the hill tribes. Just as importantly, it meant that Comrade Tuan had to leave his phone and tablet at home. And I must admit that, because we had come together with meteoric force only to be torn asunder so soon afterwards, there were some dark moments when I resented him for leaving me and wished most fervently that it was I who was journeying westward, if not with Comrade Tuan, then in his place. But to my credit, I was quick to extinguish these unbecoming sentiments and direct my energies to more constructive tasks.

In particular, I realised that we had been reckless, elevating our personal desires over the objectivity and far-sightedness of our leaders. It was not for us alone to determine our compatibility as boyfriend and girlfriend; we needed the Party's blessing.

This involved compiling personal histories that detailed our relatives and ancestors back at least three generations, noting their occupations and any activities that might be judged as either pro- or counter-revolutionary. Father had a contact at the public records office, so I had little trouble accessing the information that I required. My side was straightforward. After reviewing the personal histories that my parents, uncles, aunts, grandparents, great uncles and great aunts had compiled over the decades, I proudly confirmed that my bloodline was impeccably red. There was not a hint of jaundiced yellow republicanism, enemy collaboration or class betrayal. In fact, I believe that the health of my ancestral roots can be traced back at least 30 generations, all the way back to the Great March South when we liberated what is now Central Vietnam from the Cham.

With that accomplished, I turned to Tuan's personal history, which was far more difficult to put together, particularly because his father had worked for the Public Security Office, so details of his background and life were confidential. However, relying on the personal histories of other relatives, I pieced together that Comrade Tuan's mother (who he never mentioned) had suddenly left Vietnam when Tuan was small and was now thought to be in New Zealand. This would usually be a stain on both their records, but to my relief there was an explanatory note from the Public Security Office exonerating Tuan's father of his wife's treachery. An investigation deemed her departure to be 'spontaneous, mad and incongruous. It was impossible to predict by even the most vigilant of cadres and impossible to prevent by even the most attentive of husbands.' Otherwise, from what I could find, Comrade Tuan's history was unblemished. I even confirmed that, as he had once boasted to me, he was a descendent of one-time Prime Minister Pham Van Dong. Just as prestigious was his working class and revolutionary pedigree. Comrade Tuan had an uncle who farmed pigs near Cam Ranh Bay, a second cousin once removed who was a union official for a state-owned tobacco company and his great grandmother had participated in a rubber plantation uprising in the 1930s.

My scrupulous research helped me to cope with Comrade Tuan's absence. It was as if I was becoming more familiar with him one official document at a time. And by the end of the process, I was sure that I knew him better than he knew himself and that I could trust him with my affections.

At that stage, there was also little doubt in my mind that the Party would approve my application. However, because I could not find the appropriate form, I compiled a spreadsheet with accompanying coloured bar graphs that clearly indicated how the agrarian, industrial and activist components of our personal histories lined up almost perfectly together. When I showed this to Comrade Tuan after his return from Laos, he said it was like a game of Tetris in which all of the components of our lives had been brought together to achieve the highest possible score.

Unfortunately, both the Secretary of the District People's Committee and the regional head of the Youth League showed little interest in appraising my application. The former asserted that Party approval for such unions had not been necessary since the American War. The latter was flippant and lewd, suggesting that he knew of only one way to consummate a relationship and that if Comrade Tuan and I wanted his assistance in this regard then he would happily watch to see if we were doing it right. To both I stipulated that if they had any doubts, then Comrade Tuan and I could begin our relationship on a probationary basis with monthly reviews. After only glimpsing at the documentation and data that I had spent so much time compiling, they proceeded to sign and stamp my application. Comrade Tuan and I were officially a couple.

Comrade Tuan's return, this time by bus, was delayed by two days because of a landslide. He was still recovering from a bout of malaria, but was otherwise healthy and high spirited when we were finally reunited. The trek had indeed left him sinewy and square-jawed. I was pleased to see that the weight loss had accentuated his dimple. When we embraced for the second time, my head fit neatly into the cavity of his chest and my arms reached easily around his bony waist. Never have I known a more tender moment.

Finally, Comrade Tuan's housekeeper, Sister Bay, answered the door.

'Have you been waiting long? I was up on the roof putting a load of washing on the line. Can't hear a thing from up there.'

Sister Bay was Tuan's second cousin and had helped raise him, which is why we referred to her affectionately as 'Older Sister'. She was the sixth of nine children and had left her village just outside of Hoi An as a teenager to go work for Tuan's father in Hanoi. Despite having lived in the city for half her life, Sister Bay retained her salt-of-the-earth candour along with a heavy country accent that is at times hard for me to understand.

'You look like you've seen a ghost. Is there something up?'

'Hello, Sister Bay', and after removing my shoes I kept my eyes downcast so that she did not see the mark from my father's assault. 'Is Comrade Tuan at home, I have to see him, as a matter of urgency.'

'Is there anything that's not urgent with you two?'

'Is Tuan upstairs in his room?'

'I think so. I was out at the market and then down here for most of the morning. I went up to see if he needed any laundry done, but he didn't answer his door and I dare not disturb him. He told me that when he's working on a design he often gets into "the zone". Apparently, he can't hear or see anything except for what he's concentrating on. "Don't come in, even if it's an emergency", he told me, "It will break my train of thought". Anyway, you just head up there and go right on in. He won't mind you breaking his train of thought and busting into his zone.'

'Thank you, Sister Bay.' Although I had more pressing matters on my mind, I made a mental note to convey my disappointment to Comrade Tuan about closing his door. He was surely aware of the dangers of drawing a distinction between the private and the commons. Closing his door was the first step to him locking himself up in his room for years like so many young Japanese Hikikomori hermits. It would rightfully attract suspicion.

On the occasions when we had worked in his room composing socialist realist poetry and organising events, we always kept the door wide open so that everyone would know that we were upstanding and had nothing to hide. Although lately it was not unusual for our legs to be touching under his desk and, once a task was completed, for us to kiss.

So again I was gliding along the tiles in my socks, but whereas this morning I almost expected my father to betray me, there was no reason for me to suspect Comrade Tuan of anything untoward. In fact, it would be accurate to say that since coming into my life, Comrade Tuan had amply filled the role of socialist exemplar that my father had vacated. And so, as I thrust open the door and stormed into his spacious bedroom I did not know what I craved most: his political acumen or rock-hard embrace.

It was then that I saw him as I never thought I would, slovenly reclined in his chair. His head was cocked back, almost as if he was in pain. But the expression on his face reminded me of pictures that I had seen of opium addicts lying on their sides smoking pipes. His eyes were slightly shut and his mouth softly open, in contrast with his tightly wound right fist, which was not poised in the air, but rather pointing downwards with the butt of his palm rubbing vigorously at his crotch.

All of these sights, as unusual and disturbing as they were, retreated into the background when I saw what was on the computer screen. As I recollect those images, I am again overcome by a sickening sensation. There were four separate windows open on his monitor. In the top left there was a picture of the famous-and-good-for-nothing-other-than-her-bust Elly Tran, as she emerged from a swimming pool in a bikini. In the top right was a video of a voluptuous black woman with a platinum blond wig bent over a piano. Her gargantuan breasts dangled so low that they bashed upon the keys. A scrawny white man with a moustache wearing only a bow tie defiled her from behind. Next was a database of some sort with rows of dates and times and columns that I later discovered were headed, 'duration', 'filth rating', 'excitement', 'copulation' and 'notes'. In the final window there was what I initially thought was a benign Doraemon cartoon, but the blue cat had a grotesquely large penis which he had inserted through a fish. The end was being bitten by a pink cat on all fours with a balloon tied on her tail that had the number '18' on it.

With his earphones firmly on, Comrade Tuan did not hear me enter the room. But when I gasped, he swivelled around and swore, and then he saw me and he knew that I had seen him. I could not help but witness the shameful shaft emerging from his pants. Comrade Tuan almost fell backwards as he swivelled away from my gaze and reached to his laptop to close all those windows, 'Ah, Comrade Kim Lien, I was not expecting …'

In clumsy desperation he yanked the earphones out of the socket, the audio suddenly blasting out from the household speaker system: a cacophony of grunting and squealing; the smashing of piano keys; and electronic simulation of howling cats. I made a move to the flashing control panel to turn the sound off, but Comrade Tuan collected himself enough to press the mute button on his laptop, and then he turned off his monitor.

Comrade Tuan sat upright. There was silence. I turned away from him and heard him zipping up his pants. Silence again, but I could still make out the faint hum of the fan from his hard drive and I knew that all the portals to those depraved universes were still very much open. After a few deep breaths, I turned around to face him.

'Comrade Tuan. What are you doing? Whatever it is, you must desist immediately. I need to speak to you about something of grave importance. Something …' and I was struggling to hold back the tears.

'Yes, ah, Comrade Kim Lien. I wasn't expecting you. I was just doing some work. There's a ground-breaking project that I'm assisting the Cultural Office with. It involves gauging the impact and *modi operandi* of toxic foreign culture on the minds of our young compatriots. Let me explain …'

He could see the tears falling down my cheeks just before I turned away from him again.

He rolled his chair forward and took hold of my elbow, urging me to turn around, but I dared not, worried that he wanted me to sit on his lap. His touch made me squirm.

'I don't know what to say. I don't want to deceive you. There's no point anyway. You are as familiar with my work program and calendar as I am. I'm sorry, so very sorry.'

'What for, Comrade Tuan? Are you sorry that you have been caught? Sorry that I know? That I know what you do when you're alone? I trusted you, Comrade. I compiled and examined your personal history. I thought I knew you. I thought …'

'I have let you down. I'm sorry. But I am still Pham Minh Tuan, Student 353256 of Chu Van An High School. Believe me, Comrade Kim Lien. Nothing has changed between us. All I need is a little re-education. That's all.'

'What about all those speeches and articles that you wrote for the Youth League newsletter? The ones about the Western cultural invasion of Vietnam being as threatening as the American invasion of the 1960s? What about the article on the perils of Hollywood escapism and the need for us to engage with the real world, the socialist realist world, the world the Party in all its benevolence and wisdom has constructed for us? I relished those articles, Comrade Tuan. I believed in them, and in you.'

I faced him again as he moved back to his desk and was staring into the blank monitor.

'Have you done that sort of thing, those sorts of things in real life? Is that what you want to do to me?'

'No. Of course not. Never.'

'What were you thinking of when we kissed in this room, Comrade Tuan? Were you thinking about that sort of thing? What about that time we kissed on your scooter as the sun rose over the Hai Van Pass? What about when we kissed after eating guava at the base of Minh Mang's palace? Or last month when we were listening to our favourite folk song "Saigonese Girls Carry Ammunition for Liberation Forces"? Or last week when we were watching the Vietnam Sea in My Heart concert? Or when we went to watch the *Like Living with History* documentary about the 60th Anniversary of the Battle of Dien Bien Phu?

What did those kisses mean to you Comrade? What am I to make of them now? Now that you have cheated on me and Vietnam? Is there anything else or anyone else I should know about?'

'No, no, never. I have never been with anyone. You know you are my first and only girlfriend. You know that. You must believe me. You're everything I've ever wished for, Kim Lien.'

'Then why? Why do this? Tell me Comrade. You must be honest. Tell me everything. For the sake of the Party, for us.'

'I really don't know. I know that this is another universe, Comrade', and he flung an accusing finger at his laptop. 'A universe in which I am not myself. Please, believe me when I tell you that I always mean what I say and write. It's just that sometimes I don't have the strength to live up to my words. But from now on, I will. I will because I want to be with you, but not like this. Not in a disgusting, foreign and demeaning sort of way. Believe me.'

'Why? Why should I?'

Comrade Tuan stood again and walked to the far side of the room. Facing out the window, holding his hands behind his back, his chin upwards. He took a little while to respond.

'There are weaknesses and contradictions in all of us, Comrade. I'm not sure what yours are, but I know they're there, perhaps lying dormant just under the surface. But that doesn't matter to me. What's important is that we help one another scrutinise and work through our contradictions so that we can progress. I know I have hurt you Kim Lien, but I am begging you now to help me.'

We sat in preparation for criticism–self-criticism, not in Comrade Tuan's bedroom, but downstairs in the sitting room with the French doors wide open and the mid-morning sunshine flooding in. Neither Comrade Tuan nor I had ever participated in the criticism–self-criticism process, but we had studied it in communist texts and I had once written an essay on how Stalin's criticism–self-criticism or *samokritika* helped to unite and renew the Soviet Central Committee. Although I was not sure of the mechanics, I knew from news reports that criticism–self-criticism was a public process that allowed cadres who had made mistakes to correct them, while encouraging others to avoid committing the same errors. Both Comrade Tuan and I were well aware of Uncle Ho's proclamation that it is only when 'a party has the courage to clearly identify, admit and address its mistakes, that it can make steady progress'. And so we started in good faith, confident that with sufficient candour, guidance and determination, Comrade Tuan would make steady progress.

Sister Bay was less enthusiastic about the process but, after sustained lobbying from me, agreed to oversee it as a representative of the proletarian and agrarian classes. She also prepared the tea and biscuits.

Once I had reported to Sister Bay the facts and showed her the laptop with the incriminating images, we were ready to proceed with Comrade Tuan's admission and self-evaluation.

'I don't know where to begin', said Comrade Tuan. 'It's complicated, and there are many shameful details that I find hard to recount, let alone disclose.'

'You must try, Comrade Tuan', I said. 'You must combat the conspiracies and distortions that you have contrived to justify your waywardness.'

'I know, I know that this is for the best, that it is for my own good, and for the good of the fatherland. And I know that I have not thought clearly and acted righteously for some time now. I suppose I have confused what is good with what feels good and sacrificed the Party's principles for my pleasure. Saying this out loud, before both of you, helps. But it's also painful. It makes me wonder whether I am no better than all of the young people who I have castigated for being easily misled.'

'This is positive', I said with stern encouragement, 'a move in the right direction. It should be painful, Comrade, arduous like your march to Laos, but ultimately salutary.'

'Excellent, so let's leave it there', Sister Bay chimed in. 'It's not all that complicated is it? Basically, your girlfriend caught you wanking over some naughty videos. Terribly embarrassing. You'll try not to do it again. And we'll try our best not to think about it. So there's no need to discuss it any further. Now, we can all get on with our day. If you two will excuse me, I have more laundry to do.'

'Wait, please Sister Bay!' I pleaded to her as she got up to leave. 'I know this seems trifling to you, but if criticism–self-criticism is to be successful, we have to do it properly. We need your wisdom as a worker and one-time peasant. Comrade Tuan and I have lived in towns and cities for almost all of our lives. Despite our best efforts, we do not have the moral compass and insight that you developed from a young age cultivating rice and looking after animals. Please be patient and give this a little more time.'

'You can have until the end of the spin cycle.'

'Thank you, thank you again Sister. Now, Comrade Tuan you're aware that you have violated a number of laws, most notably, the Decree on the Management, Provision and Use of Internet Service, and the Ministry of Culture and Information's regulation prohibiting the use of the internet to destabilise social order and impair cultural values. You have accessed sites that, if they're not blacklisted, certainly should be. I assume that you're aware of this Comrade Tuan?'

'Yes, but I am grateful to you for reminding me.'

Sister Bay interjected again but was more forgiving of Comrade Tuan than I had expected. Indeed, at that stage she openly defended him.

'The only problem I can see here is that young Tuan has got his satisfaction from his computer when he should have got it from you, Kim Lien.' She was still holding a feather duster that she pointed at both Comrade Tuan and me accusingly.

'Now, it's only natural that *you* would feel hurt, but remember that he hasn't cheated on you, at least not with a person. You're acting like those pictures are somehow real, but they're just fantasies, strange and sick perhaps, but harmless. And, since you're keeping me here against my will, perhaps you will let me be as frank as possible. Is that okay with your honour?'

'Yes, always. We appreciate it.' I said to her.

'If you want him to stop doing what he's doing then why don't you satisfy him a little more? Unless there's laws against that too now? Mind you, I'm not talking about anything indecent or kinky, just a bit of rubbing in the right places and a spit and polish where it's needed. Given that you admire life in the rice paddies so much, I can assure you that I was doing that sort of thing behind the pandanus palms when I was much younger than you. It's just a bit of fun. It's natural. Animals do it all the time.'

Seeing my discomfort, Comrade Tuan intervened, 'Please, Sister, the fault lies wholly with me. It is I who have been weak and misguided. I am the one to blame. I mean, I have been doing this to myself since before I met Comrade Kim Lien. It has nothing to do with her.'

But Comrade Tuan's attempts to shield me from Sister Bay's criticism had little effect. It dawned on me that I too was being scrutinised and exposed in the process of criticism–self-criticism. The question at hand was not just whether Comrade Tuan had failed in his duties as a revolutionary boyfriend, but whether I had failed in mine as a revolutionary girlfriend.

Suddenly I was weeping again, ever so softly, but weeping nonetheless.

And then Comrade Tuan was beside me on the divan, his hand resting on my shoulder.

'I am sorry Comrade Kim Lien. Sister Bay is well-meaning but totally wrong. You have done more than enough to satisfy me. Please know that there is nothing that you could have done to stop me from watching those videos.'

Without looking at him, I wept some more, and wondered, 'What would Uncle Ho do in my situation?' I envisaged him, foot outstretched, flying through the air and kicking the bulbous nose of a French Legionnaire. And then I saw him standing by a pond serenely stroking his wispy beard as B52s dropped bombs all around him.

I removed Tuan's hand from my arm.

'I am fine. Please do not concern yourself. Sister Bay is right. Every question must be asked, every action scrutinised and every solution considered. No one is exempt from criticism in the same way that every plant in the field must be treated if the crop is to flourish. Please continue with the process. I would prefer it if you did so from your own chair.'

'Yes, certainly', said Comrade Tuan as he retreated. 'As I was saying. It started before we were officially boyfriend and girlfriend. Before we even knew one another.'

'Exactly when, Comrade? What was it that made you want to defy the Party and defile yourself? When did you first lose control of your senses?'

'Believe me when I say that I have asked myself this question many times over. My answers have never been wholly satisfying, but perhaps with the benefit of criticism–self-criticism they will improve. Well, there have been times when I believed this irrepressible urge, this fire in my loins, my carnal recklessness, was natural. Perhaps I was pre-programmed to start masturbating on a particular day, do it a few thousand times, and then stop. But as a committed Party member and socialist, I knew that I could not adopt such a fatalistic outlook. I had to believe the will, properly motivated and directed, has no limits. Look at Uncle Ho who was so wedded to the nation that he had no need for a wife or family of his own.'

'Get to the point, boy!' said Sister Bay. 'She wants to know when did you first jerk your bird?'

'Yes, I was getting to that. I can trace the problem, my problem, back to *Suddenly I Wanna Cry*.'

This was not the answer that I had expected.

'But how can that be? We saw a few re-run episodes together and agreed that, while not being strictly socialist realist, the soap opera makes a positive contribution to the national spirit. We had mutual admiration for the street vendor Truc. We agreed that it was popular culture of the highest order and deserved all its accolades. How could you possibly twist something so virtuous into something so, so dirty?'

'You've got me stumped too.' Sister Bay admitted. 'From what I remember, there's a few bikini scenes and half a bra is flashed in the whole series. Hardly anything to get excited about nowadays.'

'These are incisive lines of inquiry. I will do my best to address them. Let me stress, *Suddenly I Wanna Cry* itself is harmless, or at least I think it is. But, because I was not alert, it served as a Trojan horse for debauched cultural forces to infiltrate my consciousness and overrun my entire being. The first time I watched the show, my passions were stirred by messages of virtue; but by the end of the re-run season, something had changed. I started to lust after the heroine, Truc, and then the actress that played her, Tang Ha. And let me confess to you Comrade Kim Lien that after we discussed the show — its plot, production values and social outcomes — I proceeded in quiet moments to stain the cultural analysis with many strokes of my palm.'

'I'm afraid I don't know what you mean, Comrade Tuan.'

'I'm afraid that I do', said the ever prescient Sister Bay.

'Possibly, I do not understand myself. But with you and Sister Bay here to guide me, I can start by recalling the progression of events that brought me here, down to where I am now. As I said, when the show first aired, I was enraptured by it and by Truc: her independent spirit, incorruptibility and penny pinching. But somewhere along the way, I'm guessing around the 25th episode, I developed an erotic desire for Truc. The way that she flared her nostrils at injustice, the vigour with which she performed her morning backbends and the tiny triangle of exposed flesh above the waistline of her pants and between the slit in her long tunic, sparked a flame in me that all my reasoning could not extinguish. I told myself that she was good and pure, and so if I wanted to see more of her, then that too was good and pure.'

'Where are you going with this?' I asked.

'Please bear with me. And know that it was with much anticipation that I awaited the release of Tang Ha's first feature film, *Beautiful by the Centimetre*. It took all of my will power to not see it at the cinema after it was released. Somewhere deep down — and this is crazy I know — I was convinced that I had a one-on-one relationship with Tang Ha, and watching her with others in the room would be like I was sharing her with them. I read the online reviews, all of them scathing. It was base, uncivilised and worse than pornographic. Yet this was not enough to stop me, part of me hoping that all the critics were wrong, another part fervently wanting to discover how right they were. Finally, I found a bootlegged version online. And I remember waiting for it to download with immense excitement and titillation.'

'That was a goddamn awful film', asserted Sister Bay. 'I watched the first 30 minutes confused, swore for the second 30 minutes, and then changed the channel without seeing the end.'

'Your response was spot-on, Sister. And the critics and popular reviews were right too. The amazing thing is that I agreed. The film was senseless and obscene. In online forums, Tang Ha was accused of being a no-good tart who had forgotten where she came from. Once-devoted fans proclaimed that they would never again watch anything she was in or buy anything that she promoted. One even expressed her intent to commit suicide because *Suddenly I Wanna Cry* had given her a reason to live and this film had taken that away. Of course, it was not long before Tang Ha apologised for her rash misadventure. Apparently, she had never really liked the role, but had been badgered by her agent into taking it on, and in so doing had lost touch with her true self and her fans.'

'But Comrade Tuan, this is neither interesting nor related to what you are being criticised for.'

'I don't mean to digress, Comrade Kim Lien. The point is this. Even after enduring the film and agreeing with every scathing comment, I watched *Beautiful by the Centimetre* again, taking note along the way of the most offensive and pornographic scenes. And then, with a click of the mouse, I revisited those scenes: the one from the opening credits when Tang Ha is getting dressed while a white rabbit sits on her bed; the bikini shoot in which she is arched over rocks with ocean suds rolling over her; and the infamous up-the-skirt soccer match in which she continually falls over while playing with neighbourhood ruffians. Over and over I viewed those excerpts so that even now I can trace the curvaceous line of her panties. I knew that what I was doing was depraved, but I couldn't help it. Each time, I promised that this was the last time, then just once more. Before I knew it the sun was breaking through my curtains, and the stark morning light informed me that I had not only wasted the night, but also spilled my previously untapped semen at least four times over. After meticulously cleaning the shame from my work station, I deleted the video with a decisive click.'

'Well done Brother Tuan', said Sister Bay, 'especially on the cleaning.'

'But the next night, as much as I needed sleep, I downloaded *Beautiful by the Centimetre* again and went directly to the scenes that I knew so well. Not long afterwards, I was searching through the night for more pictures of Tang Ha: Tang Ha at the Vietnam Television Awards; Tang Ha driving Vietnam's first-ever Audi A6; studying hotel management at a Singaporean University; as a lesbian lady assassin; and as a judge on Masterchef. I suppose I was compiling a personal history of sorts, but I had little interest in her past and there was no direction or purpose to my research; I was trying to get an instant fix. Many times over I deleted my internet browser history so as to cover my tracks from myself, but I always found my way back to those websites and was on the lookout for others. It was as if I was in a dream in which I could see myself the whole time, I could see that in my rapacious consumption of that young woman, I too was becoming consumed, by the insidious forces of advanced capitalism, and by my own sordid subconscious. But I could not stop. I could not break free.'

'This is progress', I said, trying to encourage him. 'I believe I am just starting to understand your malaise, Comrade Tuan. But I do not see any pictures of Tang Ha on your computer.'

'That was some time ago, Comrade. You see these images and the urges that they excite are like a drug: if you want to maintain the effect, you have to increase the dose. Nowadays I am more nostalgic about Tang Ha than aroused. Her bras and bunny rabbits don't do much for me anymore. Now it's all …'

'You don't need to go into details, Tuan', urged Sister Bay. 'I really wish I had put the washing machine on a quick cycle because this is getting more and more screwed up.'

'Rest assured, Sister Bay and Comrade Kim Lien, never have I been drawn to anything that harms animals or children. And I'm not into violence. My depravity has boundaries, or at least I think it does. You can see from this database that I have compiled to keep track of my viewings.'

As I scanned the database I could not help but gasp and balk. There was an abundance of material from the US – *Stop or my MILF will Shoot* and *Forrest Hump* – and many references to videos made by one-time fascist powers: *Japanese Mangabang* and *Fritz and Franjo's Argentinian Escapade*.

That was when Comrade Tuan started to shake and sniffle.

'I know that your stomach is churning with disgust. No doubt you think I'm a freak. So very often, I've thought that about myself. But surely I am not alone in suffering from this malaise. Maybe there is a fifth column in all of us, constantly conspiring to take hold of our bodies and minds. I've done my best to suppress it. And I have tried to be perfectly clean in public life, perhaps in part to make up for the filthiness of my private hours. I wish I could be pure like you, Comrade Kim Lien and Sister Bay, you who have the same face in all places and live by the same set of principles at all times.'

'Don't drag me into this', insisted Sister Bay.

'But I still don't comprehend why, if you knew what you were doing was wrong, why you didn't just stop. Cut your internet connection or something?'

'I tried, I tried, I swear to the spirits of my ancestors and all the founders of the Vietnamese Communist Party that I tried. But once this noxious culture has taken hold of you, it is not easy to break away. Particularly now that there are so many access points. Now that the smartphone and tablet are always there, awake and attentive to your every whim in an instant, with millions of colluding little pixels that can take you to anywhere that you want to go and do anything imaginable. How can our reasoned selves possibly intervene against such access, such permissiveness? Nothing can fasten down our urges as they leap from one fantastic world to another. I can't count the number of times that I have sat down to work on something that's meaningful to me and urgent for the nation, but have been lured away by those senseless little gif pics and video snippets. Five minutes of reprieve from everyday life turns so quickly into 40, and then 140, until suddenly there's no reprieve from your reprieve.'

'You are making excuses Comrade Tuan. There's no sign of effort in what you recount, only weakness.'

'But I *have* tried. Last year I decided to log my wantonness in this database. There's a separate database for each month. You can see from the graphs that I've made progress, albeit jagged. During times of stress, exams and what not, I tend to be more decadent. But overall, my perversion has clearly declined in both frequency and offensiveness, particularly since you came into my life, Comrade Kim Lien.'

And it was then that I started to fathom the extent of Comrade Tuan's condition. There were more databases. I was only seeing the tail of the beast.

'That's what you've been doing this whole time up there?' exclaimed Sister Bay. 'I should have realised from all the tissues you were using. Kim Lien is right, this has to stop. At the very least, you can do your own washing from now on.'

'As you are my witnesses, I promise that it will, I swear to 18 generations of Hung Vuong Kings. No more. We will find a better filter for my computer. Comrade Kim Lien, you can set the password and keep it from me. I'll buy a new phone, an old phone, without high-speed data. It will be just like when I was on the Ho Chi Minh Trail, when I was losing weight and sleeping soundly. Sister Bay can sleep in my room to keep watch if need be.'

'No chance of that', she said with both her feather duster and head shaking vigorously.

'Both of you can see what I'm willing to do. I will rectify myself, become a new person. And not just because you have caught me out. Comrade Kim Lien, you have witnessed already how I have started to address my sickness. When you stormed into my room I was not using my tender palm to defile myself but rather my unforgiving fist. I have found this technique dampens my arousal and helps me to retain my energy and focus for revolutionary ends. Look here at this week's records, I have not ejaculated for over two days.'

'These are positive signs, Comrade Tuan, and bode well for your reform. They'll all be taken into account when our superiors at the People's Committee, Ho Chi Minh Scouts and Youth League review your case.'

'What do you mean, Comrade Kim Lien? We are now undertaking criticism–self-criticism. The process has been proper and thorough. Sister Bay is here to attest to that fact. I have repented, without reservation, and am beginning to see myself in a new light. What reason is there to take this any further? Why inconvenience others? Comrade, I was hoping we could go back to the way things were.'

'I agree', said Sister Bay. 'Be reasonable, Kim Lien. The boy's suffered enough. He's sorry. Let it go and I'll keep an eye on him.'

'That's very generous of you, Sister Bay, but this is only a preliminary hearing, the first informal stage in a long process. We cannot leave it here. Above all, we must elevate collective need over individual expediency. Social evils must be reported in full to the Party. How else can it register and regulate what is going on in the nation? How will others learn from Comrade Tuan's mistakes if they are not made public? How will Comrade Tuan learn? How can he control traffic when he cannot control himself?'

'I will control myself, I guarantee it. And I will be an even better Party member, more committed, more sacrificing and more proactive. I have had this condition, this weakness, for some time now and still performed my traffic duties perfectly well. For heaven's sake, Kim Lien, I was the one who taught you.'

'Everything that you have achieved to date as a Party member must be reassessed. In any case, the rules are clear: there can be no exceptions, especially for Party members. I have not been able to raise this with you both, but I have reason to believe that my father is deeply involved in corrupt dealings with a foreign company. He too makes exceptions for himself; that's the problem: everyone wants to be the exception. Well, not anymore. Not here. Not when I'm concerned. I have noted the facts of this case and your confession which I can forward to you both for confirmation before sending them to our superiors. I will, of course, enclose as evidence all of your databases. As for your computer, I ask that you pass it on to me or possibly to your father, as he will be able to dig up your browser history from your hard drive so that we can determine whether you are telling the whole truth, particularly with respect to children and animals.'

With this Comrade Tuan became defiant. 'I've told you everything, Comrade Kim Lien. There's no need for this to go beyond this room. It would be useless, counterproductive even. Sister Bay, tell her, please tell her.'

'Okay. Okay. You don't have to worry about me. I'm never mentioning this to anyone. Even if I did say something, no one would listen. You two are the only ones who give a stuff about what I think, which is touching, I suppose, but also very odd. So listen to me Kim Lien, no one cares about what I think as a proletarian-peasant or whatever you reckon I am. And no one cares that Tuan here gives himself a polish every now and then. So just leave it be. He's not the exception. He's probably just a normal guy. Sure, you deserve better than normal. But if we all lived by your laws, Kim Lien, we'd have to turn every school into a courthouse and every other building into a prison. There'd hardly be a man left in the street. So if you want my advice, let off some steam if you have to, but the best thing to do after that is kiss and make up.'

'With respect, Sister Bay, I cannot follow your advice and still call myself a patriotic Party member. And to be frank, there's nothing for Comrade Tuan to fear, at least from the Party. The Vietnamese state does not threaten anyone and no one threatens the state. The law is there to direct and protect us, and it is a most benevolent master, even to those who flout it like Comrade Tuan. He has set his own rules for a long time now, and to what effect? Self-mastery has made him a slave, a slave to temptation. The law will rectify and liberate him. It is the only way. Remember what Uncle Ho said about criticism—self-criticism? He said that we should not be concerned with losing prestige? "Faults are like a disease", he said. "Failure to acknowledge your faults is like not taking your medicine. Failure to criticise another cadre's faults is like refraining from giving him his medicine."'

'But Kim Lien, I thought you cared for me', said Comrade Tuan. 'We're a couple, a unit. We have to look out for one another. You must realise what this would do to me? I would lose all of the respect that I have worked so hard to foster since coming here. I would be ridiculed. It would ruin my career, my entire life. How could you do this to me?'

'I do care for you, Comrade Tuan, like no one before. But these are revolutionary times and so our personal whims cannot come before and above the needs of the Party. You're right about how much you have progressed in terms of self-awareness, just in this last hour. Imagine what you can achieve after re-education under the guidance and support of expert cadres? You will be a new person. Whatever you risk losing, you will surely gain tenfold afterwards. And who knows, the Party in all its wisdom, may well approve our relationship once you're reformed; in which case I'll be waiting for you.'

'Listen to yourself, Kim Lien!' And suddenly Comrade Tuan was like a caged beast lashing out at its captor. 'I opened up to you and Sister Bay. I told you all of this in confidence because I trusted you. So that you could help me. Because I thought you would understand. Do you think that anyone else would? How could the Party geriatrics possibly pass judgment on something like this? They don't understand the pressures that we young people are under, to be new and old, left and right, to always be looking forward to our bright future while also venerating the past. They don't understand what the internet and social media has done for us, to us, for that matter. But, if you insist on telling anyone, tell my father first. He will put a stop to your scheme, more for his sake than mine. And do you really think I should go to a re-education camp for this? I visited one of those camps on my trek to Laos and I can assure you that nothing good – new or reformed – comes out of them. You want me to waste away in the highlands with drug addicts, paedophiles, violent criminals and traitors? I haven't harmed a soul. What's fair or just about that?'

With some of his composure regained, Comrade Tuan asked Sister Bay to leave so that we could speak privately.

'Listen, Kim Lien, I've betrayed you; I'm sorry for what I've done – that you found out in this way. You are proud and it hurts. And believe me that there is no stronger motivation for me to change than to see you suffering like this. But don't betray me just so that you can have your revenge. And that's exactly what you would be doing by reporting this business – betraying me. The choice is simple. If you do this for me, I'll be forever grateful. My already considerable camaraderie and admiration for you will grow. And together we can achieve anything, become the Defence Minister and General Secretary, even. But if you continue down this path, I will never forgive you, and you'll discover exactly how thin and fragile the line is between love and hate. I will turn all of my energy to refuting your accusations and ruining your reputation, just as you seek to ruin mine. I will say that you are a jilted, crazy girlfriend and that it is you who is in need of re-education. My father will support me and even your father will not be able to protect you. I'm sorry if I sound threatening. Know that this is not my preference, and it is not my choice to make, it's yours. You say we have no choice as cadres. Maybe you're right, but we're not just comrades, we're also people, who care for one another. Or at least that's what I hope. I'm not going to pressure you – take some time to think about this – but don't just think about what's right according to the rules. Listen to your heart, or at least take it into consideration, along with what Uncle Ho would do.'

Ordinarily, as I ride the bus to the soccer fields, I am totally focused on the game I am about to play and how I want to play it. It doesn't matter whether I am surrounded by people jostling to buy tickets, bickering over seats, eager to get home for the night. Always, I am calm. I like to stand with my soccer bag secure between my legs and my feet firmly planted on the straps to protect it from thieves. The more intense and uncomfortable the setting becomes, the more conscious I am of the need to be composed. I visualise the ball coming at me from every angle and see myself scrambling and soaring to reach it. The ball lands with a thud into my padded gloves or flies into my chest, where it is immediately wrapped up. Sometimes I can only get a finger on it, but that is enough to deflect it from the goalmouth. Before the game has even begun, I anticipate the wave of relief that comes over me as the final whistle blows and I look up to see a glorious '0' beside the opposition team's name on the scoreboard. Sometimes I imagine there is no one else on my side, that I'm a team of one, the indispensable goalkeeper.

But this afternoon was out of the ordinary. This afternoon I dashed to get a seat at the back of the bus. Feeling the rupture of each stop, start and bump, I clutched on to my bag. For the entire journey I brooded over the choices forced onto me this morning by my father and then by Comrade Tuan. Self-doubt and loathing – of them and the world at large – had consumed my revolutionary spirit. So much so that when I reached the fields, I struggled to get off the bus. For the first time that I can remember, I did not want to play football, the pride and passion of my life, second only to the Party.

It was still well before kick-off when I lumbered into the change room but, because I am usually the first one there, my arrival was noted and deemed worthy of condemnation.

'What happened to Mother Superior Goalkeeper?' asked our flanker in her usual snide manner. 'What did you say to us after the last training session? On and off the pitch, we have to be timely, efficient, disciplined. 'Rust-free screws' – that was it – 'rust-free screws in a finely tuned machine. Who's out of tune now, Goalkeeper?'

I apologised to her, curtly so, before making my way to my locker. Unlike other lockers that were plastered with pictures of pop stars and celebrities, mine was adorned with only three icons: the national flag, a photo of the Vietnamese team goalkeeper and a picture of the Head of the Defence Forces with his fist thumping down on the table during a maritime dispute with China. Usually these images would give me a final inspiring jolt before the game, but today I hardly noticed them. Instead I was drawn to the bareness of my locker, both inside and out. And I returned to the sour and gut-wrenching sentiments that had engulfed me on the bus. Despite everything that I had done to honour my father, Comrade Tuan and my team, no one took me seriously. For all my calls for 'Solidarity, solidarity, more solidarity!', I remained on the outside.

I thought of how Trung Sisters United had all but collapsed when I joined them three seasons ago. Back then, a marginal loss was a victory. The Trung Sisters were mocked as unworthy opposition, striking practice for the rest of the league. We had no uniform or logical formation on the pitch. Training was haphazard and any ferocity was directed inwards. Symptomatic of the team's plight was that no one wanted to keep goal. Most of the team tried to avoid playing up front too because they hardly saw the ball, but anything was better than being subjected to wave after wave of merciless attack, only to be held responsible for yet another defeat.

And so I announced at a training session that I was giving up my natural and well-earned position on the left wing to become the full-time goalkeeper. This was received with general applause, but I did not take this as a vote of confidence. Some of them were simply relieved that the goalkeeping duties would no longer be rotated and others were eager to see me fail.

'It will take time, but I am determined to act as a vanguard from the backline and show how, both as individuals and as a team, we can make ourselves anew. My aim is for Trung Sisters United to be not only competitive in this league, but dominant. I ask that you too make this your unwavering objective, not because it is easy, but rather, because it is gruelling. As Uncle Ho said, 'Nothing is too hard; just set your mind to it, and it will surely be done.'

During that first season I dedicated my body, mind and soul to the science of goalkeeping. Staying up late into the night, I read instruction manuals and biographies, and dissected videos of all the great keepers like Schmeichel,

Seaman, Kahn and Hong Son. Before I went to bed, I visualised my goal zone as if it was the Chi Lang Pass through which China had for centuries tried to invade Vietnam only to be driven back by patriotic heroes. The midway line on the pitch was the 17th Parallel, which we were determined to transgress at all costs. And the enemy half was the Dien Bien Phu Valley into which our haughty foes had become besieged.

In my dreams, my small stature was no impediment to me rising to the heights of national and even global adulation. Heartened by the fact that goalkeepers do not peak until late in life, I fantasised that the national goalie position would soon be mine to have and that I would hold on to it forever.

In my favourite dream, I lead Vietnam to victory in the World Cup finals, becoming the first ever goalkeeper to do so with a clean sheet. The final comes down to a penalty shootout that is so finely balanced that the goalkeepers are called upon to face one another. The hulking Chinese villain – carefully chosen from a billion other candidates and then cunningly engineered for the singular task of goalkeeping – shoots first. She launches a twirling and conniving ball towards the edge of the goalmouth, where my hands are already waiting. Then it is my turn to approach the 11-metre line. After sensing that she has committed to the right, I kick the ball hard and straight. Despite her best efforts, the Chinese goalie can do little more than watch it fly into the back of the net. And then the crowd that has filled the makeshift stadium in Ba Dinh Square at the base of Uncle Ho's mausoleum rises up in unison with the nation to cheer Vietnam, the host team, and its first-ever World Cup victory. Amidst this adulation, I resist the temptation to impersonate aeroplanes or dance around the corner flag. And my teammates know not to leap on top of me. Instead, with my fist raised high, I stand like Fansipan Mountain, singular and tall, just as Ho Chi Minh had done when he declared national independence. Vietnam's time has finally come, no longer just a slayer of great powers, now a great power in its own right.

Of course my efforts and dedication did not yield immediate results, but with each match, I improved. By ignoring the extravagant boot scooting antics of strikers and concentrating on their minute hip movements, I could predict with great accuracy what they were going to do. Increasingly, I pressured my opponents into kicking the ball too early and missing the mark. Before long I was known and even feared for my aggressive defence, my propensity to move forward and attack those who sought to attack me. And, after a time, I could feel my hands expanding and mutating so that they came to perfectly fit the gloves into which the fate of our team rested.

As I improved and transformed, so did my team. They were driven first, by the satisfaction of avoiding defeat, and then by the thrill of triumphing over others. Our training sessions picked up in intensity with the vainglorious forwards eager to test their goalscoring skills against me. My defenders united in the knowledge that they were building their walls on a firm foundation. Yet, astonishingly, I could still not develop a rapport with my teammates. There was never a ready-made place for me in huddles. And whenever we faced a set play, they resented my shouting at them to get into position. This did not bother me as I reasoned that for a team to succeed, obedience is more important than affection. And after intense consideration, it struck me that in soccer the goalkeeper is the essential outcast, that she is part of the team, but also separate from it. She wears a different uniform, lives by different rules and moves in smaller circles. When she saves everyone from falling, the most she gets is a pat on the shoulder: 'Good work, goalkeeper.' Despite putting her body on the line every time she laces up her boots and straps on her armour, the goalkeeper is almost never invited to celebrations and outings. At some stage, I decided that this suited me just fine.

There was an especially memorable moment in our second season when our opponents, the Con Dao Convicts, strategised that, while my leap was impressive, I could not come even close to reaching the crossbar. And so every Convict shot at goal was either lobbed over my head or directed into the upper edges of the goalmouth. We conceded one goal in the first 20 minutes and at half-time were fortunate not to be further behind. After the break, the Convicts came out beaming with confidence, while we had fallen back on our heels. It was clear that not only this match, but the entire season was at stake. If we lost in this manner, the message would soon spread that there was a chink in my armour and therefore a sure-fire way to beat the Trung Sisters. I had to send a different message, make it known to all that there were no heights that we could not reach and that we would do whatever it took to win.

My opportunity came when one of my defenders was caught out of position, leaving the Convicts' number nine open. On receiving the ball she sent it soaring up towards the corner of my goal with the force of a North Korean rocket. I propped back, then took a run-up and planted the front end of my boot into the lower back of one of my defenders who was loitering on the goal line. It was as close as I have ever come to flying. I soared so high that I hardly had to stretch my arms to catch the ball, and while I could have hung on to it, I decided to push the ball over the top of the goal. This meant conceding a corner, but it allowed me to hang on to the crossbar so that all could witness the indomitable grimace on my face. After daintily descending to the ground, I brushed off the protests from both the Convict forwards and my crying defender: 'Whose side do you think you're on, goalkeeper?' Evidently, she did not know the value of sacrifice.

By the end of my first season, I had been knocked unconscious three times and the Trung Sisters United finished in third last place, which was a creditable result given where we had come from. Last year we failed to reach the semifinals, but only barely. Particularly impressive was our performance in the last match of the regular season against the eventual champions, the Au Co Angels, who we defeated 1–0.

For us to improve further, I knew it was necessary for me to control more than just the goal line. And so I approached our manager with a detailed proposal outlining why I should take on the responsibilities of captain. As always, he was frightfully relaxed about the affair (the manager was only really doing the job because he was courting two of our midfielders). 'Fine. As long as you sort it out yourself', was all he said.

With his approval, I contacted the flanker, who was our existing captain, and whose father happened to work with mine. In my text message, I pointed out that she had done a reasonable job but, from my tally, had missed over a quarter of the training sessions, and so it would be best for the team if she stepped down in favour of someone who could set a better example. The flanker asserted that she had 'seen this coup coming', but acquiesced with, 'Whatever your father and his Princess want, they get.' When I offered her the vice-captaincy, she answered, 'Never, and don't bother asking anyone else.' Again, this suited me, because now the red armband was mine alone.

During the off season I introduced a mandatory attendance at training and incorporated fitness, skills and formation work into every session. These sessions became progressively harder throughout the season, which led some of my sisters to protest that they needed to rest and taper off before a match if they were to perform at their peak. My response was that pacifism and weakness had no place in sport-as-war-as-life.

On the field, my plays were commonly criticised for being overly defensive, relying on disciplined ball retention and striking only at opportune moments when the enemy was fatigued and ill-focused. The flanker said that my style of football was so boring that it made the Italians look like Brazilians. But I was vindicated by success, and the realisation midway through the season that we were premiership favourites.

Our run of victories brought newfound challenges and conflicts. Most controversially, despite my team spirit, I had never sung the team song nor participated in post-goal celebrations because they were derived from Psy's 'Gangnam Style'. In fact, I tried to outlaw both as they reflected an affinity with cultural surrender rather than sporting triumph. But I simply could not get my teammates to comprehend this. Nor could I get them to see the virtue of singing the national anthem, 'The Song of the Advancing Soldiers', both before and after each game. One night, kept awake by my frustration, I got up and sent my sisters an email.

To: Trung Sisters United Division 2
CC: the Manager

Comrades,

Of late I am pleased to see that we are winning, but what concerns me as captain is our team culture, which is in many ways impoverished and feeble. It is not a winning culture. This is because it is based on the shifting and slippery stones of individual desire. Often I have witnessed your obsessions with passing fads from distant lands. Often I have overheard you profess that you are training not for the team's glory, but to trim your thighs or to firm your buttocks so that you can fill your jeans in a way that draws improper attention. This behaviour will lead to vice, not victory.

Both on and off the field, we must be motivated to achieve real victory. A real victory emerges from a real culture. This culture is close and familiar to all of us. It is the culture that has fought off Chinese imperialism for millennia. It is the culture that resisted against, and finally triumphed over, French colonialism. It is the culture that reunified the nation in 1975, curing it of Republicanism. It is the culture that acted when the rest of the world was too timid, liberating the Kampucheans from Pol Pot's murderous grip. Since 1986 it is the culture that has renovated our economy and society for a post-industrial world. Continually dynamic and yet always secure, it is the culture of a rising dragon. It is the Vietnamese Communist Party's culture, which the heroic, intellectual Truong Chinh described as 'national, scientific, and mass-based'. My sisters, I ask you, why has this eternal culture, this winning culture, this culture of patriots, gone out of fashion? And, just as important, what must we do about this?

We must identify and defeat the contemporary enemies of this winning culture. In the past century, the three enemies that were identified and defeated by the Party were illiteracy, poverty and invaders. Now the nation faces three new enemies. They have infiltrated every team in this league, ours being no exception. And it is because of the pervasiveness of these enemies that we must be vigilant and ever conscious that together, and only together, can we prevail.

The first enemy is not the blindness that comes from illiteracy, but the blindness of indifference. Too many youth are indifferent to our glorious past, indifferent to the dire challenges of today, and indifferent to our glorious collective future. They are trees without roots, duckweed floating aimlessly, not knowing which direction to take. This leads them to be callous towards themselves and everyone else. Ultimately, it leads to oblivion. Surely, you know of youth who are so indifferent to the world that they resort to mutilating themselves, purportedly in order to feel. And there are other youth who lash out at society, like the 17-year-old from Bac Giang who remorselessly slaughtered a family for their jewellery. How long before we are like those Chinese who have no qualms about manufacturing poisonous baby formula? In times past, when our enemies were at our gates, we always had the courage to drive them away. Now that our enemies are within us, they are far more difficult to face.

The second enemy, rampant individualism, is a close cousin of the first. I know many of you think that being an individual is the same as being free. Maybe you want to be liberated from the expectations of old people, the pressures of your community or even the guidance of the state. But you should know that this sort of individualism is contrary to correct thought and proper action. It breeds anxiety and anomie, rather than independence and liberty. You must remember that liberty is not the same as license. True liberty does not give us license to squander the inheritance that our ancestors have fought and died for. It does not stand by as people do damage to others and themselves. The Party understands this and it understands that no individual or living thing can prosper in a vacuum. And so the Party is dedicated to making Vietnam 10 times more beautiful, within our lifetimes, for our benefit, and for those who come after us. It is only in this context and in this Way – the Party's Way – that as individuals we can flourish and be free.

False idols are the third enemy that keeps us from becoming new people. I hope all of you remember Nguyen Trai's famous assertion that Vietnam has never lacked heroes, but has also never been short of enemies. This remains true today. What has changed is that our enemies are far more familiar and attractive to us than our heroes. All of you, I know, are drawn to pop stars, models, actors, athletes and figures who have no value or status other than that based on their celebrity. I urge you to recognise that they are more deserving of caution than admiration. They are the enemy. Many of you who sat the university entrance examinations would have addressed the pressing question: 'Deference to real cultural idols is a wondrous duty, but going mad over false idols is a national tragedy. Discuss.' I am proud to say that I achieved perfect marks for this question (and can email to you my essay upon request). But I was disappointed to discover that many of you were offended by this question and felt as if you were being forced to lie about your deep affection for K-pop and J-pop in order to get into university.

False idols are key elements of the poisonous foreign cultures that have invaded our country. These cultures are like hallucinogens that lure and then trap young people into nightmarish states of semi-consciousness. The action films from Hong Kong crammed full of special effects; the senseless frivolity of Bollywood extravaganzas; the inane romanticism peddled by so many Korean chick flicks. They are not grounded. They have no foundation in our reality. They offer us no better knowledge of our material condition or how to improve it. Instead we are left with a yearning for greater spectacle and ever more falseness. They make us passive and compliant to foreign forces that want to keep us down and run us over.

So I want to promote a movement that starts with us, the Trung Sisters United, standing up and emphatically returning to the source. We must esteem and imitate those who are truly worthy of esteem and imitation, the idols that have made Vietnam an exemplary nation and its people so proud and strong.

If you agree with me, and I know you will, it is not enough to sit by your computers and nod your heads. We must confront falseness with truth. We must respond to this cultural invasion by going on a cultural offensive, an offensive in which every blog, tweet, SMS, like, instant message, avatar, mash up, gif, Snapchat and email is a bullet directed straight to the heart of our foes.

Most immediately, we must praise the everlasting artistry of the national anthem and reject Psy's 'Gangnam Style', which will be blown away by the next gust of wind.

For independence, freedom and happiness, The Goalkeeper.

After several more emails and an extended team meeting we formally decided to keep the Gangnam celebratory dance, but replaced the song with a modified version of, 'It is as if Uncle Ho was here on this day of great and joyous victory'. It was tolerable compromise, at least for a season or so. Out of good faith, I even learnt how to do the dance, which helped me to grow a little closer to my teammates. And so, we sang and danced our way through the regular season, finishing on top of the ladder, sweeping through the semi-final with a 3–0 win, and coming into the Grand Final against our rivals, the Au Co Angels, as raging favourites. The tragedy, of course, is that this game was scheduled for the same day that I would discover my father and Tuan's crimes. My crime relates not so much to the fact that we lost, but rather to the fact that I willed it.

My usual pre-match pep talk takes around 15 minutes, but this afternoon it boiled down to, 'Let's get this over with'. We lost the toss, which I took some satisfaction in such was my impulse for self-destruction. As I took my position in goal, it was as if I was watching the game on a big screen and had no interest in it whatsoever. The teams were unfamiliar to me and the stakes were measly. Football itself seemed utterly futile and absurd. I mulled over my father ingratiating himself to foreign businesspeople, selling hectare after hectare of my homeland, sipping champagne while overseeing peasants being forced from their farms, speaking Mandarin as if he were a Chinese agent. And I envisaged Comrade Tuan in all manner of compromising positions: wedged between Elly Tran's colossal breasts or chasing a pink cartoon cat with his zipper open and his fist rubbing his crotch.

It was fortunate in a way that for most of the first half, my goal line was not threatened. But invariably the Angels counterattacked. Their number ten delicately received a pass on her chest and brought it down to her feet. She pivoted as if about to dash out to the flank, but then turned inwards to get past my defender. The centre forward stormed down the corridor directly at me, the last line of defence. Like a startled buffalo, I started to sprint at her. Having left my goal line far too early with no eye for the ball whatsoever, the striker could have scored by simply lobbing the ball over me. In retrospect, I wish she had done so. Instead she kept coming, which allowed us to get close enough for her to see the unbridled madness in my eyes and for me to be invigorated by the scent of her fright. As it turned out, she sprayed the ball sideways; however, this was of no significance to me. Something in me had snapped. I was convinced that she wanted to do more than just score a goal in a game of soccer. She aspired to humiliate me and upset everything that I believed in. And so, with a steel-hard hip and shoulder, I barged into my enemy. She was slightly taller and broader than me, but it would not have mattered if she was the size of an elephant or as loveable as a baby bird, such was my intent to destroy.

What lingers in my mind is the sensation of feeling her ribs shudder and hearing the wind escape from her lungs, just before she flew back and fell to the ground. In the still and silent moment that followed, I had a monstrous grin on my face.

Then I heard the referee's whistle and the crowd jeering. Ten Angels were screaming. I could sense the pounding of their boots against the turf as they stormed towards me. Looking down at the wheezing striker, I noticed that I had somehow come to rest my foot on her pony tail. She caught my eye again and tried to roll away in fear, but my studs had dug into her hair. She let out a piercing screech with the air that was left in her lungs. The barrage of Angels crashed into me and forced me to the ground, threatening to stomp my body to a pulp and kick my head to the other side of the Perfume River. Throughout all of this, my teammates remained huddled together on the other side of the pitch.

When the referee finally dispersed my opponents, he reached into his pocket and pulled out a yellow card before pointing to the spot for a penalty kick. This evoked further howls of protest from the Angels, who were convinced I should have been sent off.

As I returned to the goal box the umpire whispered to me, 'What's gotten into you? You wouldn't be on the pitch if I didn't hold your father in such high regard.'

The number ten eventually recovered and insisted on taking the penalty kick. As she lined up for the shot I felt truly guilty for assaulting her. However, I was also still enraged, confused and full of self-pity.

She elected to drive the ball straight at my head and must have had been both exultant and terrified to see that the only force acting upon me was inertia. At the last millisecond I moved my head, more out of instinct that any desire for self-preservation. At the same time my gloves went up and I caught the ball. However, because there was no body mass or spirit behind this effort, the ball emerged from my grip and fell down behind me before dribbling into the goal. Again, I heard gasps of horror, this time from my team. The Angels and their supporters hooted and cheered. Their number ten sprinted past me to grab the ball and as she made her way back to the centre line sneered, 'Eat shit, bitch. That won't be the last.'

She was right. I let in three more goals before the half was over and, like the first goal, they were largely self-inflicted. In the change rooms at half-time I sat slumped against my locker. The manager and my teammates tried everything to revive me; screaming abuse at first, then feigning sympathy, asking what had caused my spiritual implosion and promising to help me. They asserted that we were on the verge of glorious victory and that we would rise up from the depths like a golden phoenix. 'Nothing is too hard', one of my defenders reminded me, 'just set your mind to it, and it'll happen!' The flanker was more honest. She whispered to me that everything I'd invested in the team would amount to nothing if we didn't win the match. 'Everyone will know that you've played the cruellest prank on us – getting our hopes up and dashing them at the last minute.'

I was not stirred by their efforts. Instead, I removed my captain's armband and flicked it to the flanker. The manager commanded me to hand over my gloves and jersey, which I did without protest. We conceded four more goals in the second half as I sat at the end of the substitute bench, enduring abuse from both my teammates and the opposition. It struck me that the people who I had tried so hard to unite around me were so eager to unite against me.

With five minutes to go, as the Angels were randomly passing the ball around, I left. I stumbled through the alleyways to a shabby café on the banks of the Perfume River, with beach chairs outside and prowling bar girls within. I nursed a black iced coffee until I was certain everyone had left the soccer fields, then made my way back to the main road for the last bus home.

As I staggered into my street, more out of habit than will, I ran my eyes over the two banners that hung over the entrance to my street: 'The citizens of Vy Da Hamlet strive to maintain cleanliness and order', and one of Ho Chi Minh's sayings, 'Love other human beings, as you would love yourself'. Some time ago I promised myself I would meditate upon the Party's banners every time I passed under them and do my best to carry them out to the fullest. My crime is that tonight I have no love for other human beings or for myself.

Overcome with both fatigue and frustration, I drag myself out of bed again and sit at my computer. I attach to the email Comrade Tuan's offending spreadsheets and enclose a link to the recording of my father and Mr Kuang's dealings in my cloud account. A cursory look at my inbox reveals several invective-filled messages from the Trung Sisters. I include one from the flanker and one from our manager as evidence of my defeatism.

The only thing left to do is to press 'send'.

I cannot do it. Not right now. Perhaps protocol demands that I present a hard copy to the authorities. Have I included all the necessary recipients? Should I cc my father and Comrade Tuan? Have I made a mistake?

So once more, I am in bed holding on to that dreadful green body pillow, wearier than before, yet unable to sleep. In frustration, I fling the pillow aside and lie flat on my back with my palms facing up, making every possible effort to relax.

It occurs to me that I still have my soccer socks on, pulled up over my shins. Using the big toe from one foot, I hook on to the top of the sock on the other leg and drag it off. It's then that I feel it; the titillation of my toenail rubbing against the inside of my leg. The sensation lingers. I do it again, this time with the underside of my toe, but find that this is not as effective. I return to using the tip of my toenail, sliding it up the inside of my calves, knees and thighs.

Before I know it, my hand is reaching into my shorts, furtively searching for a way to get back at Comrade Tuan for his thousands of sordid misadventures, my fingers are driven by the need to prove I am not, as my father believes, a naïve little girl. Unsure as to whether the Party approves of masturbation, I have previously refrained from doing it. Now, however, a wet, pleasing sensation tells me that everything is permitted. I consider whether auto-stimulation is counterproductive to sleep, but trust that my rousing apex will be followed by a slumber-inducing trough. After a promising start, I begin to lose rhythm and direction. And so I try imagining the Party General Secretary; not as he is now, but back when he was a young and slender soldier. I envisage him standing on the shores of one of the Paracel Islands, his shirt half open and pants rolled up, whistling a valiant folk song. This has no appreciable impact.

And so I turn my thoughts to a recent documentary in which a startlingly handsome young actor plays Le Van Tam, the boy martyr who doused himself with petrol before charging into a cavalcade of French legionnaires and striking a match. Visualising this heroic explosion will surely set me off. However,

I am less enthused with him than with the General Secretary. In desperation, I conjure up memories of Tuan after he had returned from Laos when he was as thin as an egret, but this only makes me feel bitter and frustrated.

I resolve to try again later. For now, I remain alert but not aroused, both hands palm-up on the mattress, totally unsatisfied.

From the city lights creeping under the window blind, I can make out the silhouette of a gecko on the ceiling in the corner of my room. It is the same gecko that has skirted around my bedroom for the last few days. I warm to it. That lizard seems like one of the most stable things in my life, as it was here with me before the ruptures of today and is more likely than any teammate, friend or relative to be with me tomorrow. Both of us are somehow stuck in the corner of a vast and uncertain universe. I wonder if our destinies are tethered. Maybe the gecko can guide me. Perhaps we can be comrades.

And so I designate the horizontal edge of my ceiling the 'People Axis', along which my loyalty to my father, Comrade Tuan and my teammates can be measured. The vertical edge is the 'Principle Axis', indicating my dedication to Party values, which are tightly bound to my own. The idea of reducing this day and my life to two dimensions and relying on a reptile to determine my fate makes me cackle like a mad scientist.

I will go wherever Comrade Gecko takes me.

As I wait for my steadfast friend to move, I encounter another unexpected turn: I find myself praying. I pray earnestly and vigorously but, as was the case with masturbating, this is my first time and so I do it with reckless abandon. Clamping my eyes shut and my palms together, I pray to my ancestors and to all the venerable heroes in Vietnam's 5,000-year history, beseeching them to look over me. Although I have always disapproved of the superstitious Cult of Ho Chi Minh, I pray to him for guidance so that I might make the right decisions, emphatically so. To Buddha I appeal for mindfulness in the hope of eliminating my desire and suffering, if not in this life, then the next. I pray to the Jade Emperor to guide me along the Way and, despite my rejection of Jesus' defeatism, I ask him for advice on how best to redeem the wrongdoings of all those around me. Above all, I pray that Comrade Gecko will make the right move and somehow show me that my life has meaning and direction.

I open my eyes to find that the lizard is still in the corner: immobile, indifferent, resisting me.

Chapter 5
The Student

01:20.21

With every glance at my watch time seems to slow down. I tell myself this is because I am bored, frustrated and cold. I remember from a textbook on quantum physics that time is radically variable but flows evenly as long as we remain relatively still. In my mind, however, it's the stillness that's the problem; that sense of being fixed in one spot forever.

Finally, after over an hour of digging, my grandmother's coffin is ready to be raised. My father and my two uncles heave it out and place it before the small crowd of family and friends that has gathered for my grandmother's reburial. Father gently prises open the lid of the teak veneer coffin, which he had crafted himself. I inch forward and stare at the first corpse I have ever seen. My grandmother's skeleton is black and almost comically small. A layer of grit covers the bottom of the coffin – all that's left of her flesh and organs. Her burial shroud and clothes are caked with mud but largely intact. After removing the shroud, my father turns to my grandmother's gloves. The long violet-coloured gloves that once shielded her arms from the summer rays and winter chills are now washed-out shades of pink. I am surprised at how well they have retained their elasticity as father stretches them before turning them inside-out so that grandmother's wrist bones and knuckles tumble out like misshapen marbles. I thought that this part of the ceremony would be gruesome and sickening. Instead, I am unmoved.

Father cradles the blackened skull in his wide hands, carefully scooping out the grime from the eye sockets with his fingers. As he removes the dirt and clumps of wispy hair, a fracture opens up along the forehead and the skull suddenly breaks into two. Some of the onlookers gasp, sensing this is a horrible omen. But Father is unfazed. He places the piece of cranium on the ground and continues using his thumbs and fingers to brush the soil from each cavity and crevice of the skull. Everyone around me is reassured by the steadiness of his gaze and the sureness of his gestures. Some of them comment that my grandmother and those looking on from the next world in judgement would also approve.

The swaying fluorescent bulb hanging over my father cuts out and we are engulfed by night. Again there are gasps. Only one person has a torch. An outbreak of cigarette lighters and mobile phones raised in the air make it seem as if we are in an enchanted forest surrounded by glowing nymphs.

I take the opportunity to close my eyes. I listen to the wind battering the tarpaulin sheets on the makeshift A-frame tent sheltering my father and the gravesite. People behind me use the anonymity of darkness to grumble about the bitter cold and unholy hour. Lorries rumble away from one of the nearby concrete quarries. Seconds later, someone restores the clip connecting the bulb to a truck battery. I open my eyes to see my father running his hands along the length of a blackened thigh bone, as if nothing has happened.

Latecomers appear, navigating their way across the rice fields and between headstones. Many have tied white sashes over their foreheads to show that they are still in mourning. The clean white bands glow on top of vibrant scarves wrapped around their necks and faces. I suspect that anyone who looked on us without knowing our sombre purpose would burst out laughing. This suspicion is heightened when the multicoloured mummies are joined by figures that glide in wearing motorbike helmets and plastic ponchos to protect them from the blasting wind. They look like astronauts leaving for another planet, or maybe aliens visiting this one.

I am struck by the banality of comments accompanying this sacred event.

'Is that a leg or an arm bone?'

'Surely that's too small and blunt to be a rib?'

'Are my hips anything like that?'

But soon enough I find myself emulating those around me, trying to label the bones as they emerge. What else is there to do?

A turtle emerges from the dark and starts to dawdle across the dirt mounds of the gravesite. Again, there's inane speculation about what this all means. Is it warning us or welcoming us? Has anyone seen this particular turtle before? Are they nocturnal? Why is it tottering about here? I suspect it was simply making its way from pond to pond and was attracted to the light. The turtle retracts into its shell as my uncle picks it up and moves it on its way.

Oblivious, my father scours the bottom of the coffin, salvaging everything down to the minute toe bones and teeth, which he cups in his hands as if they are precious gems. I have long admired his strong and unfaltering carpenter hands, the first ever laid upon me.

I think back to when I was six or so and was playing in the river with my friends. I had wandered into deep, fast-flowing water and plummeted so quickly that I had no chance to scream out for help. My arms flailed as I sank. When I made contact with the riverbed I tried to leap up for air, but the sand gave way. As the sunlight receded and I lost all sense of where I was and what to do, I felt my father's hands around my arms, hauling me up to the surface and throwing me over his shoulder before marching back to the shore.

A few years ago when the river flooded I recalled this event to my father, who had no recollection of it. When I said how shocked I was that he had forgotten he replied, 'How can you expect a father to remember every time that he saves his child's life? Between you learning how to crawl and getting your motorbike licence there were hundreds of times when I had to step in to save you from catastrophe. There's nothing unusual about that. Your sister has needed much more rescuing than you. Your mother and I are still trying to save her from drowning in one way or another. Parenting is about giving, saving, and making a life for your children. You probably don't know what I'm talking about. But you'll find out someday, when you have kids.'

By 02:42.42 all the bones are arranged on a plastic sheet. The conspicuous pieces of dirt and putrefied flesh have been brushed off so that the ritual washing can begin. At this point I notice a pause in my father's efforts. No one else registers this because they are focused on the skeleton, not close enough to see, or they don't know him as well as I do. His deep, long breath followed by a slight tremble tells me he is a little nauseous, reluctant to continue.

My father began charging himself with rice wine at the banquet before the ceremony, and had drunk steadily throughout the evening. He is under great pressure to get everything right, convinced that a single mistake could have drastic consequences for his mother's soul. And then there is the propriety of thoughts and sentiments that has to be maintained because, as far as he is concerned, his mother's soul can see straight into his. Father recently reminded me that the umbilical cord connecting him to his mother was buried in that same field, as was the cord that connected me to my mother. This symbolised the enduring bond between our people and the countryside. I wanted to tell him that if he really wanted to do something useful with our umbilical cords, then he shouldn't have allowed them to be eaten by worms and bacteria. I wanted to explain to my father what I learnt in biology class, about how umbilical cord blood is a rich source of stem cells that can be used to treat diseases, repair injuries, improve the immune system. Instead, I cast my eyes to the ground and nodded. 'Yes Father, I know.'

Throughout the ceremony everyone solemnly pays their respects to my grandmother. Many recount the hardship she endured raising three boys on her own. My grandfather was killed somewhere in the Central Highlands during the American War, with no one to wash and honour his bones. She had picked and sold betel nuts for a pittance, laboured in the rice fields, risked her life to reach black markets and, in the 1980s, took a job in a plastics factory when she should have been preparing to retire. Somehow, she always managed to come home in the evening with something for her family to eat, even if it was their only meal that day.

The congregation is convinced that whatever is conveyed to my grandmother now, with her bones laid out before us, is as important as any words they had uttered to her when she was still alive. Twice I have heard people solemnly recite the proverb, 'Final impressions upon the deceased must be righteous and proper, for they are everlasting.' But surely it is far better to make an impression on people when they are still alive. It is absurd that I have to remind myself of this. Gratitude, resentment, esteem, anguish, adoration and all other sentiments mean nothing to the deceased.

It also seems ridiculous to me that so many people are guided in their beliefs by folktales and proverbs. No one knows the author of these proverbs and even if they once offered some insight into the human condition, this doesn't mean they have any relationship to the present. It's as if a few lyrical lines, repeated often enough, transform into a law of nature. Whatever happened to scientific rigour, double-blind trials, healthy scepticism? It occurs to me that a million proverbs do not amount to an ounce of reliable knowledge.

02:56.52

The wind dies down just as my father begins to wash the bones. He appears focused and tranquil, even though I know he's in the middle of a cyclone of sensations and memories.

I have seen that face many times. His eyes are softly creased, his jaws are moving gently back and forth as he purifies and revives his mother's remains. This is his workshop face, the face with which he planes doorframes and girders, chisels rooftop decorations and varnishes coffee tables. It is the face that dovetails with the words of advice he has often tried to pass on to me. 'You can't perfect the past or dictate the future. So just devote yourself to the task in front of you. If you can focus on what is at hand, then the shelves, table, house or whatever it is you're building will come together as planned.'

I am not a capable or enthusiastic carpenter. My hands are not like my father's. And although he has never urged me to follow in his footsteps, I sense that he always wanted me to appreciate what he did for a living – our living – if not show some aptitude for woodwork. Now, as I watch my father undertaking this sacred task, I begin to grasp a small part of the skill, patience and exactitude it requires.

His cleaning moves from the large bones to small ones, starting with the femur bones, then the hips, ribs and vertebrae, followed by all the tiny pieces that must be sifted in plastic colanders. Last, he turns to the broken skull. There are no sponges or implements. Cloths are used, but only delicately to pat dry the remains; everything else is done with his bare hands.

The first washing takes place in spring water scented with pomelo leaves. The water was ordered by the crate and came out of dark green glass bottles with pictures of snow-capped mountains on them, a brand I haven't seen before, but can identify as lavish. From this my grandmother's soul is prepared for revival. A second, final rinsing takes place in a receptacle brimming with homemade rice wine. From this solvent, rich with all the sustenance and joy of my village surrounds, it is thought that my grandmother is sent into the beyond with the assurance that she will never be left wanting.

As the washing draws to an end, my mother prepares the small metal casket that will permanently house the bones. The burnished black casket is adorned with silver dragons symbolising the ascension of the spirit. My mother lines it with red cellophane and votive offerings of faux gold taels and oversized US dollars – more money than my grandmother had ever possessed in her life. On top of these flashy offerings, Mother sprinkles a handful of plain cooked rice from the banquet the night before. She grows frustrated as she tries to remove the grains sticking to her woollen gloves. My mother has several layers of clothing on, two scarves and a face mask, in stark contrast to my barefoot father, whose sleeves and pants are rolled up as if he had just discovered treasure on a tropical island.

Hardly a word passes between my parents throughout this part of the ceremony. Each of them knows what is to be done. Their silence masks a great discord.

'Talk some sense into your father!' was how mother had begun a phone call to me just over a month ago. 'He still insists on doing the exhumation himself.'

'Well, I agree he shouldn't do it, but I don't see why anyone should either', I said to her. 'But there's no use trying to convince him. He's not going to change his mind.'

'You know the Daos up the road? They just reburied their grandfather a few nights ago. I asked them how much it cost to hire professionals, less than 2 million dong. I would pay 10 million. But your father won't listen.'

She went on praising the benefits of hiring specialists. They'd be proper and thorough, and they would do it quickly. Most importantly, it was the safest option. Mother was frightened that the soul caller had miscalculated the date for the ceremony and they would disinter my grandmother's body only to discover that it hadn't fully decomposed. She had heard that this commonly occurred, largely because people were not as skinny as they used to be and soul callers not as skilled. Father would then have to strip away all of the flesh with his hands and a knife which was, in her view, repulsive and risky. Stories abounded of disease after such ceremonies.

But my mother's major concern was supernatural in origin. There was a very thin line in her mind between commemorating and desecrating the dead, a line that mortals could never accurately gauge. An undetected morsel of rotting flesh or slight ill-positioning of the bones was enough to offend greatly those from the other world, and thereby attract their wrath. She had read newspaper articles about a family who had captured and eaten a snake that was resting on their ancestor's grave. The family hadn't realised that the snake embodied the spirit of their forebear who was informing them it was not time to move on. The agony inflicted upon the deceased was duly transmitted to the living family members who were, in the following months and years, dragged into the underworld in freakish ways. Above all, Mother wanted to hire the team of professionals as insurance; they would assume liability for committing a grievous crime against my grandmother.

I could tell from my mother's voice that she was growing more and more distressed, and so agreed to speak to my father.

'I will do it the way my father and his father did it, not the way that some people prefer to do it today.'

I had never heard my father come so close to yelling.

'How can we pay *others* to carry out *our* duties? Your grandmother gave up everything for me, for us. She never shirked a thing in her life. And now you're telling me that I should not do this for her. It is not like your grandparents do not have any sons. There are three of us, all able-bodied and devoted. If I do not do it, one of your uncles will. They would never hire "professionals", as your mother likes to call them, as if they are doctors with degrees. Your mother acts like your grandmother was infected with cholera and has been festering in the grave. She died of old age, and even then it took three strokes. So what do we have to fear, except disgracing ourselves and her memory? Do you understand what I am saying, Son?'

'Yes, Father. Mother and I are only worried about you. We love and respect Grandmother too but …'

'We didn't abandon her to the care of others when she was old and infirm. We didn't dishonour her then, in her final years, and we will not dishonour her now. So don't ask me to bring in strangers with rubber gloves and boots to tramp all over our ancestors and pretend it is the best thing for everyone. Only I can do this. I alone.'

03:16.13

I am deeply doubtful, not so much about whether to side with my mother or father about who should be doing the reburying, but whether it should be done at all.

Specks of rain appear on my glasses and gusts of wind are mounting again. Whereas before my lips were dry and chafed, now they're so numb that I can barely feel the mucus running from my nose down over my lip and into my mouth. I rue forgetting my gloves. The cold has trapped my hands in my pockets, barring me from wiping my chin. I shuffle my feet and run on the spot to get warm, but this draws my father's attention. He stares at me menacingly before shifting the bones to the driest spot under the tarpaulin sheets.

A family friend with a penchant for the obvious remarks that reburials would be much easier during the daytime. But everyone knows that that is not an option. The world of the dead is negative, nocturnal – not the positive light-filled world of the living. For this reason, the fire lit before the ceremony is kept small and at a distance from the gravesite. Here the ephemeral needs of the living make way for the demands of the deceased.

'But what does this negative world nonsense really mean?' I ask myself. 'All this fuss over auspiciousness and inauspiciousness, the finicky details of divination and paying respects to the dead. Does any of it matter? If by some off chance the spirits of the dead prefer the night, what's wrong with exhuming them at seven or eight o'clock, right after dinner? What's sacrosanct about the smallest hours of the morning and the coldest months of the year?'

Of course it is fruitless to ask. I know the answer already. It's the catchcry of people across the countryside, village elders in particular: 'Because ancestors are there to be worshipped. Because filial piety is the first and most fundamental virtue. Because it has always been this way.'

I vaguely recall a folktale about the earnest peasant Dong Tu, who was so poor that together he and his father owned only one garment, a loincloth that was worn by whoever needed to go to the market. When Dong Tu's father became very ill he informed his son that as much as he dreaded the thought of dying, at least Dong Tu would no longer have to face the indignity of scurrying around unclothed. But when the time came to bury his father, such was the young man's reverence that he could not bear the thought of allowing the old man to leave this world as naked as the day he had entered it. And so Dong Tu dressed his deceased father in the loincloth and resigned himself to nudity and shame. Instead of going to the market to sell his wares he stood in the river and fished, trading his catch with boats that went by, never emerging from the water until the end of the day when no one could see him.

Even as a young boy, I was convinced that Dong Tu was more deserving of ridicule than praise. But in the story, if I remember it correctly, he is royally rewarded for his sacrifice, receiving the hand in marriage of a beautiful princess along with an enchanted staff, hat and bowl, all of which help him to establish a magisterial kingdom.

I think back two decades to when I watched my grandmother as she piled plates of food onto our ancestral altar in preparation for my grandfather's death anniversary: dishes of spring rolls; steaming hot sticky rice; crab-mince soup; lotus shoot and jelly fish salad; piles of biscuits; and a sumptuous array of carefully arranged fruit. As a young boy I was drawn to a glistening bunch of plump, purple grapes.

'Grandma, is this all for Grandpa? How can he eat so much in one go?'

'It's all for him, my darling. Not just for now, but for the entire year. Don't worry though, once we have made our offering and he has had his fill there will be plenty left over for us. He was a generous, not gluttonous man.'

'But everything will be cold by then. And sticky rice is better hot.'

As my grandmother strained to remove the plastic from a packet of incense sticks, I locked my index finger and thumb around a fat grape. When grandmother finally looked up I mischievously asked her, 'What if I had just one of these now, Grandma? What would *he* do?'

My goading provoked a soft, crinkled grin from my grandmother.

'You may not know it now, my darling, but life can be hard, sometimes very hard. And during these times we all need to believe in something or someone. Otherwise we would simply give up. Me, I believe in my mother and father and my grandmother and grandfather. I am grateful to them for all the sacrifices they made and the wisdom they have imparted to us. Most of all, I worship your grandfather. Although he was taken away long before you were born, I have faith that he is still looking over us. I know he cares for me and for our family, and especially for you.'

'If he cares for me then he won't mind me eating a grape or two. He would be happy to give me a whole bunch!'

'We don't pay our respects to our ancestors so that we can get something from them, child. At least I don't. Of course there have been occasions when I wished that your grandfather could come back and make all of my troubles go away and riches would rain from the sky. But that's not what I have ever truly asked for. As it happens, I don't really ask your grandfather for anything. In the short time that we were together, he gave me more than enough love for a hundred lifetimes.'

'Why do you go to all this trouble if you don't get anything?'

'When I pay tribute to him I feel less lonely. I get a sense of who I am and where I belong. And it's from that sense of being and belonging that I find the strength to get through my days.'

Hearing this, I loosened my grip on the luscious fruit, but did not let it go entirely.

'So let me tell you this, my precious grandson. Your grandfather deserves some respect and restraint. He is worth believing in. He is worth letting your sticky rice go cold. And to be honest, I'm not sure what he would do if you plucked that grape and ate it. But I know what I'll do if you don't get your paw off it this instant. I'll give you a smack on the bottom that you won't forget for a very long time.'

Reflecting upon that moment with Grandma, I am reminded of how faithful and resilient she was. She must have had chances to remarry. From the few pictures I've seen and stories I've heard, she was very beautiful and much admired. However, I do wonder whether staying true to my grandfather was worth the loneliness and hardship. And I question the great pressure placed on widows to remain loyal to their deceased husbands. I suppose Grandma made a reasonable case for ancestor worship. And if one is going to thank any spirit, then one's genetic and material forebears constitute a logical choice.

But this is the best of bad arguments. I am not a child anymore who is easily frightened and persuaded. I have lived in the city and can support myself. My life and my destiny are self-made. I have come across other faiths with their own compelling logics and convictions. Most importantly, I know the value of science over superstition, not only in terms of accuracy, but also in openness, fairness and efficiency; my education in civil engineering and urban planning provides me with all the confidence and identity that I need.

I'm not sure how much the ceremony has cost my parents, but my cousin Truong confided, 'Good thing Aunt Lien sent us all that money. Otherwise your parents would be in serious debt.'

My father's cousin Lien owns a chain of nail salons in the US and comes back to Vietnam every couple of years. I haven't spoken to her or her husband since I was a boy, in large part because her visits have turned into bidding wars in which relatives and friends seek cash handouts or loans for small business ventures, school fees and home renovations. She also funded the reconstruction and upgrade of my father's family communal house and altar after it was damaged in a storm. And while everyone shows their gratitude to Aunt Lien for 'remembering her roots', I suspect she could never give them enough money.

I've overheard a few of my older relatives taking credit for my Aunt's success. 'It's only because we have honoured our ancestral spirits and tended to their graves that she has had such good fortune and success. If it wasn't for us, she wouldn't have gotten anywhere. She wouldn't have her own house to live in, let alone four of them to rent out. She wouldn't have ever made it out of the country in that rickety little fishing boat.'

My parents have never sought anything from Aunt Lien and I don't think they asked her to help pay for the reburial ceremony. They didn't have to. She would have found out that the ceremony was taking place and known exactly what was expected.

As father continues to clean and organise the bones, I occupy myself by tallying up all the things my parents and aunt have had to pay for. The money they saved by not hiring grave removalists was significant, but they still had to pay the soul caller to determine the day and time of the exhumation. The truck battery and transformer that supplied them with light look brand-new. Copious amounts of water and rice wine have been consumed by both the living and the dead. The major line item is catering. Mother and the women of the village undertook some of the preparations and cooking, and will clean up, but much food has had to be brought in, tables and chairs have been hired for the pre-ceremony dinner and the morning banquet, which looks like it will rival a wedding reception.

With these calculations done, I evaluate the effect of ancestor worship on my village and Vietnam; how throughout the country ever more land is being taken up by cemeteries. The problem is made worse by the opulent tombs intended to show off the prosperity of the occupants' family. Often there is jockeying over favourable *feng shui* locations overlooking bodies of water, but where the soil is not so moist that it would make it uncomfortable for the ancestors. Fortunately, the cemeteries around my village are modest, although a handful of 3-metre-high marble headstones have been erected. The local authorities decided to thwart grave-grabbing and conspicuous displays of wealth by standardising the plot size and recommending that people choose from a small selection of gravestones. I've heard some villagers have grumbled that this is an act of impiety against their ancestral spirits and an infringement of their human rights.

I know from my urban planning studies that by far the most heated confrontations between the living and the dead occur when new housing developments and roads demand that cemeteries be relocated, moves that are accompanied by public uproar and unrelenting media attention. And while I feel for the families who are forced to disinter their relatives, I can't think of a viable alternative for a country growing in population and shrinking in arable land. How can we allow the deceased to encroach upon those of us still above ground? Otherwise, it will be like the zombie films I've seen, except that the dead wouldn't even have to leave their graves to reap havoc on the living. I make a mental note to choose cremation when my time approaches.

'Don't forget to factor in the opportunity costs', is the lesson that has stuck with me from high school economics. 'Remember', my teacher liked to say in English, 'time is money.' At first I didn't think much of this saying because I knew many people in my village who were largely idle and had a great deal of time on their hands but no money to show for it. But through the notion of opportunity cost I realised that it is not so much the amount of time that matters but what people do with it. And as a result I've come to believe that far too much time-as-money is wasted in Vietnam on worshipping the dead. I consider the impact of General Vo Nguyen Giap's death on national productivity. Hundreds of thousands of people descended upon his house and millions more took part in mourning ceremonies across the country, some of them weeping as if he were a close relative. Then there was the two-day-long national funeral that must have brought government to a standstill. General Giap was a great leader and patriot, but this suggests to me that he would not have wanted his death to damage the country. We should have devoted more to celebrating him while he was alive and far less to commemorating his death.

As I apply this thinking to my grandmother's reburial I grow increasingly frustrated at how the conveniences of the spirit and soul are inconvenient to the mind and body. None of us huddled around the gravesite tonight would get any work done the next day, and I suspect most of us will need another day or more to recover. I can feel the harbingers of illness coming on: phlegm is building up in my throat and chest; there is an insistent weariness in my limbs; my head is light and dizzy. Hopefully it's just a cold. If by chance I can get a seat on the bus back to the city, then I will try to rest so that I can return to work the next day.

The soul caller obviously didn't take my work into account when he chose a time for the reburial. He should have known I'm in the middle of an internship with an international civil engineering company and that I've been working long hours in the hope of turning this opportunity into a prestigious career. Or perhaps he did know. Perhaps he knew how important it would be for me to impress all my bosses in these last few weeks so that I stand out from the other interns. Perhaps the soul caller was determined to make this ceremony as difficult and costly as possible. And maybe that's exactly what my grandmother and all the spirits of the dead desire – to impose themselves in the most impractical way on the living. But I shouldn't unduly credit the soul caller with this foresight, nor discredit my grandmother's memory. I refuse to tie myself up in this lie.

It was necessary, however, for me to lie to my German supervisor as to the real reason why I needed a day off to return to the village. 'It's for my cousin's engagement ceremony ... a really close cousin, like a brother.'

'Do Vietnamese often have engagement parties in the middle of the week?' my supervisor asked, more out of curiosity than suspicion.

'I'm not sure. It's just a lucky day, I suppose.'

03:21.23

What frustrates me most about the reburial ceremony is how much fuzzy mysticism is dressed up as fact and law.

Protruding from my father's shirt pocket is a piece of paper upon which the soul caller set out precisely when and how each part of the ceremony was to be performed. This program has to be followed exactly, but by whose clock and measure I'm not sure. A different soul caller would no doubt provide totally different instructions. Yet such is my father's faith in this mysticism that he committed the program to memory, reviewed it just prior to the exhumation, and keeps the paper close to his chest in case he forgets something. It is as if he is following a recipe of delicate ingredients and complex techniques, and one mistake will ruin the entire meal.

From speaking to my friends, I know there is a wide variety of bone-washing practices. Some people insist that relatives of the deceased must be crying as the coffin is opened so that the ancestor knows she or he is still missed. Others prohibit crying outright as a fearful affront. The washing can use any number of medicinal concoctions, often wine, and sometimes just water.

As my grandmother's bones emerge from their wash, relatives and friends cluck and coo as if they are greeting a newborn baby. 'Oooh, the bones are so beautiful and youthful looking!' Minutes later they argue over whether black, gold or white bones are most auspicious and appealing.

When I told my friend Binh, who is of the Tay minority, that I was attending a reburial, he said that compared to him I was getting off lightly. When Binh's grandfather passed away they had to refrain from haircuts and sleep on the ground for 40 days. 'It would have been even worse if I had a girlfriend because we wouldn't be able to fuck for 100 days after the mourning period! Anything that might be pleasurable was banned. Going to the dentist or sitting exams was totally fine.'

I wish superstition was confined to minorities, old people and the countryside. But I have seen too many fellow students flock to temples to pray for good marks before examinations. And a recent experience with one of my flatmates, Nga, also suggests that it is on the rise.

'Here, put this garlic in your bag and keep a clove of it in your pocket at all times', commanded Nga as she thrust a bag of bulbs at my chest.

'And remember, you're not setting a foot back in this place until you perform this ritual, properly. No short cuts!' On the pavement in front of our building Nga showed me what I had to do on my return. Nga struck a match and lit the end of some scrunched up sheets of newspaper. She then leant forward and passed the flaming torch from hand-to-hand around her knees twice, before throwing it on the ground and hopping over it. This would ensure that malevolent souls and nasty omens didn't follow me back from the cemetery. I hastily kicked the smouldering paper into the gutter and stamped it out.

'Okay, okay, I'll do whatever you say. But for your sake, not mine.'

I figured that this would be less trouble than facing Nga's wrath. Yet I remained uneasy, not so much at the idea of carrying out this contrived ritual on a bustling street, but rather at my sense that the vast majority of passers-by would know exactly what I was doing and whole-heartedly approve.

'Answer one thing for me, Nga. You've studied chemistry and biology. You're going to be a nurse next year. How can you know all about germs, vaccines, sickness and surgery – how can you know why people live and die – and believe in this?'

'There are lots of things that nurses and doctors can't explain', she said with an index finger raised. 'Science and medicine can't prescribe anything to improve our essence and soul; they probably never will. So I'm not taking any risks when it comes to the eternal afterlife. And neither should you if you know what's good for you. But look, I don't care what you think, as long as you hold on to that garlic and do as I say.'

While I can live with Nga's lack of concern with reconciling science and spirituality, I find it much harder to suffer my Uncle Candy's sermonising. Candy acquired his nickname because of a long-running lust for sweets. He's not really my uncle and sometimes I wonder how he and my father have remained close friends since childhood, given their dispositions are vastly different and Candy has almost no personal qualities or achievements to speak of. He has never married and has barely been to school, which is more Candy's fault than anyone else's. I have never known him to be employed or to seek a proper job. He has no credible trade or skill and stays with any relative or friend who will take him.

Uncle Candy has hardly ever left the village and has no desire to do so. One of his many mottos is 'My village is good enough for me', which is to say that those who leave are snobs and sellouts. There are many people in my village who think this way, but what makes Candy intolerable is how staunchly he voices his views.

I remember a young Japanese anthropologist coming to our village once to study the impact of urbanisation. Candy followed the man and his translator incessantly, presenting himself as the local historian and expert in everything from ceramics to ethnic minorities. Without any research or evidence, he asserted that the region had played a pivotal but unacknowledged role in Vietnam's ancient history. Just before the anthropologist departed, Candy made an effort to pull the young man's penis in the avuncular sort of way that he did to me when I was a young boy. This custom is thankfully waning in the countryside, but not in Uncle Candy's mind. I imagine that the young scholar returned to Japan and published articles about the buffoonery and barbarism of my village. I can only hope he gave the village a different name.

With everyone busy preparing for the reburial ceremony, my mother sent Candy to pick me up from the bus station. I would have preferred to hire a motorbike taxi, but could not refuse Uncle Candy, who scurried up to me as I stepped out of the bus.

'Good to see you, boy! It's been too long since you've been back.' As usual he reeked of rice wine and tobacco and spluttered his words without removing the cigarette from his near-toothless mouth. Candy was wearing a war veteran's pith helmet and rubber tyre sandals despite never having been in the army.

'I see you're still as soft and pale as silken tofu. Those glasses make you look like a pansy too, but that's what you get for staring at the books and the computers all day.'

'Greetings, Uncle Candy. It's good to see you. It's been a long time. I hope it hasn't been too much trouble for you to pick me up.'

The thing about me and Candy is that although I have little respect for and nothing in common with him, I am fond of him. And I think that he has always cared for me as his nephew. I haven't forgotten how he secretly used to share lollies with me because my parents thought such indulgences would make me unruly. But it wasn't long, primary school perhaps, before I realised that Uncle Candy was not as wise and accomplished as he professed to be. I quickly became convinced that I was smarter and better than him at most things. My determination from a young age to leave the village and attend university made it even more difficult for us to connect. And now it is clear to me that Candy manages his insecurities about going nowhere and doing nothing by mocking people like me who want to make something of themselves. As infuriating as he is, I know that Uncle Candy otherwise means well and I have come to feel more than a little sorry for him.

'This is your first reburial, isn't it, boy? You know, this is my fourth this season.'

As we weave around lorries on his wheezing old motorbike, Uncle Candy lectured me non-stop, often looking back to make sure I was listening and then thumping me on the thigh with an instructive fist.

'I'll tell you something about reburials and ancestor worship that few people dare to say. All that stuff about paying respects to our loved ones is utter bullshit! I've spoken to people in the know, fellows who've looked into this sort of thing long and deep, all the way back to China and Taiwan. And they tell me it's not about worshipping the dead at all. You know what it's about? It's about protecting *us* from *them*.'

Uncle Candy's phone rang. 'Fuck. That's probably them trying to silence me.' He reached into his trouser pocket and switched it off.

'Listen to me, boy. Why do you think all the bones have to be stripped of flesh? It's because meat and muscle is the stuff of our world. We're saying to them, "Please, please relinquish everything from this world – your money, authority, fame – and in return we'll help purify and push you across that horizon that never ends." Why do you think we give 'em all that fake gold, cars and credit cards? Everyone likes to think it's because we love them so much and want them to be warm and happy? Fuckin' bullshit! We burn all that fake crap so they don't take the real stuff from us! People are nasty and envious and when they're dead they're even worse. The dead resent us. They resent that we're living better now than they ever did. Above all they resent that we're breathing fresh air while they're choking on dirt.'

'Yes, Uncle Candy.'

'I don't want to scare you or anything. But you're old enough to know what it's all about: life, death and all that shit. I know this is hard for you to grasp. You haven't been to a reburial before. All you know about is computers. But listen to me carefully. Trust me on this. One hundred per cent. You boy, are a prime target. They want nothing more than to take your youth, talent and future. Are you listening, boy?!'

'Yes, of course I am, Uncle.'

'And believe me when I tell you this ain't gonna be a good night for anyone, living or dead. I don't like the scent in the air. Can you smell it? This morning as I left the house the first person I came across was a woman, she had a face like a monkey's arse, and then it was lady after lady until lunchtime, all of 'em arse-ugly. That's a bad omen. No doubt about it. I'll be there tonight, of course, to support you and your father. But there'll be a sizeable space between me and your ol' Gran.'

True to his word, I can see Uncle Candy standing at the back of the small crowd wearing two face masks for added protection from the cold and the malevolent spirits. With his thick poncho and pith helmet, he's better prepared than most when the specks of rain turn into splotches.

Silently I curse myself for not challenging Uncle Candy outright. My grandmother was beautiful, caring and kind when she was alive. Why would her spirit be otherwise? Why should someone who sacrificed much when she was living want to do others harm once she was gone? The purpose of the affair was apparently to defame, not remember.

I am all for commemorating people, especially my Gran, I think to myself in the icy rain. But a small gathering of people who truly knew and cared about her – isn't that enough? We could pay our respects by reflecting upon the ways she affected us and everything we had learnt from her. We could look at pictures or watch videos – in the comfort of a living room – that would revive more faithful memories than anything that could be conjured up through hours of bone washing. The costs to her descendants of the commemoration – actual and opportunity – would be minimal, and there might even be a few benefits of getting together and remembering her life now gone. Wouldn't she have appreciated this?

03:58.53

There is widespread agreement that my grandmother's spirit is pleased by the arrangement of her bones – so pleased that she has commanded the wind to die down and the rain to stop.

Gran has been cleansed – 'given a new shirt', as the saying goes – rebuilt and ready for her next journey. Her skeleton is now tightly packed in her final casket, which is about the length of my arm and two handspans wide. The leg bones are tucked under the hips and the ribs are laid out over the spine and upper arms. Her skull has been pieced together and sits on the top with the mouth closed. I can't help but be impressed by the completion of this intricate puzzle.

Briefly, before the casket is closed for good, my mother summons my younger sister to see our Gran one last time.

I have not had the chance to speak to Linh since returning to the village. As my sister makes her way past the mourners, I notice that her sandals elevate her to my line of vision. I can see her long lashes and glittery pink-and-purple nail polish under the dim fluorescent light. She is wearing a body-hugging cardigan that barely buttons up that my mother had threatened to throw out.

'You look like you're heading out to a karaoke club in the city rather than sending off Gran', I tell her.

Linh's pouty bottom lip suggests she is in no mood to be lectured. I ruffle her cola-coloured hair, 'It's good to see you, *em*.'

Linh and her entourage arrived late, a little after 02:00. They had been sipping green tea and energy drinks at a café in town before playing cards and losing track of time. Linh commonly stays up until the early hours of the morning, so if the exhumation is testing for her it is not because of the timing.

She and her gang kept their distance from the gravesite, their mood seeming to sway between mild curiosity and repulsion. After about half an hour they could no longer tolerate the wintry gales and the tedium and retreated to a nearby gravesite surrounded by a low white wall. There they rolled themselves up in rattan mats, using a wool blanket for the innermost layer. With the wall as a buffer against the gale, the young 20-somethings have managed to rest and even sleep. Whenever the wind swirled from that direction, I heard the faint sound of snoring along with a tinny pop song playing from someone's mobile phone.

Linh certainly lacks decorum. Yet no one who knows what she has been through could rebuke her. It is enough that she is here. When it comes to loving and caring for Gran, she has proven herself many times over. Indeed, Linh has had more affectionate and challenging times with Gran than anyone.

As a young child Linh adored Gran, who in turn treasured her only granddaughter. Gran listened to her make up tales about princesses, swans and fairies with boundless patience and interest. The young girl slept more nights in Gran's bed than she did her own. They shopped and chatted with a natural easiness even after Linh became a teenager whose primary concerns were clothes, music, movies and boys.

This all changed when Linh was 17 and Gran suffered her first stroke. Gran survived and recovered physically within weeks, but her mind was mush. Whereas before, Gran's poignancy and wisdom was only occasionally punctuated by senseless blather, now the opposite was true. It was not long before her condition deteriorated to the point that, when no one was watching, she would wander out of the house and into the fields. The first time we found her sitting in the mud cackling at a toad. The second time she made it much further and was fortunately rescued by a passing motorist who found her half-dressed cowering by the freeway.

It was clear that Gran would need full-time care. My mother was busy in the fields and my aunts had factory jobs and families to look after. Our cousins had either moved away or were deemed unsuitable for such duties because they were boys. Linh was the first and only candidate for the job.

The fact that Linh had seen this coming did not lessen her despair. She had only just finished high school and made it clear to all that tending to Gran would prohibit her from going to university – it would ruin her life.

My mother responded with a callousness peculiar to mothers and their daughters. 'What's all this talk about university now? You never cared about your studies before. You've never even expressed a desire to do anything but watch movies and listen to music. So here's a chance for you to help your family, at least until you find a calling, or until it finds you. If you really want to attend university, you can always apply next year or the year after. Think of it this way. You need to have someone to look after to help you stop thinking about yourself so much. It will make you a better woman and prepare you for motherhood. It will be good for you.'

At the time, I thought it only fair that Linh should look after Gran in the same way that Gran had once looked after her. However, I didn't say this to my sister, who was inconsolable. My parents did not know then, but for the first time in her life she had started seeing a boy. Much later she would confess to me that such was their grief that they considered catching a bus to Hai Phong and finding someone who would marry them. Then, like so many others, they would leap off the Bai Chay Bridge and forever be wedded together in the waters 50 metres below.

The first three months took a heavy toll on the household. Gran screamed and slapped the dour young stranger with whom she was, once again, sharing a bed. She did not recognise her granddaughter or occasionally thought she was one of her daughters-in-law. Both of them were cranky and prone to hysteria. Linh rough-handed her grandmother as she changed her clothes, a task that had to be carried out after every meal and mistimed toilet trip. If Gran couldn't sleep, then neither could Linh. To make matters worse, the neighbours complained about the hollering, hooting and old revolutionary songs that Gran sang in the middle of the night, standing in her nightgown with her fist up in the air as if it was 1954 again.

After a few weeks, Gran's large wooden bed was moved into the living room to give her a little more sunlight and space. This also brought her closer to the bathroom and made it easier for guests to visit her. The drawback for Linh, however, was that she had even less privacy than before. So when my father erected a swinging metal gate over the front doorway to prevent Gran from darting out, it was Linh who felt she was at once on display and imprisoned.

Gran aged years in a matter of weeks. Her skin had the texture of jerky, yet it was as translucent as sago jelly, with every vein and sinew visible. Her back became heavily bowed and the left side of her face ceased to function. The family's fear that she would wander away quickly dissolved as Gran lost all motivation to leave her bed.

Linh was at best uncaring and at worst cruel. There were times when Grandma refused to eat or take her medicine and Linh too easily relented. She allowed children in the village to come inside and gawk at the ancient figure who was, for them, more dead than alive. When young boys concocted stories about all the horrible things Gran must have done to deserve such a fate, Linh said nothing. The children especially liked it when the old woman sat up after lying on her side, as it took several seconds for gravity to restore shape to the flattened edge of her face. Under Linh's watch, the village boys dared one another to touch the old woman's limbs, shoulders, hair, and even her dangling earlobes.

I had just started university and was distressed by my parents' reports of events at home. Linh had hardly spoken to me since I left. But then, about five months into her ordeal, I was surprised to get a call from her. She asked me how I was going and what it was like living in the city. Linh told me that both she and Gran were doing better and revealed an astounding incident that had taken place late one evening as she was changing Gran's underwear.

'I don't know who you are', the elderly woman pronounced, 'but I know that I love you.' Upon hearing this confession an exhausted Linh hugged her grandmother and sobbed, not out of self-pity, but from affection. Gran put her arms around her granddaughter and lightly patted her on the back, and stroked her head and said, 'Don't worry. Everything is going to be fine, little girl.'

Gradually, the relationship between the two women was restored and even developed. While there was no miraculous change to Gran's condition, her posture and energy improved. She regained her appetite, in part because of a game Linh devised in which she hid food in and around the house for her grandmother to find.

Before I returned home for the summer, I told Linh I was eager to spend time with Gran so that she could have some respite. I expected her to run out the door as soon as I arrived and head straight for the newly constructed shopping mall. This she did, but not before carefully explaining to me how Gran liked to be fed, how she needed to be turned over now and then, and how to calm her if she woke up and was frightened to see me instead of her. Fortunately my grandmother slept peacefully that night. I, on the other hand, hardly slept at all. Throughout the evening I stared at Gran's face lying centimetres from mine. I was petrified by the prospect of being the last person to see her alive. Each cough and wheeze seemed terminal, and the silences were worse because I thought she would never make another sound. It occurred to me that this must be what it was like to have a newborn and concluded that I was not ready for parenthood.

The following morning, wearing her new jeans, Linh said to me, '*Anh oi*, I'm used to looking after Gran now. You've been studying hard and rarely come home. Go see your friends and spend some time with our family. Leave Gran to me.' At that moment, I felt the greatest admiration for my little sister, while also suspecting that she didn't fully trust me.

That summer I witnessed an astonishing tenderness between Linh and Gran. Now, it was the granddaughter who sat and listened to her grandmother's stories with uncommon patience. And while Gran was utterly dependent upon Linh, she gave her granddaughter an impalpable yet precious gift: a sense of purpose and perspective, perhaps something to believe in.

I returned one evening from a night out with friends to see Linh sound asleep, but Gran sitting up with her tiny withered feet hanging out of the mosquito net and her hands resting on her rotund belly. Through the net I could see her ancient face flecked by the moonlight. Gran turned to me but looked right through me. She had no idea who I was but at the same time seemed to perceive much more. It was as if the son of her eldest son was a fleeting speck in a cosmos within a cosmos, a reality that she, in her final days on earth, was starting to fathom. I scuttled off to bed, awestruck by what the elderly can achieve and wondering how many of these encounters my sister must have been privy to.

When Gran died, two strokes and almost a year later, Linh was desolate. It happened quietly at night, while she was lying by Linh's side. The village awoke the next morning to Linh's wailing, which overwhelmed the loudspeakers broadcasting the news and regulations.

On the day of Gran's funeral my sister remained inside the house, the gate over the front door recently removed. My parents thought her grief was so great that she would faint or fall ill during the ceremony.

Now, more than 1,000 days later, Linh has come to look in on Gran one last time.

'Are you okay?' I ask my sister.

'That time's over, Gran's gone. I don't need no ceremony to tell me that.'

04:42.44

The mourning of my grandmother is almost over. The casket has been transferred to the final resting place beside my paternal ancestors. Now the men sit around the fire, which has been stoked to a roaring height. All of our white sashes are cast into the flames. The incense sticks that we maintained throughout the night have all burnt out. Once again bottles of rice wine are brought out. This time the wine is not to garner fortitude, but to be drunk in celebration.

My weary father encourages the men to have a drink with him. Because I don't have a family of my own, I am not offered any wine. Father is flanked by his brothers and Uncle Candy, who is now pleased to be the centre of attention. Uncle Candy tells them about the recent reburials he has been to and of others in the distant past. He recollects how there were times after the American War when the government looked down on all banquets and ceremonies as distractions from the material needs of the workers and peasants.

'But they could never stamp out reburials. In a country where so many soldiers have lost their lives and have not yet come home, it's impossible to sever the living from the dead', he says.

Without a hint of fatigue, Uncle Candy recites a poem by Tu Nguyen Tinh he has learnt by heart.

> Who dares step out in this month?
> This month of rain and shivering cold,
> This month reserved for reburial ceremonies.
> Who dares return to the countryside?
> To move loved ones to new homes,
> Where incessant pain goes hand-in-hand,
> With a sense of life powerless.
> Together we take the plunge,
> But in those final moments, we drift apart.

'That's enough, Candy', says my father. 'It's time for all of us to go home.'

We thank everyone for coming. My sister and mother leave to prepare the morning banquet.

There is one remaining sacrifice, one further exhibition of discomfort in this world so that my grandmother might be more comfortable in hers. My father and I must sleep at the foot of her new grave. At this stage I'm so exhausted that the prospect of resting anywhere is inviting.

Together, my father and I gather all the tarpaulins and lay them wet-side-down. He finishes a bottle of rice wine before falling to the ground. 'Say farewell to your Gran', he murmurs. 'And remember this when the time comes to farewell me.'

I am not one for dramatic conversions, yet Father's appeal has a powerful impact on me. Whereas before I felt detached from the reburial ceremony, suddenly I begin to fathom its significance. I understand that much of this night is about me.

And I start to see how entire epochs have converged upon the spot that I occupy. The smouldering fire; the surrounding rice paddy; the factory lights on the horizon; the layer of concrete dust that covers everything in my village; the mobile phone in my coat pocket constantly sending and receiving signals that connect me to billions of people. I also apprehend the efforts of those close to me to harmonise these criss-crossing worlds with a sense of the transcendent.

The soul callers, fake money, incense smoke, spring water and white sashes are all there to help me grasp that I will someday be in my father's place, and then in my grandmother's.

Entombed within layers of plastic I place my arm around my father, who lies soaked in icy perspiration, shuddering in a half-foetal position. I close my eyes and allow sleep to come to me just as night begins to drain from the sky.

Postscript
The Other Turtle's Tale

While writing this book, I often turned to a Vietnamese friend and colleague for advice. After reading 'The Professional', he hazarded: 'You're Maria Pham, aren't you?' My friend was convinced that I had made myself a character in the book in the same way a film director might take on a cameo role. As he saw it, Maria Pham revealed the true me as an expatriate who had reluctantly returned to his birthplace only to find himself adopting the culture and loving the country. My friend was right. I am Maria Pham. But there's more to my relationship with this book, and with Vietnam, than that.

'Every character is me', I explained to him. By which I meant that they not only do in the stories as I have done in real life, but also that they often think and feel how I thought and felt. Like the Sticky Rice Seller, I've made up stories about people as they go by in the street, wanting to get to know them and for them to know something of me. The Ball Boy and the Professional's struggles against conformity and obligation very much align with mine. At times, I'm as insufferable as the Goalkeeper. And, like the Student, I have sought to reconcile the present with the past and whatever lies beyond. Other characters are also me, depicting everything from my obssession with gadgetry to my pursuit of mindfulness in a world of distractions.

However, none of the characters are closer to me than the Turtle of Hoan Kiem Lake, who embodies how I lived in Vietnam and how I've studied and written about it. That is, as if I was dreaming; as if I was part of the action, as if I somehow knew that it was all a dream, and as if I was all the while observing events from the outside unable and unwilling to intervene. Allow me to explain.

I was part of the action in Vietnam during an extended visit from early 2011 to mid-2012. My intentions during this time were to experience all that I could of my birthplace, to relearn the language so as never to forget it, and to eat out as much as possible. I was successful on all three counts, although I had to cook once during the Lunar New Year when my favourite food stalls were closed. During my visit I took on many trades and identities. I spent time with street vendors, motorbike taxi drivers and ball boys. I dined, drank, sang karaoke and went on spiritual pilgrimages with corporate flyers and government officials. I attended weddings, concerts, exhibitions and rituals, and spent much time with students lounging in cafes, bars and bookshops. For a while I was an editor, activist and student. I was even a lecturer. Whereas newcomers are often horrified by the traffic in Hanoi and Ho Chi Minh City, I was able to walk, pedal, and ride with a degree of surety and comfort. Near the end of my time in Vietnam, strangers asked me for directions and I could show them the way.

These experiences compelled me to write this book about the everyday wonders of contemporary Vietnam. In so doing, I had to be ever conscious of the dreams and visions of the Vietnamese people. I had to gain an appreciation of how their and my cultural heritage animates Vietnam today. The vital literary works that informed each chapter are set out below.

'The Sticky Rice Seller' echoes a famous poem by the salacious yet much revered Ho Xuan Huong (1772–1822). A concubine and then widow for much of her life, Ho Xuan Huong compares the fate of women to sweet dumplings: moulded by the hands of men, just as likely to float or sink, yet able to preserve their inner essence. My translation of 'Floating Dumplings' is as follows.

> My body pure white,
> My fate gently rounded.
> Rising and sinking
> With mountain streams.
>
> Whatever hands
> Shape me.
> My heart remains
> Red and true.

The opening story of this collection explores gender discrimination in Vietnam, acknowledging how women often negotiate their social roles and contest their subjugation. Almost instinctively, Mai blends her mother's and boyfriend's expectations with her own desires for affection and belonging. 'The Sticky Rice Seller' also considers some of the ongoing cultural tensions between North and South Vietnam, which have been largely taboo for Vietnamese writers and researchers since the end of the Second Indochina War. The varied and dynamic tastes of the sticky rice seller's customers reflect the complexity of dialects, outlooks and values stretching from Ca Mau and the Gulf of Thailand to Lang Son and the gateway to China.

'The Ball Boy' is a rough remake of Vu Trong Phung's (1912–39) modern classic, *Dumb Luck*, which tells of an impoverished young man named Xuan (Spring) who finds fame, popularity and love among Hanoi's Francophile tennis playing community. Mistaken as someone of high culture and intellect, Xuan's sun-bleached red hair is deemed stylish by the city's *nouveau riche*. Xuan's admiration for high society and desire to be part of it is affirmed when he falls into good fortune. Thu, on the other hand, makes his own fate and sets his own standards. He turns his exile into a platform for advancement and savours conflict as an opportunity to assert himself over others. The ball boy Thu screams out to minorities to reject orthodoxy, to rejoice in all that is different, to never cower in the shadows.

'The Professional' turns upside-down the values and virtues espoused in Vietnam's most esteemed literary work, 'The Tale of Kieu'. Nguyen Du's (1766–1820) 3,254-verse poem tells of a star-crossed heroine who sells herself to save her family and then denies herself happiness so as to protect her true love's integrity. In contrast, the cut-throat businesswoman Kieu has contempt for Confucian duties and patronising Westerners. Nguyen Du's Kieu is incessant in her self-sacrifice, while Kieu the professional is incessant in her self-interest. As a result, both of them are never at ease with themselves or others. The major issue that this twenty-first-century tale seeks to deal with is the moral and civic indifference (*vo cam*) that has beset many of the Vietnamese super-rich and which shows signs of spreading throughout society.

'The Goalkeeper' pays tribute to Pham Thi Hoai's (1960–) award-winning novel, *The Crystal Messenger*. Hoai's story tells of the social and sexual coming of age of twin sisters from the perspective of the more reserved and plain-looking of the two as she watches people go by from her window. The book was banned in Vietnam and Hoai left the country in the 1990s. In part this was because it was an incisive allegory of Vietnam's tribulations as it emerged from a cloistered post-war era to encounter alluring but unsettling forms of capitalism and Westernisation. Most controversially, the narrator's suitor is a stalwart party cadre named Quang who happens to be a dwarf. For all his efforts and virtues, Quang is ultimately thwarted in his quest for love and respect. Like the dwarf and other true believers in the Vietnamese Communist Party, Kim Lien's earnestness and rectitude cannot make up for her emotional and aesthetic limitations. Many of the Goalkeeper's proclamations have been adapted from the speeches and letters of prominent revolutionaries and point out the corrosive effects of corruption and excessive consumerism in Vietnam. In a conflicted socialist-oriented market economy, Kim Lien stands out because she believes everything the Party says, and attempts to live by its principles and rules without compromise.

Finally, 'The Student' is informed by the idea of taking my father as a young man out of the 1950s and 1960s and placing him in Vietnam today. Back then, my father's move from the countryside to the city sparked in him a stridently modern outlook. From the time that he first touched ice as a small boy right up until he helped to design the South Vietnamese electricity grid, my father believed that his life and his country were moving ever onward and upward. This tale is told in my book about my parents and twentieth-century Vietnam, *Where the Sea Takes Us: A Vietnamese–Australian Story*. The student Kien is also eager to catapult himself and Vietnam into tomorrow and in so doing sever all associations with ancestors and superstition. My father's progressive zeal was blunted by the fall of Saigon and subsequent events that compelled us to leave Vietnam. Kien has a far more positive confrontation with resurgent tradition and is drawn back to his home soil, which he comes to regard not solely as a place for vanquished ghosts and macabre rituals, but also as a source of spiritual nourishment and meaning.

For all my efforts to engage with Vietnam's literature and people, I am now and probably always will be as much an outsider as I am insider. This is not such a bad thing. It grows in part out of the fact that, having left Vietnam as an infant, I have no childhood memory of it. I am also on the fringe of Vietnamese youth culture and youthfulness more generally. Being in my mid-30s, this book captures my last chance to hang out with a demographic that increasingly confounds and outpaces me. Like Hoan Kiem's antediluvian turtle, I often find myself amazed by Vietnam's exuberance and dynamism, and also a little anxious about the pace and direction of change.

Returning to Vietnam as an academic has also contributed to my detached dream-like state of being. Archetypical social scientists seek to set themselves apart from the objects and forces they research. To this end, I found it useful to wake up early in Vietnam to watch people. The light and air are clearest in the morning. This is when people are on the move, doing their exercises and preparing for the day. Often they are not fully awake or wholly cognisant of their surroundings. They are too preoccupied to pay much attention to me, which allows me to pay more attention to them. Roughly speaking, 5 to 6 am is the hour of the social scientist in Vietnam, when one can best observe others without influencing or being influenced by them.

Of course, *Vietnam as if...* is not standard social science scholarship. This raises the question of why I have chosen to represent my research as fiction as opposed to fact. By 'fact' I mean the Western tradition that famously grows out of the meditations of the seventeenth-century French philosopher René Descartes. Descartes tried to discern truth by severing his mind from everything around him – his body, culture, history and other people – all of which might be illusion or dream. It is largely from this example that the social sciences came to associate truth with the qualities of detachment and purity.

Importantly, the ways that Westerners have come to know the world align with the ways that they have sought to conquer and control it. And so, French colonists were disdainful of Indochinese culture and history: the natives had no libraries and were therefore not literate. They were clumps of clay – as one Governor-General of Indochina stated – that Western civilisation would mould into humans.

An even more extreme derivation of Cartesian thinking is evident in the way that America managed its Vietnam War. In *The Best and the Brightest*, David Halberstam tells the story of the 'whiz kids' who were recruited from academia and industry into the highest levels of government so that they could apply the latest scientific methods to the counter-revolutionary cause in Indochina. Again, Vietnam as a country and people – even the instructive history of the French occupation – were wilfully ignored by American managers of war, who busied themselves collating statistics about enemy behaviour, the territory and their resources. In the end, being detached from the Vietnamese only made it easier for the best and the brightest to carpet bomb, spray toxins and drop napalm upon them. And so, putting aside scientific fact in favour of fiction is not merely a matter of style or method for me. It is a deeply political and ethical endeavour.

Others have turned to storytelling after linking detached truth to acts of horror. Indeed, there is a vast body of work on how the social sciences took a 'narrative turn' in the 1980s. The exponents of this turn sought to destabilise grand narratives such as Marxism-Leninism and liberal capitalism, which they associated with disastrous social engineering projects and the unprecedented concentration of political and economic power. Instead, they espoused micro-narratives that were more intimate, situated and radically egalitarian. In the social studies literature, this shift can be seen in the proliferation of academic articles in which the identities, biases and backgrounds of both the researcher and the researched are not set aside, but brought to the foreground by way of autobiographical and biographical vignettes. While I am indebted to this narrative turn, *Vietnam as if…* also represents my turning away from it. This is because the push for narratives has become rather predictable and stale; there is now a ready-made way to use and think about stories and a formal language with which to talk about them. To the extent that the narrative turn has become part of an academic discipline, it has abandoned the creative flair that makes it worthwhile.

So my rationale for this book was simple: if I was serious about stories as scholarship, then I should write a few. I was also compelled by the belief that scholars can strive to be public intellectuals who not only describe social change, but also inspire better forms of it. In this regard, stories are particularly useful because of their potential to operate in a democratic fashion, whereby writers do not so much dictate messages to readers, but rather conjure scenes and scenarios which readers can occupy, contemplate and complete at will. Good literature, as an expression of enlightened social science, must therefore entice readers to slow down, to savour the story and to make it their own – a process that the old Turtle of Hoan Kiem Lake would endorse.

Of course, to promote fiction as a valuable form of truth is not to suggest that all scholarly writing should be replaced with storytelling. There are dangers and drawbacks in fiction. Most notably, it arguably asserts an arrogant truth that cannot be probed, verified, contested. Thus, a key purpose of this postscript in laying out the influences and reasons behind these stories is not to force the reader to interpret them in a particular way, but rather to humble their truth claims and to pry those claims open so that they can be scrutinised. There will be people who enter these fictional worlds only to find that they are distorted, exaggerated, and seem nothing like Vietnam as it is. Even so, I maintain that it is important to imagine Vietnam as if … In fact, I would not conceive of it in any other way.

With respect,
Kim Huynh

References

Nguyen Du (translated by Huynh Sanh Thong), *The Tale of Kieu* (New Haven: Council on Southeast Asia and Yale University, 1983).

David Halberstam, *The Best and the Brightest* (New York: Random House, 1972).

Pham Thi Hoai (translated by Ton-That Quynh-Du), *The Crystal Messenger* (Dunedin: University of Otago Press, 1997).

Kim Huynh, *Where the Sea Takes Us: a Vietnamese–Australian story* (London; New York: Fourth Estate, 2007).

Vu Trong Phung (translated by Nguyen Nguyet Cam and Peter Zinoman), *Dumb Luck: a novel* (Ann Arbor: University of Michigan Press, 2002).

www.ingramcontent.com/pod-product-compliance
Lightning Source LLC
Chambersburg PA
CBHW061140230426
43663CB00024B/2974